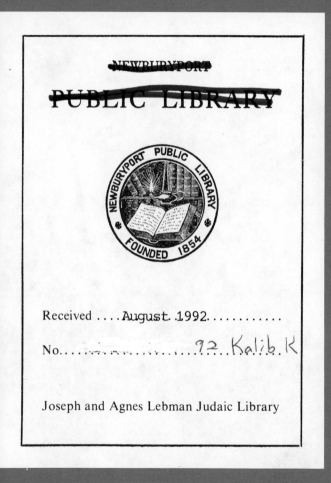

THE LAST SELECTION

The Last Selection

A CHILD'S JOURNEY THROUGH THE HOLOCAUST

BY

Goldie Szachter Kalib

WITH

Sylvan Kalib and Ken Wachsberger

The University of Massachusetts Press

AMHERST

Copyright © 1991 by
Goldie Kalib, Sylvan Kalib, and Ken Wachsberger
All rights reserved
Printed in the United States of America
LC 91-3869
ISBN 0-87023-758-6
Designed by Jack Harrison
Set in Weiss & Sabon by Keystone Typesetting, Inc.
Printed and bound by Thomson-Shore, Inc.
Library of Congress Cataloging-in-Publication Data

Kalib, Goldie Szachter, 1931–
    The last selection : a child's journey through the Holocaust / by
Goldie Szachter Kalib, with Sylvan Kalib and Ken Wachsberger.
        p.   cm.
    ISBN 0-87023-758-6 (alk. paper)
    1. Kalib, Goldie Szachter, 1931–
    2. Jews—Poland—Bodzentyn—Biography.
    3. Holocaust, Jewish (1939–1945)—Poland—Bodzentyn—Personal narratives.
    4. Bodzentyn (Poland)—Biography.
    I. Kalib, Sylvan.   II. Wachsberger, Ken.   III. Title.
    DS135.P63K244   1991
    940.53'18'094386—dc20
    [B]   91–3869
                        CIP

British Library Cataloguing in Publication data are available.

Contents

List of Illustrations

Foreword

For both Jews and Germans, the ninth day of November holds special significance. On November 9, 1989, as the descendants of the Third Reich celebrated, the Berlin Wall fell. American journalists broadcast live from the Wall, proclaiming another triumph for freedom; within a year the same newscasters would be reporting on the reunification of East and West Germany. In the midst of this revelry, Jewish intellectuals gently pointed out that the ninth of November was a day for mourning as well as gaiety. On the night of November 9, 1938, Hitler's regime launched a pogrom of unimaginable proportions. The Nazis burned synagogues throughout Germany, arrested prominent Jewish leaders, and attacked Jewish-owned stores. For a brief moment, the world clearly recognized the barbarous policies of German fascism; policies that led to the annihilation of six million Jews during World War II.

It is important to remember Kristallnacht and its aftermath. Yet human beings in the twentieth century unfortunately do not seem to be blessed with long memories. We celebrate the reunion of Germany without seeming to recollect that its partition was not the result of Soviet Cold War aggression. Rather, the Germans brought occupation and division upon themselves by starting a war of mass destruction and genocide. The story of Golda Szachter reminds us that some of the victims (and perpetrators) of Nazism have survived to see the "rehabilitation" of Germany. Szachter's fascinating and moving tale joins those of Elie Wiesel, Primo Levi, and others who managed to defy the odds and survive the death camps. While her recollections bring to mind those of other survivors, she provides us with a particularly interesting lens through which to view the destruction of European Jewry.

Golda Szachter was a child thrust into a nightmare. She was only seven years old when the Germans occupied her native Poland. At thirteen she joined the infamous Auschwitz death march as the Nazis evacuated the camp and fled the approaching Red Army.

Golda's descriptions of prewar life in her hometown are the nostalgic memories of a young girl who was robbed of her childhood. Through her eyes we see the destruction of her entire world. We watch her struggle to comprehend as her neighbors and relatives go off to fight the invading armies and as others are arrested by the victorious Germans. Throughout her ordeal she had faith that her father would somehow manage to protect and preserve the family. Finally, we witness her desperate fight to survive after the loss of her source of strength and hope.

Unlike most of Hitler's victims, the Szachter family was very prosperous. Although wealth could not guarantee her family's safety, Golda's father had unique resources that allowed him to prolong his family's survival. With money and jewelry he was able to bribe officials and receive special favors. Even more important, Golda's father's business dealings gave him an extensive network of Jewish and Polish Christian acquaintances who provided the family with temporary haven and nourishment. They also kept her father well informed of Nazi actions and movements, intelligence that allowed him to skillfully avoid, at least temporarily, annihilation. Golda's father acted heroically and honorably; however, we see glimpses in her story of resentment by Jews not blessed with the resources at her family's disposal.

Golda could not have survived the Holocaust without the help of Polish Christians who hid and protected her. Her memoirs provide us with a particularly good and personal view of the complex nature of the Poles' response to the murder of the European Jews. Numerous Polish Christians risked their lives to help Golda and her family. Some were willing to risk execution in return for handsome rewards by Golda's father. Others were guided by ideology, as was the case of a young Communist who became something of an older brother to Golda. Some, however, seem to have been primarily motivated by nothing more than a simple moral belief that murder was wrong and should be resisted. Sadly, while some Poles came to the aid of the Jews, others remained indifferent to their plight and some even collaborated with the Nazis. Golda and her Polish protectors lived in constant fear of anti-Semitic neighbors.

The Nazis murdered one million Jewish children. Through Golda we are given the opportunity to learn something about their terrible experiences. As we witness, with the recent reunification of Germany, the final end of World War II it is important not to lose sight of the war's victims. Golda's book deserves to be read carefully.

AARON BERMAN

Preface

On April 15, 1945, I, along with my sisters Rachela and Irka, my cousin Rivtche, my mother, and sixty thousand other Jewish prisoners, was liberated by the British army from Bergen-Belsen. Less than a month later, on May 8, 1945—the day the Germans surrendered to the Allies in Europe—my mother died in a makeshift hospital set up by the British. She had survived nearly two years and seven months in Starachowice labor camp and Auschwitz. She had survived the infamous Death March to Bergen-Belsen. Unfortunately, by the time of our liberation her health had deteriorated to a point where she would never recover. She was buried May 9 in a mass grave inside the camp following a mass funeral service.

For the next four years, the others of us, along with my Uncle Leib'l, the only other survivor from our previously large family, remained in Bergen-Belsen. In fact, practically all the liberated internees, unwilling to return to Poland and unable to immigrate to Palestine or the United States because of stringent quotas, remained there also, essentially stateless and unwanted in what now became a Displaced Persons camp in the British zone of occupation.

In these camps a new life slowly emerged. Living quarters were provided in small apartments that formerly housed German soldiers; food and clothing were provided by Jewish and non-Jewish international organizations. Soon, a group of soldiers from the Palestine Jewish Brigade of the British Army arrived and organized schools as well as groups representing all Zionist political persuasions. Through these efforts, education of the young, halted during the war, was resumed.

Old friendships from home and from the concentration camps were renewed, and new friendships were formed. There was much socializing, partying, singing, and dancing to songs of an emerging Jewish national homeland. Adults learned professions and engaged in business beyond the camp confines. Many met future spouses. Numerous marriages and births took place.

Meanwhile, through the efforts and under the influence of soldiers and teachers from the Palestine Jewish Brigade, significant numbers of our friends joined illegal immigrations into Palestine. After Israel became a state on May 19, 1948, others then chose to immigrate legally.

We were among those who passed up that chance, even after statehood. Still feeling the pain of the war years, we did not find alluring the prospects of a hazardous and difficult life in the new Jewish state. When the United States Congress passed the Displaced Persons Act of 1948 and opened up opportunities for one hundred thousand Jews from the camps, we chose to emigrate there instead. We were assisted in being among the first to register for emigration by Shmiel Weintraub, a lifelong friend of our family who was now a member of the Central Jewish Committee of the Bergen-Belsen Displaced Persons camp. After approximately one year's wait, we were notified that our turn had come. One week before departure, we visited Mother's grave site for the last time. On September 13, 1949, Irka and I arrived in the United States. Rachela, Rivtche, and Uncle Leib'l arrived separately.

In the United States, we were assisted by the Hebrew Immigrant Aid Society in becoming acclimated to our new lives. By 1954, all of us had found our life partners and were married. Between the years 1953 and 1959, each of us was blessed with two children. Life went on. We were preoccupied with shaping our new lives: establishing careers and businesses, bringing up children, providing for their education and careers.

In August 1984 I visited Israel with my husband, Sholom (Sylvan's Hebrew name by which I call him). It was thirty-five years since I had left Bergen-Belsen with my surviving family members. In that time, none of us had returned to visit Mother's grave site, so Sholom and I decided that during the return leg of our trip we would stop over in Amsterdam and from there make the journey to Bergen-Belsen. From Amsterdam, on Tuesday, August 21, we boarded a 7 A.M. train to Hannover, West Germany, the closest major city to Bergen-Belsen. Two hours later, we entered West Germany.

The first words I was to hear in German were spoken by a uniformed German official, who asked to see our passports and railroad tickets, and I wondered how a Jew would have felt in this same situation in the 1930s, when Hitler came to power. No Jews *could* have been here from about 1940 or so through World War II. How would the German officer or the German passengers have reacted if one had been discovered? What do they think now? How many of them or their older relatives were Nazi soldiers, officers, murderers? I remarked to Sholom how the sight of the German in uniform, speaking in German, reminded me of countless scenes from my youth. Sholom was hardly surprised.

As the train rolled on through the towns and villages, we saw lovely landscapes all about and small, carefully maintained European-style houses, many with steep red rooftops, along clean and beautiful narrow streets, some with shops, and many flourishing industrial buildings, all seen so brightly on this idyllic sunny morning. How much of this picturesque land under God's eye is drenched with innocent Jewish blood, I wondered. How much of this wealth was plundered from innocent and helpless Jews? Did the natives living here now have any compassion for their Jewish neighbors who were forced out of their homes, and whose wealth was confiscated, and who were shipped off to the death camps for extermination and cremation? Did these onetime neighbors perhaps aid or take part in the atrocities? Were these beautiful buildings erected over land once used for synagogues, religious schools, or cemeteries?

By noon, we were at the main Hannover railroad station. As we descended from the platform, we saw a huge complex of services with colorfully lit signs and service quarters, all filled with the bustling activity of people hustling to and fro amid a continuous flow of conversation, all in German. I couldn't help imagining the same setting during the war and prewar eras, when huge ostentatious Swastika flags would have hung from the four sides of the enormous, high ceilings, and uniformed Nazi military personnel would have stalked arrogantly about the station in tall, shining boots, generating terror in the heart of every Jew.

From Hannover, we took a half-hour train ride to Celle, a little town approximately thirty kilometers from Bergen-Belsen. From Celle, we took a bus to Bergen, roughly five kilometers from Bergen-Belsen. The bus ride gave us an even clearer view of the rural German countryside. Curiously, Sholom now said aloud what I had been thinking silently: "Look how beautiful and clean everything is here. I wonder how much was paid for with plundered Jewish wealth."

In Bergen we hailed a taxicab and instructed the young lady driver to take us to Bergen-Belsen. When we arrived, I told her we wanted to go to the Jewish Cemetery. Not knowing where it was, she stopped the cab and asked a passerby, an elderly woman in her sixties, for the cemetery's exact address. The woman told us there were two. Which did we wish to visit, our driver asked. We said we didn't know, so she contacted her taxi office by cab-phone. We were disheartened when her office confirmed the existence of two different places. Upon hearing that we wanted the onetime concentration camp site, our driver took us to a place with beautifully kept grounds. Four workers, two men and two women, were working on the property, as sprinklers liberally watered the surrounding flowers and foliage.

Sholom walked first past the workers and into a somewhat circular, curved stone structure, in search of directions to the cemetery. In this building, however, there was but one rather large room, with panels containing museumlike exhibits and some twenty-five young and middle-aged tourists who were viewing the displays with intense interest. Expecting no help from them, Sholom next approached the workers, showed them the snapshot of Mother's monument, and asked them for directions. They replied that no cemetery there had such monuments and pointed to a door next to the main building, where a permanent caretaker resided.

The caretaker was a gray-haired man of about sixty-five. When Sholom showed him the photograph, the man replied that the grave was most likely in the "other cemetery." Our driver then took us to what appeared to be a military camp, where her employer was waiting for us in his cab. We followed him into the camp to what looked like an entrance gate of a cemetery. Assuming confidently that we were at the right place, we stepped out of the taxi, paid our driver, and asked her to return in forty-five minutes. As she drove off, her employer escorted us through a gate. On the other side were but three standing monuments—and none was Mother's.

We protested that there had to be more, but our escort, a resident of the area for forty-three years, insisted he knew of no others. Noting our anguish and disappointment, however, and sympathizing with our predicament, he offered to drive us, free of charge, to the British military headquarters within the camp. There, he consulted with an official and showed her our old snapshot. In clear British English, the official insisted that the grave was at the "other cemetery," where we had already met disappointment once.

With sinking hearts, we returned to the first cemetery and went directly to the caretaker's residence next to the museum. When the elderly gentleman saw us, however, he merely reiterated what he had said earlier. But when our escort showed the caretaker the photograph of Mother's monument, the elderly gentleman explained that the museum site was the site of the Bergen-Belsen concentration camp. When the British army took over the area in April 1945, he added, they encountered many thousands of unburied dead and thousands of others dying daily. They immediately set up new camps in the area of the present military camp and set up a cemetery within that compound, beyond where our escort had driven.

Heartened once again, we nevertheless found it hard to believe that not a trace remained even of a barracks of the onetime campsite. Cutting off the view of the once blood-soaked earth was a wall of tall evergreen trees, neatly maintained, forming a geometric complement to the rounded stone structure housing the museum and the caretaker's residence.

Riding back to the military camp, I was struck by the long rows of trees on both sides of the road linking the outskirts of Bergen to Bergen-Belsen. The two rows of trees formed a near-canopy, whose beauty contrasted rudely with the former death camp to which it led. Presumably, the Nazi authorities had considered it prudent to conceal even from their own faithful German supporters the full depth and extent of their crimes.

For the second time, our escort drove into the military camp, but this time he drove past the gate of the minuscule cemetery on our left. Not more than a block farther, on our right, was the entrance to the cemetery that had been set up by the British. At the entrance stood a monument that we knew, through snapshots and published photographs, to be the general monument to the victims of Bergen-Belsen. We were then sure we were in the right place at last.

We quickly proceeded to search for a monument shaped like the monument over Mother's grave in our photograph. We were amazed that the entire Bergen-Belsen cemetery—which contained the remains of thousands—seemed so small compared with even local cemeteries in the United States. It took us but a few minutes to discover that nowhere in the entire cemetery was there even one standing stone that resembled Mother's monument. In fact, more than one-half the graves had no markers at all and were entirely covered with ivylike foliage. Of the graves with a marker, perhaps half contained a flat stone with the engraved designation *Unbekannte Toter* (unknown dead person). I remembered that our photo showed a stone to the left of Mother's monument. If we could identify and locate it, we would know that Mother's grave would have to be immediately on the right side of it.

On the photo, the print was so tiny that neither Sholom nor I could make out the inscription, even with our glasses on. I asked our escort if he could make out the portion inscribed in Latin script. He couldn't—but he did identify a portion of the inscription in Polish and the names of Feldman and Herling on the stone. We imprinted those names firmly in our minds as we searched the cemetery further, now for the shape of the Feldman-Herling stone shown in our snapshot. Noting our intense anxiety and strength of determination, our escort asked Sholom, "Who are the young girls standing at the monument in the photo?" Sholom pointed to me and said, "The one on the right is she. The other is her sister." Our escort did not ask whose grave we were seeking, but he obviously understood and patiently helped us search for the grave. At last he found the only monument in the cemetery shaped like the Feldman-Herling monument in our snapshot—but the inscription was not the one we were seeking.

Now dejected, we were beginning to believe that the stone we had traveled so long and far to locate no longer existed. Gone as well, vanished into this desolate earth upon which we were standing, was any chance of finding Mother's remains.

Almost all the standing monuments in the cemetery were toward the far end of the grounds. From this general area, we were now plodding slowly down lane after lane of graves, with less than faint hope of seeing on one of the few flat stones the inscription of Mother's name. We felt almost certain that our long, expensive journey had been in vain—hopeless.

Moreover, we were beginning to feel pressured for time: it was now almost 3 P.M., and if we missed the last train from Celle back to Hannover scheduled to leave at 4:35, we would be unable to meet our plane back to the United States in Amsterdam. Already feeling frustrated and now under time constraints, we were forced to move rapidly. Our haste, we were certain, affected our search, as reading the inscriptions on the monuments became at times secondary to reading the time on our watches.

But how could we leave this awesome place without having located Mother's grave? We forced ourselves to pace slowly past one stone at a time, working our way in the direction of the front of the cemetery, determined on the one hand to read each and every inscription but, knowing we didn't have the time to read every inscription, subconsciously resigning ourselves on the other hand to the ultimate futility of our search.

Several long minutes later, I called out from where I was standing, near the left end of the front of the cemetery, "Sholom, come here." He rushed over to me and we looked down at the stone in front of us. Together we read the name of Rivkah—but not that of Rivkah Szachter.

We proceeded on in the front rows, moving toward the right. Casually we passed one particular headstone. It was flat like all the other headstones in that section so we didn't give it special attention at first. But then we looked again: on it were the names of Feldman and Herling! The next stone to the right had to be our stone. And as we took a careful look, there it was—a flat headstone with the engraving, "Miriam Rivkah bat [daughter of] Irah Szachter"—Mother's Hebrew name!

In life, Mother on several occasions had intuitions suggesting some degree of ESP. The thought now flashed through my mind: Was it perhaps her very spirit that had been drawing us closer and closer, never allowing us to give in to frustration, until at long last we had found her grave site? Sholom quickly took out a prayer book, and together we recited the prayer *El moleh rachamim* (Lord, full of compassion). We recited it inaudibly, because we were too overcome with emotion to recite it without our voices breaking. We remained there a few moments in deep meditation.

As we left the grave site, both Sholom and I experienced deeply emotional though conflicting feelings that we had been at a horror-filled place and at the same time at a most holy place. Just how and why the standing monuments in our snapshots were replaced with flat stones remained a mystery. Of far greater significance, however, was the fact that we had found Mother's grave.

Still, one question persisted and annoyed me. I was angry and indignant. How could it have come about that, in such a monstrous death camp where so many thousands of human beings were savagely annihilated, not even a trace remained of a barracks in which the victims were interned? Even a trace might have yielded mute testimony for posterity to the inhumanity inflicted by human beings against fellow human beings. Yet, I thought, there is but a cemetery of about two hundred graves. Further, of that small handful of graves, hardly more than half are identified. In these unmarked graves, and in those designated as *Unbekannte Toter,* must be the bones or ashes of thousands. Meanwhile, life goes on for the people who reside and work in the area, ignorant even of the cemetery's existence.

It is now forty-six years since I was liberated from Bergen-Belsen. Until the onset of the Holocaust, my few early childhood years might be compared to those of storybook tales of joy and happiness. Though the sequence of events that gradually led me from that blissful childhood into what might be likened to the maw of a satanic beast were shocking and frightening, the passage of time somehow mollified my conscious perception of the horrors I experienced and the colossal risks I had to dare if I was to have even the slightest chance of survival. Even at the moment of liberation, the macabre reality in which I had lived during some two thousand preceding days and nights, from my eighth year to my fourteenth, had become so commonplace, so benumbing, that I never experienced the desire to speak or write about that period of infinite nightmare.

On the one hand, the truth was so overwhelming to relate: any single incident was so entangled with details, how could I describe and communicate it fully and accurately? And if I could, who would want to read or hear so lengthy and complex a story? On the other hand, I feel even today a sense of shame, almost guilt, concerning my Holocaust years that I still find difficult to understand: to talk about that time requires that I lay bare my innermost sensitivities, yet the truth is so bizarre by any normal standards that I fear sounding incredible. In spite of these feelings, and perhaps because of them, I now feel compelled to tell my story.

In addition, forty-six years after liberation, the generation of survivors has thinned out and is growing older. Moreover, in recent years, a number of falsifiers of history have been vigorously attempting to "prove" that the tragedy never happened. Finally, I am deeply disappointed and angry that all traces of Bergen-Belsen have been erased. How thoughtless and insensitive to have removed every last vestige of evidence, so that future generations will find no visible or tangible reminders of this past.

For these reasons, I decided to tell my story to my children, to my grandchildren, to all of my family, and to all who desire to hear and know.

In doing so, I have referred to family members and friends, especially children, not by their formal names but rather by how those individuals were typically and affectionately addressed: for example, Ruchtcheleh rather than Rachel, Brucheleh rather than Bruche, Moisheleh or Moisheniu rather than Moishe, Yank'l rather than Yaakov. In addition, the spellings—or more accurately, the transliterations—of names correspond to the manner in which they were pronounced by Jews in pre–World War II central Poland. On the other hand, Hebrew words that are employed in the spoken Yiddish language are transliterated in accordance with their modern Sephardic Hebrew pronunciations as spoken today in the State of Israel. For example, *hachnasat orchim* is used rather than *hachnusas oirchim,* which was the Hebrew dialect of the Jews of central Poland. The names of cities, towns, and villages are presented either in their original spellings or as they appear on maps printed in English.

Because all our possessions were lost during the Holocaust, absolutely no photographs of the innumerable ones my family once owned exist today. I am therefore deeply indebted to my friend and townsman, the late

Simcha (Seymour) Weintraub, for some of the photographs included in this book. He emigrated to the United States only months before the outbreak of World War II and had in his possession many photographs from home, including two in this book that show members of my family: the photograph of Grandfather Nus'n Szachter and the group picture taken in Kraków in 1938 on the occasion of my uncle Moishe's wedding. The picture of Mother is an enlargement of a segment from that group photograph and happens to be the only surviving picture of Mother. The photograph of Mme Zofia Surowjecka standing in front of her house in Świętomarz was sent to me by her shortly before her death in 1961. The photographs of Sir Józef Surowjecki and Mme Surowjecka were given to me by Marysia Dekiel of Świętomarz.* The other photographs in this book were taken in Bergen-Belsen after our liberation in 1945.

Because I was so young when the events of my story took place, I needed assistance during the writing of this book from older townsmen and family members, who helped fill in many of the details I had forgotten and provided background information on the events of the time. I was extremely fortunate in being given that valuable input from my fellow townsmen Samuel (Shmiel) Weintraub and Morris (Moniek) Grossman; from my sisters, Mrs. Irene (Irka) Szachter Horn and Mrs. Rachel (Rachela) Szachter Eisenberg; and from my cousin, Mrs. Ruth (Rivtche) Ehrlich Turek. To each of them I wish to express my gratitude.

Mr. Weintraub, a lifelong friend of my family, possesses a knowledge of my ancestry that goes back two or perhaps three generations before I was born. He vividly recalls the wedding of my parents in 1923. In addition, he was able to provide details on the history of Jewish life in our hometown of Bodzentyn before and during World War II; and he is perhaps the only Jew alive who witnessed the liquidation of our hometown. He also survived all three camps in which we were interned: the Starachowice labor camp, and the death camps of Auschwitz and Bergen-Belsen.

Mr. Grossman recalls many details of Jewish social life in Bodzentyn shortly before and during the war because he was in his later teenage years then. He was in Bodzentyn from the time after my family left the city until shortly before its liquidation. Mr. Grossman also experienced the liquidation of Starachowice, as well as the life of an internee in the labor camp there.

My sisters Irka and Rachela and my cousin Rivtche shared most of my

---

*The Surowjeckis are referred to as Sir and Mme rather than Mr. and Mrs. because their Polish equivalents, Pan and Pani, connote greater respect and distance.

experiences in Bodzentyn before and during the war, as well as in Star-achowice, Auschwitz, and Bergen-Belsen. Their recollections of family members as well as family events filled in numerous gaps in my own recollections. Similarly, our commonly shared experiences during the war and in our detention in the three camps reinforced mutually recalled events and reactions. In addition, however, my sisters and cousin recalled individual episodes that were part of those overall experiences, but that were not shared by all of us, since we were not always together; on the contrary, there were hours during the day, and at times weeks or even months, when one or more of us were separated from the others. All these recollections were incorporated into my story.

Gizela Fudem of Wrocław, Poland, whom I have known since our time together in Bergen-Belsen, put me in contact with Artemiusz Wołczyk of Bodzentyn. He provided me with archival material that documented my family ancestry from 1855. Mr. Wołczyk also furnished a map of Bodzentyn, which has been adapted for this book to show the town during the period I discuss.

I would be remiss if I did not acknowledge Ms. Beth Anderson, who typed and carefully read the first draft of this text and offered numerous helpful suggestions, and Mary D. Teal of the Music Department of Eastern Michigan University, for having read the second draft and for her very solicitous recommendations. I also wish to thank the staff of the University of Massachusetts Press for the work they have done in producing this book, and especially Ms. Brenda Hanning, who copyedited the manuscript.

Last, I gratefully acknowledge the task undertaken and completed by my husband, Sholom Kalib of the Music Department of Eastern Michigan University, and Ken Wachsberger, of the English Department of Eastern Michigan University. It was through Sholom's initiative and urging that this story was reconstructed. He began by interviewing me extensively; then he and I interviewed my sisters and cousin and Messrs. Weintraub and Grossman. Following these interviews, Sholom organized the myriad facts and details and arranged them into this narrative, and thus wrote my story in my name. Ken rewrote the book in its present form. I am deeply grateful for his great talent, expertise, and dedication.

Goldie (Golda)* Szachter Kalib

---

*In Poland my name was Golda. In the United States I adopted the anglicized name of Goldie.

I

MY EARLY CHILDHOOD
IN BODZENTYN

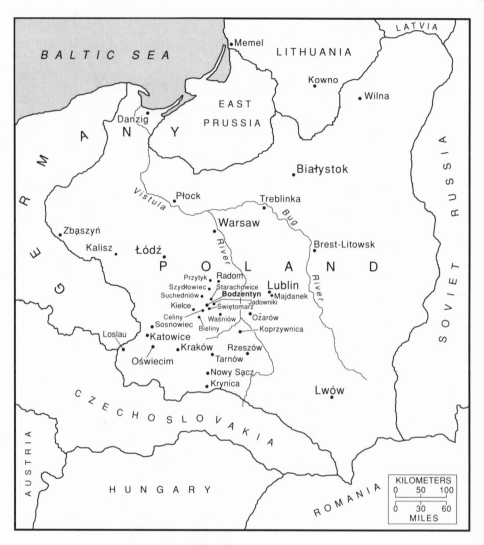

Poland, 1919–1939

1

My Hometown of Bodzentyn

I WAS BORN in a small town in Poland called Bodzentyn on December 15, 1931, the youngest of five children born to Y'chiel and Miryam Rivkah Szachter. The years of my early childhood were filled with the joy and delight that only a young child can fully experience. I was fortunate to have had the love and attention that only a youngest child can receive from parents and older siblings, grandparents, aunts, uncles, cousins, and friends. It was no detriment to my happy childhood, I must say, to have been born to the wealthiest family in town. For one who always loved nature and the outdoors, I had the wonderful luck of being raised in a rural area where splendid meadows, fields, and forests were but a short walk from our home and within only short traveling distances from our town. These are but a few of the many sources, great and small, of cherished joys and thrills that were mine in the first seven years, eight months, and two weeks of my life. They form the starkest of contrasts imaginable to the events that were to take place in the years that followed my early childhood in Bodzentyn.

Bodzentyn is located some twenty-eight kilometers northeast of Kielce and a slightly shorter distance southwest of Starachowice, almost the midpoint of an imaginary, slightly curved diagonal line connecting those two larger Polish cities. It is situated in a valley at the foot of picturesque Miejska Góra, or City Mountain. As a relatively large small town of approximately four thousand inhabitants, surrounded by dozens of farms and villages, Bodzentyn conveyed a rural atmosphere. Its inhabitants were in the main engaged in enterprises that serviced the needs of the surrounding communities, bringing into town the farmers and villagers who came to buy or sell commodities. The buildings in town were essentially shingle-roofed and wooden, with a small number of brick structures. Most were single-story buildings, and none stood higher than two stories. Cobblestone lined the streets of our little town, except for a number of muddy thoroughfares. Horses and horse-led buggies and wagons amply satisfied all local transportation needs.

I am told that a motorized bus scheduled to provide transportation from Bodzentyn to Kielce was seen in town for the first time in 1928. The event seemed so momentous that practically the entire population turned out at 5 A.M. to witness it. As the story goes, the driver revolved the crank again and again, each time more vigorously in an ever more desperate attempt to charge the motor. All his efforts, however, proved futile, as the impatient crowd grew increasingly more skeptical and cynical of the widely heralded virtues of the modern machine and its alleged superiority over the timeless, tried and tested horse and buggy. Finally he did succeed in revolving the crank and was able to start the bus. By then, however, the crowd had dispersed. No doubt, many of the townspeople were convinced that they never should have entertained the thought of replacing the horse and buggy in the first place. Except for buses going to Kielce, I do not recall ever seeing an automobile or bus in our town.

As in most towns in Eastern Europe, the Jewish population of Bodzentyn formed a community within a community. Yiddish was our mother tongue, although by the early 1930s the Polish language was beginning to rival Yiddish within the social parlance of the younger generation. While they still spoke Yiddish to parents and siblings, they now mixed Polish into conversations with Jewish friends and peers. Still, Yiddish, together with our ethnic and religious culture and our own characteristic modes of life, brought us together as a group. At the same time, however, they tended to set our group apart from the native non-Jewish host community. This separation not infrequently aroused in the native inhabitants feelings of suspicion, competition, unfriendliness, and at times hostility toward us, which in turn led more than occasionally to violence in many Jewish communities in Poland. Of the total population of four thousand, the Jewish population of Bodzentyn numbered around fourteen hundred, about three hundred Jewish families. Jewish residences tended to gravitate toward the center of town, while the non-Jewish Polish inhabitants resided primarily, but not exclusively, on the fringe areas of the city. Most residences, both Jewish and non-Jewish, were in the rear area of a shop or store that occupied the front section of a dwelling facing the street.

Jewish community life in Bodzentyn—called Bazh'tshin in Yiddish— was typical of hundreds, perhaps thousands, of Jewish towns in Eastern Europe. Like all Eastern European Jewish communities, Bodzentyn had a Jewish communal organization, elected once every two years, that consisted of a head, a secretary, and an administrative committee of six or seven, whose charge it was to tend to all Jewish communal needs. Its primary functions included providing personnel to maintain the city synagogue, the city ritual bathhouse (the *Mikvah*), and various aspects of Jewish education; coordinating numerous types of assistance to the needy in the community; and arranging for burials and cemetery maintenance by the societal group for the burial of the dead (the *Chevra Kadisha*). Its functions even included such weighty responsibilities as representing the Jewish community at the offices of the city police and mayor, when circumstances demanded.

Also like all Eastern European Jewish communities, Bodzentyn had relatively few Jewish families that were affluent or even very comfortable financially. For most, life was difficult. Children's clothes were often made considerably larger and wider than a proper fit required, for instance, so children could grow into, rather than grow out of, them. Of course all clothing, even shoes, were hand-me-downs for most families. Yet life was reasonably happy. All Jews, as a rule, knew each other through frequent contact. As a result, each Jew shared a certain closeness, warmth, sympathy, and understanding for the concerns and joys—whether financial or ethnic-religious—of all other Jews.

In my own family, my two grandfathers were both Szachters. Moreover, both stemmed from Shmiel Szachter, my maternal great great grandfather and my paternal great grandfather, who amassed much property and wealth that was passed down in parts as inheritances to his children and grandchildren. The youngest of his three sons was my paternal grandfather, Meier Szachter. Meier married Malke Zweigenbaum, my paternal grandmother, whom I never knew inasmuch as she passed away in 1933 when I was hardly two years old. I can recall only Grandfather Meier's second wife and her one younger sister. Meier and Malke had only one child, my father, Y'chiel Szachter, who was born in 1900.

My mother, Miryam Rivkah Szachter, was descended from Great great grandfather Shmiel Szachter through his oldest son Alter, my maternal great grandfather. Father and Mother were therefore first cousins once removed before marriage. Alter and his wife, Mandje Zucker, had one son and three daughters. Their one son was my maternal grandfather, Nus'n Szachter, Father's first cousin. Grandfather Nus'n married my grandmother, Irka Greenbaum. Grandmother Irka's father was the "Bazh't-shiner Rebbe" (town rabbi of Bodzentyn) until his death in 1906. A lineage such as this was, incidentally, viewed as extremely prestigious in Eastern Europe.

Mother was born in 1902, the second of ten children born to Grandfather Nus'n and Grandmother Irka. The others were: Aunts Gitteleh (b. ca. 1900), Feigeleh (b. 1904), Brucheleh (b. ca. 1906), and Dineleh (b. ca. 1908), Uncle Moishe (b. ca. 1910), Uncle Froyim (b. ca. 1912), Aunt Pereleh (b. ca. 1914), Uncle Leib'l (b. 1916), and Uncle Yank'l (b. 1919). Aunt Pereleh died in early childhood when Uncle Yank'l was hardly more than a year old, around 1920. Grandmother Irka died from complications in an eleventh pregnancy. Grandfather Nus'n remarried, but only for a short period of time. Because his second wife seemed unable to get along with his children, Grandfather decided to annul the marriage. He never remarried.

In 1923, my parents were married. As a result, Father's first cousin, Grandfather Nus'n, became his father-in-law as well. In all, my parents had five children: my brother Moishe (b. 1925), my sister Irka (b. 1927; the first child to be named after our maternal grandmother), my brother Shloime (b. 1928), my sister Rachela (b. 1929), and me, Golda (b. 1931). I am told that when Mother was pregnant with me physicians advised her to undergo an abortion, claiming that if she did not the pregnancy could place her health in jeopardy. At the time, a famous rabbi lived in the town of Ożarów, some fifty-five kilometers southeast of Bodzentyn. Mother, who had great faith in the judgment of the venerated *Ozharuver Rebbe* (rabbi from Ożarów), and who was unhappy at the thought of abortion, decided to undertake the journey there to seek his advice. Heeding his counsel, Mother sustained the pregnancy and I was born with no detriment to her health.

Jewish communal life was decidedly marked by historical religious values and mores, although to a notably lesser degree than had been the case before World War I. It used to be said that the average Eastern European Jew owned two pairs of prayer phylacteries (*T'filin*) and one pair of trousers. By the 1930s, however, concerns of livelihood and material well-being had come to equal in priority the average Jew's preoccupation with religious matters.

The centuries-old traditions and obligations as set forth in the Bible still largely controlled every aspect of daily life for all age groups within the Jewish community of Bodzentyn. The penetration of modernity, however, could be observed in a number of ways, not least of which was by the increasing number of men's faces with trimmed and shorter beards or no beards at all. Another sign of change was the open, socially accepted strolling of young Jewish men and women, especially on Sabbath and holy day afternoons and evenings, and through a general slackening of involvement on their part in traditional religious practices.

Shmiel Weintraub was an intimate boyhood friend of my mother's brothers, Moishe, who was a year or so older than Shmiel, and Froyim, who was a year or so younger. Common ages and interests brought them into each other's houses on a near-daily basis: at times they would come together at Grandfather Nus'n's residence quarters, and at other times they would come together at the yard goods store-residence of Shmiel's father, Hersh'l Weintraub, on the north side of Langiewicza Street. While it was already becoming the norm for young Jewish men to engage in religious study after (rather than before) morning services, Shmiel remembers how his mother and my own Grandmother Irka would hustle the boys out of the house in the very early premorning hours and rush them on to the synagogue for religious study. There, they immersed themselves in the sacred literature from 4 A.M. until almost 8 A.M., at which time they would pause, munch on some bagels brought from home, and be ready to join in the second (daily morning) service, commencing at the synagogue at 8 A.M.

Shmiel fondly recalls an incident that occurred in 1927 when, as a lad of sixteen, he was strolling with a young lady along a path leading outside Bodzentyn. The two young adolescents felt reasonably sure that the chances of being seen walking together would be slim indeed. To their amazement, who happened to pass by but the wife of Rabbi Hirsh Shwartz, spiritual head of the community. She stood silently, observing them critically from head to toe. Then, without uttering a single word, she proceeded on her way. Two days later, young Shmiel happened to be at the rabbi's home for a group study session. He was fantasizing that perhaps Rabbi Shwartz may not have been told of his venturesome stroll of the day before last. Suddenly he noticed the rabbi looking toward him, and he heard the rabbi wryly remark: "I hear, Mr. Weintraub, that you have already become quite a young gentleman!"

This respectful defiance of hallowed traditions was beginning to surface in part as a reaction against the continued persecution of Eastern European Jews and in part, after Poland gained its independence from czarist Russia following World War I, because of the new exposure of young Jewish minds to secular culture and public education. These factors combined made themselves felt in the rise of Zionism, in its various shades, as a form of secular political organization, for political Zionism gave young Jews hope of one day living free in their own land. Particularly in the wake of the Kishinev Pogrom in 1903, Jews the world over began thinking more seriously than ever of creating a Jewish homeland in the ancient Jewish land of Palestine. That was, after all, the biblical promised land of our patriarchs Abraham, Isaac, and Jacob, and the land toward which Jews had faced in prayer three times daily and to which they had dreamed of returning, ever since their exile at the hands of the Romans in the year 70 C.E.

With that dream in mind, Shmiel Weintraub, Uncle Moishe, and a friend, Shloime Zailes, founded the local branch of the Mizrachi (Religious Zionist) Party in Bodzentyn. To the very pious, political Zionism was considered blasphemous. Should the truly faithful not wait patiently until the Holy One sends his Messiah to deliver and lead us into the Promised Land, as had been foretold in Jewish sacred scriptures? It was therefore no surprise that Shmiel's mother was heartbroken when one day she happened to be passing a group of teenage Jewish men, and she saw and heard her son standing in the front, extolling enthusiastically the virtues of Theodor Herzl, founder of the Zionist Movement, and Chayim Nachman Bialik, poet laureate of the modern, revived secularist Hebrew language. Vexed and disillusioned, and considering her son lost to all that is sacred to pious Jews, she hurried home to commence the traditional seven-day period of mourning, known as *Shivah*, that follows the burial of an immediate member of one's family. Several oldsters of the community later demanded, "Who gave the youngsters permission to hold meetings and, mind you, unsupervised discussions and political rallies? Lord in Heaven, what is happening to our Jewish youth?" And so they ranted on, even as the more assimilated Jews of the community formed local branches of all other major Zionist parties in Bodzentyn as well.

With so many coreligionists aligning themselves with one Zionist party or another, the most pious in the community eventually felt the need to organize themselves politically as well. Thus the Agudat Yisrael Party was founded on a religious non-Zionist platform, and naturally claimed among its members the most religiously observant Jews in town, including Uncle Froyim.

It must be noted that argumentation and debate, in general, formed a popular recreational exercise for Bodzentyn Jews on issues of far lesser significance than Zionism constituted for Eastern European Jews. Many among the younger generation were educated in secular as well as Jewish subjects. Most of the older generation, however, owned few books besides the basic sacred volumes of the average religiously observant Jew, such as a *Siddur* (prayer book), a *Machzor* (holiday prayer book), and a *Chumash* (the Pentateuch), plus a few volumes of the *Talmud* (Rabbinic-Judaic Law). The one Jewish library in town, established in the early 1920s by

Y'chiel Mandelkern, a resident of Bodzentyn and an adherent of the local leftist Labor Zionist party, housed a few hundred volumes of a secularist Jewish nature. These volumes, however, were viewed as assimilationist, if not antireligious, and were shunned by the more religiously observant factions in the community. As a result, there was scanty exposure to nonsacred subjects. Nonetheless, hairsplitting, often heated controversies were always an enjoyable diversionary activity even if based on limited knowledge and even when the subject seemed hardly worth arguing about. Moreover, a group of no more than five or six persons could and did at times constitute a political party in Bodzentyn. Thus political groups in Bodzentyn included members of parties whose views ranged from the strongly political left to the staunchly political right. The party of the left, known as the leftist Labor Zionists (Linke Poiale Tziyon), envisioned a socialistic Marxist-style program for a future Jewish state in Palestine; whereas the party of the right, the militant Revisionist party (Betar), envisioned and advocated as its primary tenet a Jewish state in Palestine, consisting of both the East and the West banks of the Jordan River. This is the party that offered the greatest inspiration for many of Bodzentyn's younger generation who believed salvation would come not from prayer and messianic redemption but from one's own unequivocal, assertive, and concerted action. This attitude was shared by Uncle Leib'l as he rebelled against much of traditional religious practice. He did, however, desist from openly offending his father and older brothers, in actions or in words.

All parties held regular meetings that were advantageous to both the ideological as well as the social needs of the community, especially its younger members. In these meetings, members held discussions, sang songs, and danced to the music of the young Zionist dream. The revisionist Betar group even practiced the art of self-defense. All groups would occasionally prepare dramatized presentations on subjects of Jewish interest. However, due to low membership, groups would not infrequently be lacking in talented performers. In such cases, party rivalries and ideological differences were generally overlooked in favor of communal camaraderie, and members of rival organizations gladly made their talents available to the amateur theatrical endeavors of their peers.

The town of Bodzentyn during my time was structured around Langiewicza Street, which served as the central axis of town. This main street connected two main plazas, which were located at eastern and western ends of the street. The large western plaza was known as the Upper Plaza.

The smaller eastern plaza was known as the Lower Plaza, or Żwirki Plaza. Many side streets branched off from each of these three central localities. Small houses lining both sides of the streets coming into Langiewicza Street were owned and occupied primarily but not exclusively by non-Jewish Poles. For instance, the synagogue and the Jewish library were on one of these streets. Other side streets contained the *Mikvah*, which was attended and used regularly by most of the Jewish community, and the three-room office of the elected executors of the Jewish Community Association.

In the Upper Plaza, among the many residences and shops, were the church, the one apothecary in town, Bodzentyn's fire station, the "People's House" cinema, and the one lower-grades elementary school of the city. Continuing west and somewhat southward along a little street branching off the western plaza for about a kilometer, one passed by mostly empty lots. There were, however, the small residence and modest lumber business of one Avruhom Silberberg on one corner and, at approximately the end of that kilometer, the home-studio of the town photographer. Just beyond the home-studio was a spacious area of property owned by the town church. On this property were beautifully maintained grounds that gradually sloped downhill, leading to the remains of a fifteenth-century castle, which was said to date back to the period of King Casimir the Great. Continuing beyond the castle ruins, past a descending small hill and all the way to the western extremity of the city, lay the idyllic, picturesque Psarka River.

The mainstream of Jewish community life centered within the two plazas and Langiewicza Street. Along the perimeters of the two plazas and lining both sides of the main street were residences and combination residence-shops and residence-stores. Because Bodzentyn was a town that essentially serviced nearby farmers and villagers, most people in Bodzentyn were craftsmen, artisans, and tradesmen. Thus the principal livelihood enterprises included grocery stores and bakeries; stores and smitheries for ironware and tinware, farm tools and implements; and general notions stores for needles, yarns, and other sundry items. Yard goods stores provided material for tailors and dressmakers, who made fitted and ready-made clothes of all types, styles, and price ranges for both men and women. Other specialists made hats, caps, and wigs, as well as the tops of shoes and the soles and heels of shoes. Lumber dealers sold to carpenters and cabinetmakers, wheel makers, and wooden barrel and wooden washtub makers. In addition, there were one mill, lime stores, dealers in feathers, several taverns and tavern-restaurants, and more.

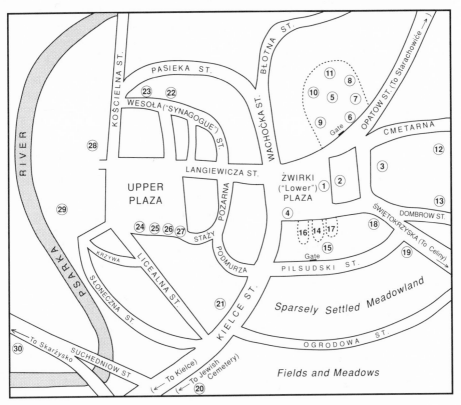

Pre-World War Two Map of Bodzentyn

KEY:

1. Well
2. Upper Grade School
3. Church Remains
4. Bus Stop
5. Courtyard of Chiel Szachter Residence
6. Nus'n and Reiz'l Perl Residence
7. Alter Szachter Residence-Store
8. Mendel "Kapushnik" Residence
9. Chiel Szachter Residence and Grandfather Meier's Bakery-Residence
10. Chiel Szachter's Storage House
11. Grandfather Meier's Garden
12. Cemetery
13. Post Office
14. Grandfather Nus'n's Estate
15. Mill
16. Jakubowski Estate
17. Sewerynski Tavern
18. Library
19. Police Station
20. Jewish Cemetery
21. Mikva (Jewish Ritual Bathhouse)
22. Synagogue and Bet Midrash
23. Mandelkern Jewish Library
24. Lower Grade School
25. Cinema ("People's House")
26. Fire Station
27. Apothecary
28. Church
29. Castle Remains
30. Town Hall

In the two confectioneries, newspapers as well as soft drinks, chocolates and other candies, and ice cream were sold up front, while in the rear young people came to sit down and socialize. Typically, they would indulge in a snack or perhaps a more luxurious "bite," such as duck or goose. Often they would play cards and even gamble. One of these confectioneries was owned by the "blind Chantche." It was located about midway along the north side of Langiewicza Street, in between though not adjacent to Hersh'l Weintraub's yard goods store-residence and the grocery-grains store-residence of our friends Y'chiel Grossman and his family.

Of the many occupations and enterprises in town, Jewish people owned the one mill and stores for ironwares, farm tools, and farm implements. In addition, Jews constituted nearly all hat and cap makers and tailors for fitted as well as ready-made clothes, nearly all the shoemakers for the upper parts of shoes, and well over half the grocery and grains stores. Jews as well as non-Jewish Poles were engaged in the other enterprises that serviced the town and surrounding areas.

The entrances to the courtyards of my own immediate family and Grandfather Nus'n's estate were located in Żwirki Plaza.

2

Our Home

Żwirki Plaza was considerably smaller than the Upper Plaza but it was a very broad area nonetheless. Walking along the western half of the Plaza, from Langiewicza Street, one encountered a street branching off to the south that was known as Kielce Street, because it served as the bus route as well as the horse and buggy route from Bodzentyn to Kielce. On the corner was the bus stop, along with the residence-shop of a Jewish shoemaker and the elegant Polish Bielawski tavern-restaurant. On the opposite corner stood what was by Bodzentyn's standards a rather large and clean-looking bookstore. Further down Kielce Street stood a Jewish butcher shop, the ritual bathhouse, and the office of the one physician in town, a Dr. Pabian, plus more residences and shops, most of which were Jewish-owned. Still further down the road was the Bodzentyn Jewish cemetery.

Several small streets branched off on the other side, northward from Żwirki Plaza. On one, Świętokrzysha Street, stood the police station for Bodzentyn's four-officer police force, and some newer brick dwellings, a number of which had lovely kept balconies, where several schoolteachers resided.

Along other streets, strolling formed a popular and widely practiced, leisurely diversion. In between the streets branching off from the eastern and western segments of Żwirki Plaza and stretching toward the southern fringe areas of Bodzentyn stood the large property belonging to Grandfather Nus'n.

Within the northern sector of Żwirki Plaza stood a well from which the inhabitants drew their water. They would come with one or two empty buckets, attach one bucket to a hook at the end of a long thick rope or chain, and lower it into the well by cranking a handle on the side of the well; when the bucket was filled with water, they would draw it up by cranking the handle again until the bucket was within reach, then remove it, and repeat the procedure. I used to delight in going to the well with a play bucket and then cranking it up and down to draw water for fun. The average family would store its water in large wooden barrels. Our family, as well as a few other more affluent families in town, employed the services of a professional water carrier, who carried two buckets at a time, hung over each end of a wooden yoke stretched across his shoulders, into our house. He then poured the water into a large, handsome porcelain barrel in our kitchen. Sometimes a wooden barrel would be left in back of our house to catch rainwater that we used for washing our hair. Near the well, along the eastern perimeter of Żwirki Plaza stood the public school building for the upper elementary grades.

Opposite the residence and property of Grandfather Nus'n, along the northern sector of the Żwirki Plaza, was a gate that led into our courtyard. Adjacent to the gate to the east was a small one-room house, which was occupied by a tinsmith named Nus'n Perl, and his wife, Father's first cousin, Reiz'l Szachter, who was known in town as Reiz'l "Shlyoch" ("Sloppy" Reiz'l). Nus'n and Reiz'l were very poor, in no small part because they had twelve children. Further, their house was always dirty because the one big room was over a hard dirt floor. The house, which had entrances from Żwirki Plaza as well as from the courtyard, served as a residence-lime store which Reiz'l had inherited from her father. After she and Nus'n were married, she continued to sell lime, which littered the entire black dirt floor. In the middle of the room, Nus'n repaired items made of tin, so that part of the floor was cluttered with tools, tin scraps, and a number of pots and pans in various stages of repair.

In front of the little house, Reiz'l sat and made wigs for the more pious women of the community. Since Jewish religious tradition prohibits a married woman from displaying her natural hair, wigs were a needed commodity for religiously observant wives, although many simply covered their heads with a tied kerchief or babushka. Hence one would see wigs placed over several dummy heads in the front of their dwelling, in addition to clusters of stray hairs on the dirt floor lying amid the lime and tin scraps. It was said that Reiz'l would continually wear her dirty apron until it became stiffened from accumulated grime, at which point she would turn it over and begin using the soft "grimeless" side of the same garment. Thus the household of Reiz'l "Shlyoch" fell considerably short of what one would reasonably describe as tidy, and her twelve children fared more or less as best they could on their own from morning until evening, practically free from parental supervision.

Adjacent to Nus'n and Reiz'l's house to the east and north was the small residence-grocery store of Alter Szachter, a distant relative of our family. His house also had entrances from Żwirki Plaza and from the courtyard, and it was slightly larger. Alter was married and had two daughters, Golda and Shprintzeleh, and two sons, Leib'l and Yoine.

Still further north inside the courtyard was the modest home of Mendel Szachter. To the townsfolk, he was known as Mendel "Kapushnik" ("Cabbagehead") because of his obtuseness. He was married and had two teenage daughters. Mendel sold dairy products from his little home in our courtyard, although there was no store area as such in his house. Indeed, he struggled to eke out a livelihood.

The courtyard was a spacious area. On the western side, opposite the houses of Nus'n and Reiz'l, Alter, and Mendel, were two family-owned buildings: the two-story house that my immediate family shared with Grandfather Meier and, to the north, a large building which was originally intended as a new residence for us. It remained unfinished, however, presumably because Father occasionally considered emigration from Poland. Instead, the building was used to store logs for our heating and cooking needs. We also stored boxes of vegetables and fruits, especially apples, jars of fruit preserves, and barrels of wine. In between the structures on the east and west was a large area where children played. Toward the far north end of the courtyard one could see little toilet houses or booths, and still farther back was Grandfather Meier's lovely fenced-in garden, where he cultivated flowers, vegetables, and fruits. We children were never allowed to trespass in the garden, but hardly a day passed when I did not manage to get in to smell the plants, pluck a leaf, or pick a flower.

Our house was the only two-story building in the courtyard, and one of the relatively few two-story structures in Bodzentyn. Grandfather Meier had inherited it upon the death of his father; our family had lived there from the time of my parents' marriage in 1923. Grandfather Meier lived in the rear of the first floor with his second wife and her sister. In the front, facing Żwirki Plaza, was his bakery store. Separate entrances led into his store and his residence.

Inside the doorway to the left of his front entrance was a stairway that led up to a second-floor landing. A kerosene lamp at the top of the stairway shed light on the landing. Walking right a few feet along this landing led to our living area. A double door was locked from the inside by two large brass bars. Upon entering through the opened doors, one stood in front of a large hall, the first of four square or rectangular main rooms on our floor. During the fall holiday of *Sukkot* (Feast of Taberna-cles), this hall area was converted into a *Sukkah*, the traditional festival hut for this holiday, by pulling a string, which caused part of the ceiling and roof to come open. At the far end of the hall stood a door leading into a large storage room.

On the left side of the hall stood a ladder leading to the attic. Although I never went up into it, I know that chickens and geese were often raised up there, to be ritually slaughtered when they were fattened sufficiently to yield substantial amounts of schmaltz. The schmaltz was then prepared and used in the cooking, frying, and baking of various meat dishes. Also stored in the attic were small amounts of wood, which had been sawed and chopped into small pieces for use in our kitchen stove.

To the right of the ladder was a door that led into our kitchen. The first feature one noticed in it was the light-colored, unfinished wooden floor. This type of floor was a distinguishing feature of a more affluent house, since by far most houses in Bodzentyn had only hard dirt floors. In the center of the kitchen stood a large wooden table and chairs.

In the near left corner from the door stood a stool, with a wooden tub set on it for dishwashing. Slightly farther along that far left wall were, first, a small picniclike table with attached benches on each side, that was frequently "my" table, and toward the center of the wall, a large wide window that looked out northward into our courtyard. A concrete sill projecting from the bottom of the window on the outside held a couple of wooden flower pots.

Along the wall opposite the door stood a strikingly beautiful, lacquered banana-colored credenza, in which our finest china was displayed. For years, Mother had dreamed of having just such an exquisite piece of furniture in that exact place in the kitchen. One day, upon arriving home from one of our summer vacations, she was thrilled to enter the house and behold this object of her imagination actually standing there in our kitchen. While we were away on vacation, Father had arranged for it to be constructed, finished, and delivered. In the two corners of the wall adja-cent to the credenza and opposite the window were the beautiful porcelain barrel that stored our water and our kitchen stove.

A door in the middle of that wall led to the large wide room where my brothers and sisters slept. This room was partitioned in the middle by a beautiful Spanish screenlike movable wall that had been specially con-structed for us by a cabinetmaker. The boys occupied the eastern half; the girls occupied the western half. We could get from one side to the other by walking around either side of the movable wall.

In the northeastern corner, left from the door to the kitchen, was a couch that was layered underneath with bedding and that opened into a double bed for Moishe and Shloime. At the western end of the room was the double bed shared by Irka and Rachela. Along the southern wall across from the door, on each side of the partition, were one desk and one kerosene table lamp. In the middle of that same wall was the door that led to our parlor room, which was the main room of our house.

The parlor room was distinguished by a heavily polished, rich-looking coral red varnished floor. In the center of this large square room, under a beautiful hanging kerosene lamp fixture, stood a large table and chairs over an exquisite reddish Persian rug. Here our family dined for our Sabbath and holy day meals as well as on special occasions when we had company.

At night, I slept in this room with my parents. Our beds were all against the wall to the far left of the door. Mine was actually a made-over cradle. Toward the middle of the wall were the two single beds used by Mother and Father. Their beds were covered with luxurious green velvet bedspreads and were separated by a nightstand. Above Mother's bed hung a framed portrait that was taken of her when she was approximately nineteen. I would often like to come out of my bed and hop into Mother's bed, which was closest to mine, and lie or sleep with her. In the corner beside Father's bed was our grandfather clock, above which sat a doll belonging to Irka.

Directly across from my bed, in the northwestern corner of the room, were a shelved linen cabinet, on top of which sat a radio with large cloth-covered speakers, and a tall, finished closet, in which we stored our long-garments wardrobe. I used to delight in rummaging through the closet, looking for Mother's old, out-of-style, fancy silk dresses, blouses, and silk shoes. I loved playing dress-up in them, and at times Rachela would join me. Rachela would take out Mother's silver mesh purse from its drawer and our playful imaginations soared as we acted out the grown-up roles of exquisitely dressed, fashionable society ladies.

Further south along this same wall was a tall, ceramic heating stove that reached from the floor all the way up to the ceiling. A heating stove of this size, style, and beauty was owned only by the few most affluent families in town. The stove was covered with four-inch-square white tiles, and it had two adjoining ornamental, lace-designed chromium doors that opened at the bottom of the front of the stove. An additional rough iron door on the inside received large chunks of coal and pieces of wood. The stove also had an opening slightly above its center where food could be warmed. The coal burned very slowly, allowing the heat to radiate for many hours, thus making this stove our primary source of heat during the winter.

In the middle of the southern wall opposite the parlor door was a French double door that led onto our outdoor balcony. This double door was flanked on each side by two windows, each of which was covered with elegant, hanging lace curtains. The balcony itself was closed in by vertical black wrought-iron bars and a railing.

When I stood on the balcony, I could look down into the center of Żwirki Plaza and over to the southern side of the plaza where Grandfather Nus'n's property was located, and to the surrounding environs. Across the horizon, I could see the mountains rising in the distance. In the summer, boxes of flowers were lined along the bottom of the balcony, interspersed with two or three boxes of chives. We used to love to pull out a bunch of chives, cut them into pieces, spread the pieces over a slice of bread and butter, and indulge in the savory delicacy.

It is within this setting and background that my wonderful early childhood years took place. Many were the moments, experiences, and events which made up those unforgettable years.

3

Joys of Early Childhood

PERHAPS the most lively event in Bodzentyn was the weekly market day, referred to in Yiddish as the *Yarid*. Early each Monday morning, nearby farmers would come into Żwirki Plaza and set up their produce on stands around the well. They would bring such livestock as cows, horses, chickens, and, less often, geese or ducks. In addition, they brought a wide variety of farm products, including eggs, butter, cheese, and sour cream, grains, vegetables such as carrots and lettuce, and berries of all kinds.

At the marketplace Jews would set up stalls, especially for such items as snaps, brushes, needles, and yarns. People would buy milk warm, directly from the cow, and then drink a cupful right then and there. It tasted marvelous. Before purchasing a chicken, goose, or duck, women would routinely pick up one at a time and blow the feathers around the buttocks area, examining and comparing the depth of fat on the fowl being considered. They naturally sought the very fattest in order to acquire through their purchase the greatest potential amount of schmaltz in the process.

The hustling and milling about and the bargaining were very lively and noisy, and continued through most of the day. After having earned well from the day's market, peasants would then shop at the local stores and enterprises. Toward evening, as the market pace gradually decelerated and the Plaza slowly emptied itself of produce and customers, the peasants closed their stalls and left town for their home farms. A number of them, however, remained in town in order to visit the taverns, especially the Sewerynski tavern next door to Grandfather Nus'n's property. There they would drink themselves drunk. Jews would make sure to be in their homes, locked in securely behind closed doors as soon as the day's market activities were through. For it was a common occurrence for drunken peasants to come out of the taverns and become ensnared in violent quarrels, fisticuffs, and general mauling before leaving town for the day. Once, after having come home, I walked out on our balcony as the sun was setting and began leisurely surveying the Plaza. Suddenly, there in the market area, I saw farmers fighting, knifing and stabbing one another, and I actually saw blood flowing from their wounds. Only after completely exhausting one another did they leave.

I remember fondly the Polish woman Zbroska, who would come twice each week, Tuesday and Thursday, to clean our house. She was a friendly, somewhat stout middle-aged woman with light brown hair and eyes. I admired how she would get down on her hands and knees and, with soapy water and a scrub brush, clean our kitchen floor so thoroughly that the wood appeared pure white and newly cut. On Thursday, she would take home most of our light, personal laundry and bring it back Friday, washed and ironed.

One day a month, however, was set aside for our heavy laundry. On the preceding day, Zbroska would come to our house, take a large, round wooden washtub made of strips of wood that were connected at the top by a circular metal strip, and place the tub on two chairs in the middle of our kitchen. She would then pour water from our porcelain barrel into two large pots, heat the pots on our stove, then pour the heated water, together with a few small chips of laundry bar soap, into the wooden tub, and allow our clothes and linens to soak overnight. The next morning, Zbroska would come again and place a washboard into the tub, across which she would rub and scrub the soiled spots on our wash. Much of our dirtier laundry, such as dish towels, was boiled in very large tin pots over our kitchen stove. When the wash was ready to be rinsed, Zbroska would bundle together as many pieces as she could into a single bedsheet by pulling together and tying the diagonal corners of first one side of the sheet and then the other. Next, she would place the tied bundle over her back and carry it all the way to the river for rinsing.

Sometimes I would go along for the fun of watching the procedure. At the river, Zbroska would immerse the wash piece by piece into the water, and with a wooden paddle she would vigorously beat out the soapy water. After wringing out the rinsed laundry, she would once again place it into a large sheet, tie it into a bundle, and carry it back to our house, where she would hang up each piece to dry. During the summer she would hang the cleaned laundry outdoors on clotheslines, but in the winter she would hang it up in our attic.

Despite the substantial hired help Mother had for housecleaning and the family laundry, she did some of her own ironing. In general, Mother took meticulous care in ordering and maintaining the family wardrobes, often sewing and knitting, and occasionally ironing fancy little dresses and blouses. She would prepare the iron by transferring a piece of burning coal from the kitchen stove into the iron; and then she would thoroughly press out one piece of clothing at a time on the ironing board. I recall once that Mother, watching closely, let me take the iron and press out a few small items. It was so much fun.

Sources of endless joy were the occasional errands Mother would send me on. I recall going to the tinsmith with a pot to be repaired. As soon as Reiz'l "Shlyoch" would see me coming with the pot in hand, she would direct me across the lime-, tin-, and hair-littered dirt floor to her husband, Nus'n Perl. I would show him the handle or hole in the pot that needed to be repaired, and he would show me where on his floor he wanted me to place the pot among the other pieces he was working on. Then he would instruct me to tell Mother the pot would be ready in a day or two. At times, Mother would send me all the way up Langiewicza Street to the apothecary in the Upper Plaza. There, I would purchase some chamomile tea, which she would then use to wash my hair because she considered it important that the natural, light blond color of my hair be retained.

Outdoors I would occasionally run into Great grandfather Alter, Grandfather Nus'n's father, whom I recall vividly and fondly throughout my childhood. To the older children in town he sometimes seemed to be an old crank, especially if they were noisy in the synagogue when he happened to be reciting his prayers. To me, however, he was always jovial and playful. He was, to be sure, up in years and hard of hearing. Nonetheless, he took pride in showing off his garden, and he particularly enjoyed catching me by hooking the handle of his walking cane around my neck. He was fond of me, and I could not help but feel his love.

I often visited the yard goods store of my aunt Gitteleh and uncle Froyim Biderman. Their three children were my cousins Moishe, Itche, and Shloime. Moishe, who was the oldest of all my cousins, was a gentle and sensitive young man who was very capable in mechanical construction. Possessing a radio was quite a rarity in Bodzentyn; Moishe used to assemble his own. It always intrigued and fascinated me to hear the music coming from his radio through the earphones he would place over my ears. Moishe's brother Itche was close to Irka's age and was highly intelligent. Shloime, the youngest, was near the age of Rachela.

The Biderman yard goods store was in the front part of their dwelling, which was close to ours. In it, they sold only exclusive fabric, several bolts of which were placed prominently in the storefront display window.

When the weather was warm, many flies would buzz along the window. I used to like to corner and trap them between the cup of my hand and the window pane. After they would buzz awhile and try to escape, I would release them and go after another bunch.

The Biderman store was a busy place. People used to buy fabrics for suits, dresses, draperies, and all sorts of other items. Uncle Yank'l frequently worked there. Irka was also allowed to help by showing fabrics to customers. Rachela used to come often to the store, where she would be given leftover remnants to make clothes for her dolls. She really wanted to be able to help out in the store too, but because she habitually chewed on pencils and on the collars of her school pinafore, Aunt Gitteleh felt she was too immature. One would often see Uncle Froyim polishing lamps as he kept a keen eye on all goings-on in the store. He would offer ideas and advice to customers who needed fabrics for particular purposes. If a desired fabric was not in stock, he would faithfully promise to acquire it on his next business trip.

One of the many customers, both Jewish and non-Jewish, who used to come into their store to buy materials was a Polish peasant woman, a Mme Surowjecka, from a nearby village called Świętomarz. She gave the impression of being a thoroughly honest and truly decent human being. My aunt and uncle liked her very much and thought very well of her. In time, she was to play a critical role in one of the most perilous periods of my story.

Of the many nostalgic recollections from my early childhood, one in particular involves my sister Rachela. Once she had a pair of shoes whose strap had been ripped off and needed to be reattached. Rachela received the money from Father to have the shoes repaired but she didn't want to go to the shoemaker, so she asked me to take the shoes for her. I, however, was not in the mood to go either. Rachela then said that she actually no longer really cared for those shoes but that they really looked good on me. If I would go and have the strap repaired, she promised that she would let me have the shoes. With that incentive, I took the shoes and the money and proceeded merrily toward a Polish shoemaker, Zwada. We often went to him to have shoes made for members of our family. His residence-shop was located on Opatow Street, which branched northeastward from the eastern part of Żwirki Plaza not far from our house. I showed Zwada the torn-off strap; he took the shoe from me and walked over to his sewing machine in the rear of the room. Within a few minutes he returned with the shoe all repaired. I paid him the money Rachela had received from Father and proceeded to stroll back home, happy with my new shoes. When I arrived home and showed them to Rachela, she told me that she had changed her mind and that she wanted the shoes back after all. They were her shoes, she maintained, and if she decided she liked them she didn't have to let me keep them. I felt deeply disappointed and angry because I believed that she had deceived me by sending me all the way to the shoemaker for nothing. So in my anger I took the shoes, ran for a pair of scissors, and cut the strap back off. I then returned the shoes to Rachela with the cut-off strap. Now she was angry that I had deliberately ruined her shoe. She said she was going to tell Father on me. And she did.

Father listened patiently to her side of the argument, and then to mine. After about ten minutes of listening, lecturing, and deliberating, he finally decided we were both wrong. He gave me more money and demanded I go directly back to Zwada and have him sew the strap on the shoe again. He also reprimanded Rachela for reneging on her promise. Father did, however, allow her to keep the shoes, but only on condition that she not repeat such a trick. Tearfully and begrudgingly, I went back to Zwada and waited for him to fix the strap. I then returned home and gave the shoes back to Rachela. Although I was angry and my pride was hurt, those feelings lasted only for the moment. Before the day had ended, we were playing together like the incident had never happened.

Frequently, Mother would send me for a few items such as sugar or salt from the little grocery store of Alter Szachter. Alter kept his sugar and salt loose in huge, tall burlap sacks that stood on the hard dirt floor. He would weigh the amount Mother wanted, transfer it to a paper bag, and give it to me to take home. I often played with his younger daughter Shprintzeleh, who was my age. One habit of hers, however, used to irritate me. Whenever she saw me coming out of their grocery store with a bag or two, she would run up and pry, "What did you get? What do you have in those bags?" She would press the bags, sometimes trying to open them in order to peek in, but the more curious she became the more obstinately I fought to frustrate her curiosity. Nevertheless, we did enjoy playing together. One game we used to play was a version of hopscotch, called "Playing Classes." With a stick, we would draw dirt hopscotch blocks on the ground. The semicircular space at the bottom of the blocks was called *Gehenem*. The penalty for landing in that space was—demotion. *Gehenem* in Yiddish literally means *hell*, but figuratively it referred to the pit one fell into as a penalty for the misstep. It seems that the harder we tried to avoid that block, the easier it was to fall in. But we had fun playing the game anyway.

Perhaps the activity I enjoyed most was going across the plaza to Grandfather Nus'n's house, and to his vast property that stretched toward the town's southern fringe areas.

4

Grandfather Nus'n's Estate

AT THE opposite end of the Plaza from our courtyard was the courtyard of Grandfather Nus'n. Inside that courtyard were two large estates: one to the west belonging to a wealthy Pole named Jakubowski; the other to the east belonging to Grandfather Nus'n. Jakubowski's property included a large sausage factory, a small farm where he raised cows and horses, and in front, a large store where large quantities of produce were displayed and sold. On the northern end of Grandfather Nus'n's property stood a large ironware store, where various iron and tin products as well as farm implements and tools were sold. An additional entrance led directly from Żwirki Plaza. The store was managed by my uncle Moishe, and was closed on Sabbaths and all holy days.

Behind the ironware store and connected to it were the spacious living quarters of Grandfather Nus'n and his four unmarried sons, my uncles Moishe, Froyim, Leib'l, and Yank'l. Aunt Dineleh also lived there and managed the house, from the time her mother, my grandmother Irka, passed away until the time of her marriage to Yoss'l Schreibman from Koprzywnica in 1933. While she was living there, she also assisted in the operation of the ironware store, answered the telephone—the only privately owned telephone in Bodzentyn—and entertained business company for Grandfather Nus'n.

The living quarters included a large kitchen, a large elaborately furnished parlor room, and a large bedroom. Although the kitchen did possess a large table and was the scene of much activity, the parlor was used as the dining room. It was also the main sitting room. Social entertainment of all types took place there. As one entered it, on the right, was a huge desk on which stood the cranked telephone. Grandfather Nus'n used to sit at that desk in the early morning hours, poring over his Talmud. On the wall to the right, facing west, was a window looking out to the Jakubowski estate. In the center of the room was a large table and chairs. On either side of the door on the southern wall were two beds, where

Uncles Leib'l and Yank'l slept, and above them hung two beautiful tapestries. Along the eastern wall, opposite the window, stood a huge lacquered iron safe and a large wardrobe. The safe was finished like an elegant piece of furniture and had a combination lock. Important business papers were kept in the safe and only Grandfather Nus'n and Uncle Leib'l knew the combination. Uncle Leib'l also kept letters from girlfriends there. When the safe was open, we children would sneak up and try to read some of the letters. If Uncle Leib'l caught us, he would run up, spank us, scold us, and then lock up the safe. The door of the southern wall led into the room where Grandfather Nus'n slept. It had been at one time the parlor. There were two beds in it. Grandfather slept on one; the other, unused one had been Grandmother Irka's when she was alive. Each bed was covered with a luxurious, medium-green velvet bedspread with a large Bordeaux flower pattern. The bedspreads were similar to those in our house, but they were older and had a less contemporary design. There were also two beautiful sofas in the room. Grandfather kept the room off-limits, probably in deference to Grandmother's memory, although he would occasionally go there with a client to transact business privately.

South of this room was a storage room that, during Sukkot, was converted into a Sukkah in the same way as our front hall was: by pulling a string, part of the ceiling and roof opened up. Behind this room was an unfinished room that contained two beds where Uncles Moishe and Froyim slept.

Grandfather Nus'n's house was known in town as the only house where everyone came. Often Polish gentry, wealthy landowners clad in elegant horsemen's attire, trousers, and boots would ride into town on handsome, leather-saddled galloping horses to meet with Grandfather Nus'n concerning matters of business. During these meetings, they would negotiate purchases and sales within his three large enterprises: ironware, farm tools and implements, and grains and flour. At other times, meetings and discussions on every current topic took place there and included members of different political persuasions. In addition, whenever my aunts, uncles, and cousins from out of town came to visit with their families, they always stayed there. Because visitors were there all the time, the house was always lively. Grandfather Nus'n was always so amiable and jovial. I loved to go over there. We children, especially, truly loved him.

In the yard behind the house stood a huge newer building that was used for storing grains. It was, however, sectioned into rooms like a house and was so large, I am told, that it was once rented out as a theater for the presentation of a silent movie that was brought to town.

In 1933, for the wedding of Aunt Dineleh to my uncle Yoss'l Schreibman, the storage house was cleared of all grains and was cleaned and prepared for the celebration. The Sukkah area behind Grandfather Nus'n's living quarters was completely occupied with tubs of water, where live carp were kept before the preparation of the meal. Some three hundred guests were invited. It seemed that the whole town appeared, including non-Jewish teachers of Jewish children as well as non-Jewish business associates. Caterers were brought in from out of town, as were *Klezmer,* folk musicians who entertained at Jewish weddings, and a *Marshalik,* a traditional Jewish moralizing wedding entertainer, sometimes called a *Badchen,* who performed rhymed rhetoric in a half-recited, half-chanted style.

Irka, who was about seven years old at the time, composed a little poem of her own for the occasion and recited it to the delight of all the assembled guests. Although I was less than two years old, I recall, as though through a vivid dream, that after the wedding meal the Klezmer musicians came to our house and played dance music in our parlor. I recall also how Father picked me up and stood me on the nightstand, holding me securely, so that I could see and take note of the musicians and the dancing. At one point, Mother came to me and gave me her beautiful silver beaded purse to hold, while she went out to join in the dancing. She was dressed in very exclusive wedding attire that had been made specially for the occasion by an expert dressmaker in Kielce.

After they were married, Aunt Dineleh and Uncle Yoss'l lived in Starachowice, where they owned and operated an ironware store that sold nails, sheet metal, and various iron products. They had two children, my cousins Irka—who was nicknamed Lalunya, which means "Little Doll"—and Moisheniu.

Behind the big storage building of Grandfather Nus'n's massive property was a large, beautifully kept fenced-in garden. In it was an orchard area where pear, apple, and cherry trees grew, along with white lilac shrubs. Also in the garden was a large birdhouse that was built by Uncle Leib'l as a hobby room for himself. Uncle Leib'l, the third son of my maternal grandparents after Moishe and Froyim, was the mechanic—the handyman of the family. Most of his time was spent in the large, separate engine room in the family mill. It was he who handled all the repairs and built and devised structures for storage or convenience. He was always seen making and doing things with his "golden" hands. Uncle Leib'l built his birdhouse in a way that required one to ascend several steps in order to enter. In it he raised pigeons; he also made ice cream for the children of the family. From that room one could reach out and fetch a pear from the tree. Here Uncle Leib'l was truly in his element.

The garden also contained an outhouse, because houses in Bodzentyn in those days had no plumbing and therefore no running water or toilets. The outhouse was kept immaculately clean. A key to the garden was needed to get into it.

Behind the garden stood a covered shack where farm implements were stored. Toward the far end of the estate was the huge family mill, which Grandfather Nus'n and Father owned jointly. Thus, Father was Grandfather Nus'n's first cousin, his son-in-law, and his business partner in three of the town's largest enterprises: the one mill in Bodzentyn, a major grains business, and a farm tools and implements export business, which made our family the wealthiest in town. Fifty percent ownership of the mill was originally inherited by each of my grandfathers. Grandfather Meier bequeathed his 50 percent share to Father, probably at the time of Father's marriage to Mother. The grain enterprise included the export of clover and a large variety of other seeds and grains to Germany as well as to numerous cities and towns in Poland. Uncle Froyim and Father were the main businessmen of the family. It was they who went on business trips to nearby cities, towns, villages, and beyond to buy and sell grains and merchandise. In addition to being Father's partner in the mill and the two export enterprises, Grandfather Nus'n also owned the town's major ironware store for local sales of farm tools and implements, which Uncle Moishe operated until the time of his marriage in the late 1930s. Uncle Froyim was also actively involved in that enterprise.

Uncle Yank'l was the youngest of my maternal grandparents' nine surviving children. Since Grandmother Irka had died when Uncle Yank'l was but an infant, he had no memory of his mother. He was raised by his older sisters, who lived at home until they married and moved on. He was a rather sickly child and not a robust or vigorous young adult, and he had no venturesome business interests or ambitions. His greatest joy and source of satisfaction lay in helping members of the family: he would always lend a hand to his older sisters when they lived at home; he would frequently go over to help in the yard goods store of Aunt Gitteleh and Uncle Froyim Biderman; he also helped in selling at his father's ironware store; at other times, he would help his older sisters by escorting their younger children.

The family businesses were voluminous and involved numerous hired workers, including a full-time young bookkeeper named Aron Silberberg, son of Avruhom Silberberg, who was a frequent visitor at our house.

Inside the huge mill building was the machinery for grinding grains into flour. In the rear was the engine room where Uncle Leib'l could almost always be found hard at work. Outdoors in the yard next to the engine room was a body of water that provided the power for the mill. In the engine room, however, was the motor itself, along with large wheels and various other pieces of machinery. When the motor was running, the mill was a very, very noisy place. Once Father took me into the mill when he was in a mood to play hide and seek with me. When I wasn't looking, he hid from me. I looked for him all over but could not find him. I became frightened, suddenly imagining myself alone in the huge, terribly noisy mill building. I called for him anxiously and was almost in tears—when suddenly he leaped up from his hiding place.

When the mill was running, which was usually until about 8 P.M., it was capable of providing power for electricity, which was otherwise nonexistent in Bodzentyn. An electrical wire, stretched across Żwirki Plaza and supported by two electrical poles, connected the top of the mill in Grandfather Nus'n's backyard to our house, thereby providing our house with electricity during the mill's operative hours. Our mill also provided electricity, for a period of time, for the upper-grades elementary public school within the Plaza as well as for the street. After a while, the city discontinued payment for the service because the cost of running the mill continuously became prohibitive, so we stopped providing the electricity. Before long, however, a Polish national electrical company, called ZEORK, began putting in electricity throughout the country. By about 1937, electrical wiring was being installed generally in the cities of Poland. For the population of Bodzentyn, this innovation was revolutionary. For our family, it only meant we no longer needed to ignite the kerosene lamps after 8 P.M.

Behind the mill and the covered shack was a large, wide yard area. Here Grandfather Nus'n had a stable for horses and several horse-drawn wagons. One of the wagons had a handsome seating area for four passengers, and so we used it for vacation travel. The other wagons were built long for the purpose of loading materials to be transported, so they had merely a small seating place up front for the driver.

Behind this yard, a new building was built to serve as both a new mill and a new engine room. The older mill was becoming obsolete because it required one particular kind of fuel that was becoming excessively expensive; the newer mill, on the other hand, could be run on all fuels used at that time in Poland for motors of that type. Moreover, the flour business was expanding and required the use of two mills to accommodate the local as well as the growing volume of out-of-town business. The flour was sold wholesale in one-hundred-pound burlap sacks that were weighed and sewn across the top by a hired worker. These bags were then loaded into wagons and delivered by workers to bakers in various towns and cities, mostly within a radius of some thirty kilometers around Bodzentyn.

Behind the new mill building stood a pair of huge wooden gates that enclosed the property of Grandfather Nus'n's estate at its outermost southern point, near the fringe areas of Bodzentyn.

There is nothing that gave me greater pleasure than to open those gate doors and go out beyond Grandfather Nus'n's property toward the outskirts of Bodzentyn. Directly behind those doors was a small village street. On one side was a factory in which seltzer water was processed and bottled, and on the other a wide, spacious meadow. When the weather was warm, I used to love to run out alone and roam about in the meadow in the open, free abode of nature. I would pick up a stick and, while walking past a farm fence, rattle it against the wire that connected the vertical wooden strips of the fence. I would sneak up to a resting butterfly and, as it flew away, run after it, trying, always in vain, to catch it. I would pick the flowers and savor the fragrance of each one, as well as the boundless expanse of fields around me.

Often Mother would take me strolling not only out there but also beyond, into the areas that I never explored alone. Together we would walk past small creeks, and I would pick the blue cornflowers that grew around there. Growing from the swampy marsh plants at the very edge of the water were the blue forget-me-nots. The smell in the air was heavenly. The freshly cut grass and bundles of hay rendered a strong and invigorating smell, especially when they were located near a stream. Because I was a slender child with a generally poor appetite, Mother would bring along some fresh, home-baked, oblong blueberry-filled cakes, as well as fresh apples, pears, or cherries—plucked off the trees in Grandfather Nus'n's orchard. She knew that out here, in nature's paradise, I would eat—and how right she was. We would often pass by a farm, where Mother would purchase a glass of milk, freshly milked from the cow, for me to drink. The warm, foamy milk tasted better here than anywhere else.

We passed by more farms, meadows, and fields that were interrupted only by small creeks, and brooks. Always flowers would be growing nearby. I felt like I could eat those wondrous fragrances of nature. How I loved the idyllic quiet and this pure, rustic atmosphere. I could never seem to take in enough.

5

An Evening at Home

TOWARD EVENING, during the week, we would generally eat our dinner meal in the kitchen. I recall one evening when Mother prepared chicken noodle soup, which did not appeal to me, at least not on that evening. I generally had a poor appetite anyhow, so when my bowl of soup was placed in front of me I stood up, stepped away from the table, and ran out of the kitchen, down the hall, past our double doors and the landing, down the stairs, and to a small space between the bottom of the staircase and the front wall of Grandfather Meier's bakery-residence.

In that little cornered-in space was a wooden box, just large enough for me to squat in and hide. It was good to be here all alone, I thought, where no one knew where I was. I fantasized how nice a place this could be for me to live in, if ever I decided to run away from home. I wouldn't have to eat when I didn't want to, and I could play all the time—when suddenly I looked up and realized that my brother Moishe had discovered my hiding place. In a coaxing, loving manner, he asked me to come back, saying that Mother wanted me to eat my supper. I insisted I didn't want to. When he offered me a half-złoty, however, I began thinking differently on the matter and went up with him. Once again Mother placed a bowl of soup—on "my" table—and, as I tasted it, I realized I liked it better than I had thought.

After dinner, when the weather was nice, I would sometimes go out-doors into our courtyard to play with some of the children of Nus'n the tinsmith and Reiz'l "Shlyoch." Because they were so poor and Reiz'l had to help earn a livelihood for the family, she was always very busy and disoriented, and their children were almost totally neglected. I enjoyed playing most with little Marmeleh, the youngest of their children, who was about two years old. Often I would bring her up to our house, where Mother or Irka would bathe her in a pan of heated water with perfumed soap and sometimes dress her in clothes that I had outgrown. Reiz'l

"Shlyoch" was so preoccupied, she would be totally unaware of the fact that Marmeleh might have been away for as much as several hours at a stretch.

Toward 8 P.M., when our electricity went out, we would make some light by turning the screw of our kerosene lamps through which the lamp wicks were extended, and we would ignite the wicks with naphtha. Hours after we had finished our dinner and long after Mother had taken care of little Marmeleh, to the amusement of us all we would suddenly hear the shrill, high-pitched pitter-patter voice of Reiz'l "Shlyoch." In her nightly ritual, she would be calling for her children, rattling off all twelve names in a single breath: "Leizerle, Yankeleh, Shmieleleh, Moisheleh, Lieber'l, Shloimeleh, Mireleh . . . Marmeleh, hurry home for supper." As soon as we heard her long awaited call, I knew it had to be just about my bedtime—which was at any time too soon for me. Once in bed, though, after a long day of much activity, I would quickly fall into a sound slumber.

I recall one occasion, however, when I had partially woken from a dream in the middle of the night. The moon outdoors reflected shadowed images in our parlor room that seemed to mesh with my dream, and I became frightened, imagining a strange presence in the room. I called out, "Oh! I am afraid!"

In a moment, Father was at my bedside, comforting me, "Why are you afraid, my Goldeleh? There's nothing to be afraid of."

"Yes there is. There's something in the room. Look!" I insisted, pointing to the strangely shaped reflection of the moonlight.

Caressing me, Father said, "Don't be afraid, my child. Watch what I will show you." He sat me up. Then he struck a match and lit the wick of the lamp. "You see, Goldeleh, there is nothing strange anywhere," he assured me as he pointed out into the dimly lit room. "All you saw were shadows of things one sees plainly in the light."

Noting that his explanation had calmed my fear, he lovingly entreated me, "Now go back to sleep, my child." As I reclined back to a lying position, he covered me. Then he extinguished the lamp, kissed me, whispered softly, "Sleep well," and went back to bed.

Soon I was back in my dreamland of childhood, sleeping contentedly as the dark night passed in peace.

6

Sabbath at Home

THE SABBATH at Bodzentyn was a special weekly event. Beginning early Friday morning, the entire day was spent in preparation for the biblically ordained day of rest. Whenever meat was being planned for a meal, and we almost always had meat on Sabbaths and holidays, the animals first had to be ritually slaughtered. We would generally purchase red meat from the Jewish kosher butcher, whose responsibility it was to carry out all appropriate kosher ritualistic requirements. When a meal of fowl was planned, we had to have the animals slaughtered by a *Shoichet,* an ordained ritual slaughterer. There were two in Bodzentyn: Moisheleh Shoichet and Avremeleh Shoichet. As a rule, the Jews in town would bring their chicken, duck, or goose to the shoichets. In deference to the wealth and social prestige of our family, our shoichet, Moisheleh, used to come to our house to slaughter the fowl for us when he was younger. In his later years, out of respect for his advanced age, Mother would often send one of us children to his house on Langiewicza Street with the fowl held securely underarm. There Moisheleh Shoichet would slaughter the fowl in accordance with the requirements of Jewish Law and then send us, and it, back home to Mother.

On one occasion, when Mother cut open a slaughtered chicken in preparation for cooking, she found a needle stuck in the fat on the inside of the chicken. This predicament posed a doubt as to whether the chicken could still qualify as a kosher fowl. In such instances of doubt, one required the scholarly judgment of a rabbi, so Mother sent me with the chicken to Rabbi Shwartz for his professional opinion. Rabbi Shwartz was an elderly man with a long gray beard. He always wore a long, black, girded caftanlike coat. When he examined the chicken, he declared it *treif,* ritually unqualified, and Mother had to prepare another chicken. Once, in another circumstance, the rabbi asked that the chicken be left with him so he could research a difficult legal question before rendering his judgment.

Later that day, I heard a rap on our main entrance door. I ran and opened the door and was greeted by the rabbi's son, who had come to inform us of his father's decision. He was a tall, slim young man whose very light skin bespoke of the sedentary nature of his daily, hours-long devotion to Talmudic scholarship. Like his father, he was dressed in a long, black coat and a black visored cap that Jews referred to as a Jewish cap. Shyly, he asked if Mother was home and if he could see her. Zbroska, our cleaning woman, had just finished scrubbing our floors, and I didn't think I should let him walk across our freshly washed floors. I noticed a rather startled reaction on his long, pale face when I, a child of but six, asked him to wipe his shoes before coming into our house.

Every Thursday evening, Mother would begin preparing our *chala*, the special braided egg bread that we ate on Sabbaths and holy days. She would prepare the yeast dough and allow it to rise overnight. She also regularly engaged the services of a baker, a hunchbacked widow named Yent'l who lived with her two daughters on Kielce Street. Mother had her bake for the Sabbath meals of a number of needy families in the community. Yent'l used to come to our house every Thursday evening to get large quantities of the ingredients necessary for making chala and other baked goods. She would deliver the baked breads to us the next day.

On Friday morning, Mother would flatten the yeast dough she had prepared the night before, knead it, and twist it in braids. To honor the Sabbath, she would also mix the ingredients for one or two types of cakes. One time, she might make up an apple cake or a coffee cake; at other times, she might make oblong fruit-filled cakes, or even a cheese cake to go with a dairy meal. Then she would take the raw chala and cake batter downstairs to Grandfather Meier's oven to bake. Often I went with her.

Grandfather Meier was a somewhat heavyset man with a long, rounded, white-gray beard, and he looked very old to me. In fact, he was about fifteen years older than Grandfather Nus'n. The children of the family felt removed from him, which was in contrast to the warm affection we felt toward Grandfather Nus'n. Although he enjoyed escorting us children into his garden, he would shout at us if he caught us going in without his permission. If only he knew how often I trespassed without his knowledge! It was not just this cranky side of his personality, however, that distanced us. There was always so much activity and fun at Grandfather Nus'n's; what was there for us to do at Grandfather Meier's? His second wife, who was much younger than he was, was not at all nice to us children. She would never let us enter the house and she shouted at us every time she heard us getting carried away in play. She showed no interest in our family and we tended to avoid her. Mother was very close to her own father, our grandfather Nus'n, and was not very interested in Father's father and stepmother. Even Father hardly ever spoke to his father's second wife. His stepmother's sister, however, was much nicer. Ester'l, about ten years younger than her sister, was dwarfish and hydrocephalic. She talked little and did almost nothing with her hands. Although she occasionally came out into the courtyard, she was almost always in the house. Her abnormally short, fat body and her disproportionately large head made her appear unusual and awkward. She was, however, neat, intelligent, and good-natured. Ester'l showed an interest in us children, and we in turn liked her. When her sister was away from home, she would invite us into the house and tell us about her life in Rzeszów. Despite the circumstances that made us prefer Grandfather Nus'n, Grandfather Meier very much wanted us to like him and, in fact, used to bribe us with a half-złoty from time to time for our affection. Still Grandfather Nus'n always seemed to win out.

Mother and I would walk through Grandfather Meier's residence-bakery, past the front bakery store area where he conducted his business to the rear of the premises. The huge oven stood on one side, his modest living quarters on the other. When we got to the oven, we would shove the mixes in to bake. Then we would go back upstairs, where Mother would busily peel carrots, cook lima beans, and prepare other foods for our Sabbath meals. She always cooked much more food than our family needed so that we could share some of it with the needy in the community. I used to enjoy watching her make *farfel* or noodles, which, incidentally, were not necessarily made only for the Sabbath. If Mother made farfel, she would knead a ball of dough, grate it, and then place the grated dough into the oven to brown. If Mother made noodles, she would take the ball of dough, flatten it with a rolling pin, spread it out into sheets, and place it on a bed to dry out partially. She would then roll up the half-dried dough and, with a sharp knife, cut thin slivers across the rolled dough to form the noodles, which were then placed into a pot of water to cook.

Yet another traditional Sabbath dish that Mother frequently prepared was *tcholent,* a mildly spiced dish that consisted of meat tucked into potato. After Mother had mixed it together, we would take the tcholent in a pot downstairs and place it in Grandfather Meier's oven to simmer overnight. The next day, we would take it out for our Sabbath noon meal. Other neighbors also placed their Sabbath tcholents in Grandfather Meier's oven to cook overnight.

Regular Friday culinary activities also included preparing fish, chicken soup, and chicken, or an alternate meat course. The appetizing aromas coming from the cooking and baking in our house and in Grandfather Meier's, as well as the hustle from the many activities that needed to be completed before sundown, enhanced our anticipation of the hallowed day of rest.

When Yent'l arrived with the chalas and pastries she had baked for us, Mother would make them up into bundles and send us children to deliver them to a number of poor or ill people so that they could honor the Sabbath without the embarrassment of having to beg for food. Nevertheless, there were others who would come and rap on our door on Friday, begging for food so they could have Sabbath meals on their tables. They were admirable indeed, despite their abject poverty, in their perseverance to observe the Sabbath in dignity. Even Reiz'l "Shlyoch" would throw sawdust across her dirt floor every Friday in the late afternoon, presumably to give her poor living quarters a clean look in honor of the Sabbath. We were also visited periodically by a wandering Polish peasant woman who used to come begging for food. Mother always dealt compassionately and generously with all in need who came for assistance.

Before sundown, we would bathe in order to achieve physical as well as spiritual cleanliness for the Sabbath. Each member of our family would place heated water into a pan, take it to a secluded corner of our house, then soap, wash, and dry him- or herself and don clothing befitting the festivity of the occasion.

During weekdays, Father would dress in businesslike suits with tailcoat, most often in a shade of gray. On holy days, however, he would dress in a special, handsome, silk, girded, long black caftanlike coat and black Jewish visored cap. As he would be leaving with my brothers for the synagogue for Sabbath Eve services, our kerosene lamps would be ignited and Mother would light the Sabbath Eve candles. Then, with a special scarf over her head, she would pronounce the benediction over the lit candles. The holy Sabbath was thus ushered into our home; its spirit radiated within each of us, as the dusk of Sabbath Eve descended over Bodzentyn.

One of the streets branching off northward from Langiewicza Street, Wesoła Street, was referred to as Synagogue Street, because at a short distance down this street stood the large town synagogue and, adjacent to it, the small prayer chapel, which we referred to by its Hebrew designation, *Bet Midrash*, not far from the Mandelkern Library farther north.

On their way to Synagogue Street, Father and my brothers would cross paths with practically the entire adult Jewish male population of Bodzen-tyn, as the grandfathers, fathers, and sons of each family would stroll along together toward the synagogue in family groups, all freshly dressed, neatly and cleanly groomed in honor of the new Sabbath. At the synagogue, up to 550 men could worship together in the main floor sanctuary. Wooden brown rails along an ascending stairway led up to the women's balcony, which had an approximate seating capacity of ninety.

In addition to all Sabbath and holy day services, the synagogue was used for the second and third of the three daily morning (*Shacharit*) services, at 8 A.M. and 9 A.M., and for the one daily, late afternoon-evening (*Mincha-Maariv*) service. The small prayer chapel next door, which seated about 80, was used for the first of the three daily morning services at 7 A.M. as well as for religious study purposes in general. The 8 A.M. service drew on the average some 125 worshipers, whereas the 7 A.M. chapel service, primarily attended by the poorer members of the community who had to be at work earlier than the others, drew some 80 attendants; and the 9 A.M. synagogue service, the service for "lazy risers," drew the smallest group of the three. The late afternoon-evening service averaged approximately 250 worshipers, whereas the Sabbath and holy day services drew from 400 to 500 congregants.

At the conclusion of the Friday evening services, people would warmly greet each other, "*Git Shabes*" (A good Sabbath to you), as they passed each other on their way home from the synagogue.

As soon as Father and my brothers returned home from the synagogue, we would gather around the table in our parlor, which was festively set over a white tablecloth, with the lit candles and two covered chalas, a bottle of wine, and by Father's seat at the head of the table, a silver goblet. Father was a tall, broad-shouldered man with a short, brown, trimmed beard and high cheekbones. When he chanted the *Kiddush,* the benediction over the wine, his brown eyes were expressive, revealing his feelings of devotion and thanks to the Almighty for the many blessings our family enjoyed.

After he had ritually washed his hands and pronounced the blessing over the chala, we would be seated and proceed with our festive Sabbath meal, which always commenced with a savory fish dish. The big carp head piece went to Father. Since Shloime and I also liked the head piece, Father would cut off a piece for each of us. We then had chicken soup, meat, and other courses, which were complemented by the singing of *Zmirot,* Sabbath hymns. A special favorite of Father's was *M'nucha V'simcha:*

M'nucha v' simcha	Rest and joy,
Or lay'hudim;	A light to the Jews;
Yom shabaton	The day of Sabbath
Yom machamdim.	Is a day of bliss.

Our dessert frequently consisted of fresh fruit. I would approach Father and sit myself on his lap, and he would cut small pieces of apple and give them to me. After tea and cake and grace, the festive meal and Sabbath Eve gradually merged into the night. The light from the kerosene lamps soon faded and went out, as we prepared to retire for the evening.

Sabbath mornings always began with attendance at the morning synagogue services—at least by the men of the family. There were two scheduled services, at 7 A.M. and at 8:30 A.M., but inasmuch as most attendants were slow to get out of bed early enough on Sabbath morning to arrive on time for the 8:30 service, that one used to start only when enough latecomers had finally come rushing in. By the time all had arrived, there would be usually four to five hundred Jews, including adherents of the nonreligious leftist Labor Zionist Party. The services constituted an enjoyable ethnic-cultural experience and pastime even for them. The more gifted local lay cantors would exert their vocal efforts in order to evoke within the congregants the true spirit of Sabbath devotional joy through their chanting of the services. Their heartfelt renditions were a source of deep spiritual inspiration for the Jews of Bodzentyn, who would frequently comment throughout the day on the emotional impact of the morning rendition of one or another of the gifted amateur cantors.

When the men returned from the synagogue, we would proceed with the Sabbath noon meal, which would be preceded by a Kiddush. On the Sabbaths when we were to have tcholent, Mother would send me down to Grandfather Meier's to fetch it. Our Sabbath noon meal proceeded with all the courses and general festivity enjoyed at Friday's Sabbath Eve meal, including the singing of Zmirot and grace.

During the remainder of the day, we avoided work or mundane activities in order to maintain the sacred character of the traditional day of rest. Mother, weary from the elaborate Sabbath preparations, would often take an afternoon nap. She would stretch out on my brother's convertible bed and in no time be sound asleep. I would continually come in to see whether she had already woken up, anticipating the possibility of going out for a stroll at the conclusion of her nap.

Father and my brothers would occasionally become involved in a game of chess. Father was an excellent player, but he consistently lost to Shloime, the uncrowned chess champion of the town, who always beat not only the members of the family but all his boyfriends as well. Once, when Shloime and a friend were deeply engrossed in the strategies of prospective moves, I grabbed one edge of the chessboard and shook the pieces out of place, causing them to topple and the game to be ruined. Shloime was instantly enraged and shouted, "Get out of here!" He raised his hand in a gesture to catch me, but I was already out of his reach, in flight, excited and delighted from having succeeded in my naughty mischief. Resigned to the situation, the two boys good-naturedly placed the pieces back on the board as accurately as their memories allowed and continued their interrupted game.

Shloime at times tried, with difficulty, to teach me how to play checkers. At other times he would play dominoes or a card game with me. I would play those games with other members of the family or a girlfriend as well.

A regular Sabbath afternoon activity for the male members of the community consisted of congregating at the synagogue for a study session. On summer Sabbaths, the session would be devoted to *Pirke Avot,* "Ethics of the Fathers"; whereas on other Sabbaths it would be on some portion of the Talmud. Another Sabbath afternoon activity at the synagogue was the *farher'n*—the public testing of the boys on their Talmudic studies of the past week. Each of the town's four Melamdim, the professional Hebrew teachers, vied to demonstrate for the community the superiority of *his* students over the students of his colleagues. Woe unto his students if they failed him!

A widely practiced activity on holy days was the afternoon promenade. When the weather was inviting, after Mother's nap, she and Father would go out strolling, either along the side streets branching off from Żwirki Plaza, where strolling was a favorite pastime, or through the fields and meadows beyond Grandfather Nus'n's property. It goes without saying that I would always tag along. Sometimes my sister Rachela and some of the other children came too.

When Father and Mother took us beyond the city limits, we would pass fields, meadows, and villages all the way into the cool dark forest, where we would encounter young Jewish adults likewise strolling, and likewise absorbing the strong aroma of the woods. They would be socializing, and on occasion flirting. As a sign of modern times, one would hear them conversing in Polish rather than in Yiddish. The forest had a deeper, more pungent fragrance than the fields and meadows, due primarily to its abundance of tall, majestic pine trees. The fallen pine needles formed a slippery surface on the ground. Blueberries and mushrooms grew in abundance there. I would sing or call out "ha-ha" or "hah-lo," and await the rebounding echo from the trees. I would repeat the procedure again and again.

On our way back, we passed Polish villagers who worked for Father; he would pause to inquire as to their welfare, and to ask whether they had ample feed for their chickens, or sufficient savings to cover a recent illness. If they complained of insufficient funds, he would offer aid and see to it that the aid would be forthcoming.

Back home, we would have a light *Shalosh S'udot,* the third Sabbath meal. As the afternoon waned, the men returned to the synagogue for the Sabbath afternoon and post-Sabbath evening services, while the women remained home. When the weather was sufficiently warm, we would sit out on our balcony as dusk descended once again, signaling the departure of the hallowed Sabbath day. Mother would sing some tender Yiddish songs. She had a lovely voice, and I loved to listen as she sang. As nightfall ended the Sabbath day, we would return inside and kindle our kerosene lamps. Soon Father and my brothers would return from the synagogue, and Father would chant the *Havdalah,* the benedictions over the wine, a spice box, and a lit braided candle, which signified the official farewell to the Sabbath, the most beautiful and special day of the week.

7

The Yearly Cycle in Bodzentyn

FALL

As was true in Jewish communities throughout Eastern Europe, the yearly cycle in Bodzentyn began in fall with the High Holidays of Rosh Hashana, Yom Kippur, and Sukkot. The fall season also ushered in a new school year, as well as the anticipation of the long winter season soon to follow. We welcomed in the new year by ordering and fitting ourselves with new clothes. Culinary preparations were essentially the same as for the Sabbath, except for the addition of apple pieces dipped in honey, which were eaten to symbolize our hopes and prayers for a "sweet" New Year, filled with happiness and good fortune. The prayers for this high holiday season are deeply solemn, as Rosh Hashana, the Jewish New Year, and Yom Kippur, our Day of Atonement, are termed the *Yamim Noraim,* or Days of Awe. On these days, Jews pray for the renewal of life in an intense awe-inspiring manner.

Our synagogue during these services was filled as on no other occasion. Inasmuch as the synagogue seated no more than six hundred men, some people formed prayer groups in private homes to accommodate the overflow. The interior of the synagogue itself was clothed in white to signify the seriousness of these holy days: the curtain covering the Holy Ark in which the Torah scrolls were kept, the Torah covers themselves, and the satin or velvet pulpit covers were all changed to white. The rabbi, the honorary cantors, and the more deeply pious men of the community all wore white prayer robes.

The services were highlighted by the sounding of the *shofar,* the traditional ram's horn, and by the singing of special traditional melodies. The Torah-reading cantillation melody was heard from the beautiful voice of our honorary synagogue *Baal Korah* (Reader of the Torah), Hersh'l Weintraub, the father of Shmiel Weintraub. The Bodzentyn Jewish community was also blessed with one specially gifted *Baal T'filah* (honorary cantor), named Yisrael Yitzchak Miodownik. Sruel Itche, as he was endearingly called, performed the primary cantorial functions of the High Holidays, including the second half of the morning services, the more prestigious *Musaf* services. With his full-length woolen *talit* (prayer shawl) draped over his head and around the shoulders of his white prayer robe, his moving rendition of the opening prayer communicated clearly the awesome mood of these holy days and his own feeling of religious responsibility toward his community and the Almighty. Hardly a dry eye could be found in the synagogue, hardly an uninspired soul.

At the conclusion of the services, as members began leaving the synagogue for home, they greeted each other with an emotionally charged wish, "*L'shana Tova Tikatevu V'techantemu*" (May you be inscribed and sealed in the Book of Life). When the men returned home, the holiday Kiddush over the wine was intoned and the wine was tasted, along with apples and honey or light pastry. Then the festive holiday meal was served.

Toward late afternoon, our family joined Bodzentyn's Jewish families in their annual stroll to the river, behind the castle remains, where the ceremonious prayer of *Tashlich* was recited and enacted. At the river, people would open their *Machzor,* their holiday prayer book, and with intense emotion they would read the prayers while ceremoniously "emptying" their pockets into the river, thereby symbolically casting their sins into the stream of water. It was thrilling to follow the crowd and pull out my pocket and shake my sins into the river, just like the older folk.

Yom Kippur, the most sacred day in the Jewish calendar year, marked the climax of the High Holiday season. Jewish tradition holds that the fate of each individual, inscribed in heaven on Rosh Hashana, becomes finalized and sealed on Yom Kippur. Thus, on the day of Yom Kippur Eve, crowds of Jews would be seen in Żwirki Plaza, piously wishing one another a heavenly verdict of good fortune for the coming year. The atmosphere was charged with the seriousness of the occasion.

During that same day, we used to enact the ceremony of *Kaparot*. Following the recitation of a prayer, a white chicken would be taken in hand, held by the legs, and waved three times over one's head, signifying that the fowl would be offered as a special sacrifice and scapegoat for that person's sins. The fowls were then to be distributed among the needy of the community. It was exciting when Mother would give me a white chicken with which to twirl my sins away. She would then supervise the procedure by helping me keep control of the fowl so I didn't become overwhelmed by its spirited wing flapping. The ceremonious atmosphere of the procedure added greatly to the anticipation of our most sacred day of the year.

Yom Kippur is marked by fasting from sundown on Yom Kippur Eve through sundown on Yom Kippur, as well as by synagogue services on the Eve and throughout the day. Because I was too young, by Rabbinic law, to be expected to fast, I was permitted to have food. My older brothers, sisters, and cousins, on the other hand, were required to fast and attend services with the adults. However, by afternoon, weary from the long day of fasting and praying, they were allowed to come home and rest for a while. I would sneak into their bedroom, swiftly pull off their blankets, and tease them by flaunting a piece of bread and butter in front of them. To me this mischief was good-natured fun, but I am certain I did not endear myself to them at that moment.

At the synagogue, Yom Kippur was climaxed and concluded by the *N'ila,* or closing service. Because the service was so sacred, it was chanted by our rabbi himself. The fast was then ended at home with a light but festive meal.

Four days after Yom Kippur came Sukkot, the Feast of Tabernacles, which commemorates the times our ancestors dwelled in huts in the Sinai Desert, after having been liberated from bondage in Ancient Egypt. This is the time of year when we converted our front hall into a sukkah, the traditional Tabernacle hut. It was an occasion of great fun and excitement for us children. My sister Rachela, and sometimes Irka, Shloime, and I, would work at decorating the sukkah. With colored paper, we would make rings and link them into chains. We would also make paper baskets, put chestnuts into them, and hang them up. Then we would stretch the colored-paper chains from one end of the sukkah to another. Part of the ceiling and roof was opened by pulling an attached rope or chain, and the top was thickly covered by leaved twigs or branches from trees, but in such a way as to allow stars to be visible at night, to preserve the temporary dwelling-hut character of the sukkah.

We would move our kitchen table and chairs into the sukkah area and eat there for the seven-day holiday period. A special delicacy of this holiday was *kreplach,* meat-filled dumplings. How much fun we children had sitting and eating in the sukkah. It was almost like eating outdoors. Sukkot is followed immediately by two additional biblically ordained holy days, *Shmini Atzeret* (Eighth Day of the Solemn Assembly) and *Simchat Torah* (Rejoicing with the Torah). The latter is the last of the fall holy days and is celebrated in a less serious and less formal manner than the others. The synagogue service is characterized by the Torahs being carried by the male adults in a seven-fold procession around the Sanctuary. It was an exciting occasion for us children. We each received a flag on a stick with an apple pierced through its top and we carried these in the Torah processions. I remember how happy I was on one particular Simchat Torah when Father put me on his shoulders and carried me in the procession.

After the fall holy days had passed, our primary attention was focused on the new school year. Schooling for Jewish children in Bodzentyn in the 1930s was much different than it had been before World War I. In those days, under czarist Russia, public schooling had been available to children of only the few, generally wealthy Jews, and education for the average Jewish child meant Jewish religious education. Jewish boys were sent to one of the three or four town Melamdim (teachers), who conducted a *Cheder,* a Hebrew school, at his house. The children spent from early morning until evening at the Cheder, with only one short break for lunch. There they received a thorough and intense education in every aspect of Judaism, ranging from prayers to Pentateuch to Talmudic studies.

Shmiel Weintraub relates how, as a young teenager in the 1920s, he once smuggled into the Cheder in the Bet Midrash a copy of a work by Baruch Spinoza, the famous seventeenth-century Jewish agnostic philosopher. Even though it was known to be socially hazardous for a youngster to be caught reading such a controversial, ill-reputed text, young Shmiel's curiosity had driven him to seek out the logic behind Spinoza's forbidden thoughts. While his fellow students were poring over a portion of their Talmuds, young Shmiel placed the small Spinoza volume over the large tractate pages of his Talmud and appeared from a distance to be deeply absorbed in his studies. His mind was, of course, devouring the taboo philosophy of Baruch Spinoza instead of the Talmud. Shmiel's concentration was so absorbed, in fact, that he failed to notice his teacher, Ber Melamed, calmly walking down the aisle, seeking to be of assistance to his students. Suddenly Ber Melamed caught sight of the forbidden volume. Trembling from disbelief and indignation, he swiftly lunged forward and grabbed the little book. With protruding eyes and expressions of anger and shock, Ber Melamed began an unceasing verbal barrage that grew into a diatribe that seemed to have no end. Who could have imagined that a son of such a pious, reputable Jew as Hersh'l Weintraub could sink to the level of reading such blasphemous trash and bring shame and disgrace to his family, his teacher, and his community! The tirade continued, stopped, and continued again and again. The scandal spread quickly as people came for various purposes in and out of the Bet Midrash that day. The furor did not simmer down until the wee hours of the next morning.

Times had indeed changed since then. After World War I, when Poland gained its independence, public schooling was made generally available to Jewish children. As a result, Jewish children began attending public school daily from early morning until 1 P.M., and Cheder from 1:30 P.M. until 6 P.M. Thus Jewish children became exposed to secular as well as Jewish-religious education. Children first attended the lower elementary-grade classes at the building in the Upper Plaza. After successfully completing these lower grades, students attended the upper elementary-grade classes—through Grade Seven—at the building in Żwirki Plaza.

For religious studies, Jewish boys were sent during afternoons to the home of one of Bodzentyn's four Melamdim, who still conducted a Cheder in the traditional manner. Despite the lack of refined pedagogical methods or even a conducive physical classroom environment, the *Cheder Melamed* almost unfailingly succeeded in imbuing each and every Jewish child with a thorough knowledge of and strong feeling for traditional Jewish philosophy and values. The student also came out with a fluent knowledge of the prayers, the Pentateuch, and as much of the Talmud as had been covered. Comprehension of the material was thorough, frequently to the point of memorization.

While Jewish education for girls was not deemed mandatory, a *Bet Yaakov* (House of Jacob) school was instituted in Bodzentyn around 1937 and was attended by all Jewish girls whose families could afford the tuition, as well as by girls from families of lesser means for whom the Jewish Committee administration made allowances. Both Irka and Rachela naturally attended. Periodically, school plays were presented in Yiddish. Often, Irka's singing ability brought her prominent roles. One play, however, involved a friend of Rachela's, one Reiz'l Winograd, and Reiz'l's sister Hadassah. The play included one role for a frog and one for an angel. The teacher supervising the play selected Hadassah, who was blond and pretty, to act the role of the angel; and her sister Reiz'l, who was red-headed, freckled, and decidedly unattractive, to be the frog. The selections were so ideally suited to the sisters' actual appearances that they evoked unrestrained hilarity among the entire class. The next day, the sisters' mother appeared at the Bet Yaakov and demanded that their roles be reversed. Further, she threatened, if her wishes went unheeded she would forbid her daughters to participate in the play. Because the Winograd family represented a major part of financial support to the school, the roles were reversed: pretty Hadassah played the frog, and unattractive Reiz'l played the angel.

My older brother Moishe was enrolled in the elementary school in the fall of 1931, at age six. Soon he began to encounter the consequences of the anti-Jewish sentiments and prejudices of the non-Jewish Polish population. Moishe's non-Jewish six-year-old classmates, and older schoolmates also, inculcated with anti-Semitic bias learned in their home environment, and by no means atypically from the church, would frequently gang up on Moishe, snicker at him, "*Parszywy Żyd!*" (You filthy Jew!), and bully him. Moishe was soon overcome with tension and began to squint nervously, so Father decided to take him out of school temporarily. Father also began making efforts to organize a Jewish day school in town. A communal meeting was called and took place in our house, with Father presiding. To his disappointment, however, far too few people were willing to invest the necessary funds for such a project. One town merchant decried: "I have only girls. I have no need for day schools." Similar sentiments were voiced by other townsmen. And so, the effort came to naught.

Not until a year later was Moishe reenrolled in school. By that time, Irka was also enrolled. Not quite six, she was actually too young, but Father and Mother felt she was sufficiently mature to begin school. With Irka attending school, she and Moishe could at least walk together, and bullying and ganging up on Jewish children was considerably less common for girls than for boys. So Moishe and Irka were enrolled in the same class and walked together daily to and from the elementary school in the Upper Plaza.

Moishe was an excellent student. He was an intelligent and responsible young lad. He read very much, and even studied foreign languages on his own. He was also skillful in drawing maps. Irka also was an excellent student, meticulous and a hard worker. Being the youngest in her class, she had to work harder to perform on a par with the best in her class. Still, she persevered, often with Father's help, and she succeeded in placing among the top students in her class. Irka also exhibited fine musical abilities. The school music teacher used to teach the classes Polish songs by playing their melodies on his violin and expecting the students to match the words as they sang along. On occasion, when he faced a class incapable of learning a particular song in that manner, he would call Irka out of her class to sing the song to them—even though they were older than she was.

In the fall of 1934, six-and-a-half-year-old Shloime was enrolled. Rachela was five years old by that time, and she wanted to be able to go to school in the worst way. "Irka started school at five, so why can't I?" she complained. Although Father and Mother felt Rachela was still too immature, she would not take no for an answer. She shouted and demanded, "I want to go to school! I want to go to school!" Then she stretched herself on the floor and worked herself into a temper tantrum, kicking her little feet with all the strength she could muster, again and again on the floor, as her face reddened from frustration and anger. She protested and cried, "I want to go to school! I am mature! I want to go to school!" She seemed so determined that Father and Mother began having second thoughts on the subject, and they soon gave in to her demand. Fortunately for Rachela, Mother, always sensitive to Jewish folk superstitions, preferred the children to be attending school in twos anyhow. She feared an "evil eye" peering on as many as five children from one family attending five different classes.

The next day, Uncle Yank'l escorted Rachela to school. The authorities, however, apparently sensing Rachela was too young, maintained that children had to be six years old in order to be admitted. When Uncle Yank'l claimed Rachela was six, in fact Shloime's twin (!), they replied he would have to bring Rachela's birth certificate. Uncle Yank'l countered that Rachela had no birth certificate, and indeed none of the children of the family had one. Rachela was admitted on the condition that a certificate eventually be brought, and she was enrolled in the same class as Shloime. Their teacher periodically reminded Rachela about the verification, but in time the subject was dropped, and Rachela succeeded in having her way.

Shloime was truly a brilliant boy and an avid reader. He loved to read practically anything and everything. Although he particularly favored books on mathematics and the sciences, he had no aversion to reading the comic strips in the Polish daily newspapers, especially Tarzan. Undoubtedly his inclination toward mathematics and the sciences was somehow related to his near-genius abilities as a chess player.

Rachela was terribly eager to act like and be as mature a student as her older classmates. So, even though she was but five years old when she started school, she stubbornly insisted that she practice her writing only with ink. Understandably, there were ink spills everywhere: on her desk, on the floor, on every table and tablecloth in the house. Over time, however, she grew into an excellent, methodical, and thoroughly conscientious student.

Since I was the youngest child in the family, and in our parents' judgment much too immature to begin school at six, I was not enrolled in the first grade until I was almost seven years of age, in the fall of 1938. Unlike Rachela, I was too preoccupied with the joys of play and with childhood in general to even realize I wasn't beginning school at the same early age as my brothers and sisters. When I entered first grade, I was overwhelmed by the requirements of discipline: sitting quietly at a desk, being continuously attentive, and having to follow instructions. The children of my class sat at typical school desks, whose tops each had a carved-out hole for an inkwell in their upper right corner. We sat at those desks as our teacher, Mme Krogulcowa, began to teach us the alphabet. She would also read children's poems and stories to us. However, I longed bitterly for the freedom I had been accustomed to, and for my family and friends with whom I preferred to be playing, and I began to cry. I pleaded, "I want to see my sister. I want to go home." Unable to assuage my distress, Mme Krogulcowa sent for Rachela from her fifth-grade class. When I saw Rachela, I felt better. She talked to me and calmed me; that is, for the time being.

In those early school days, this situation repeated itself rather often. Once as my teacher was reading us a poem about a wild mushroom, my mind wandered off to those wonderful wild mushrooms and blueberries I loved to discover in the forest during our memorable Sabbath afternoon strolls. Suddenly I was shaken back to attention by the angry sound of Mme Krogulcowa's voice. "Miss Szachter," she thundered, "why are you not paying attention to the poem being read to you?"

I was too frightened to answer.

She then commanded, "Come up to the desk."

Apprehensively and sheepishly, I obeyed and walked up.

"Stretch out your hand," she demanded. She then lifted a ruler from her desk and slapped my opened hand.

Humiliated and smarting from the slap, I began once again to cry. And once again, frustrated and unable to cope with my immature patterns of behavior, Mme Krogulcowa called for the assistance of Rachela, who was by now becoming impatient and less sympathetic with me, since every time she was called out of her class to console me she was losing precious moments in her own classes.

Gradually I became acclimated to school life until I actually enjoyed the feeling of importance that being a student in school gave me. I even recall enjoying learning to write the word "Mama" with clay. Slowly Mme Krogulcowa succeeded in communicating to me the alphabet as well as the elementary basics of Polish reading, writing, and arithmetic.

One part of the school program I always enjoyed was recess. What pleasure to be momentarily released from the rigors and discipline of the classroom. Still, recess was not without its problems. Each girl in our school was required to wear a little black dress that buttoned in front and that had a small white collar. Mother did not like the way I looked in that outfit. Because of the wealth and position of our family in town, she was allowed to dress me differently from the other children, as she pleased, so I attended school wearing white embroidered organza see-through pinafores that tied at the shoulders into a bow. Once, when it was already cold outside, I wore my new jacket and hat during outdoor recess. The outfit had been bought in Krynica, a health resort Mother visited often. The jacket was of a style and quality that was worn only by children of wealthy families. It was made of a light-colored, suedelike sheepskin leather that was fur-lined and embroidered. The hat was woolen and of a matching light beige color. One of the girls in my class, to the delight and amusement of the other children, pulled off my hat and laughed haughtily. She scornfully ridiculed the way I was dressed differently from the other children and the different manner in which my hair was worn loosely with a tied ribbon. Although she eventually returned the hat to me, the incident was reported to the school principal, a liberal man who recognized the envy as well as the underlying anti-Jewish prejudice inherent in the mischief. The girl was eventually punished, but unfortunately other anti-Jewish manifestations erupted often and at all school-age levels, particularly against boys. One favorite taunt was *Żydzie Bejlisie* or Beilis Jew, a reference to Mendel Beilis, a Jew from czarist Russia who was accused—and eventually found innocent—of murdering Christian children for ritualistic purposes.

After school, we would return home for a quick lunch. In the afternoons, the boys would be in Cheder and the girls in Bet Yaakov from 1:30 until 6 P.M. Then, after the evening meal, young children generally stayed home for the evening and remained occupied with school work until bedtime. Older teenagers, especially boys, might meet in the Plaza or on Langiewicza Street. A boy might escort a girl, either for a walk or for a visit to one of the confectionery stores, where groups of young people would spend time leisurely together and socialize during the early evening hours.

WINTER

As winter came to Bodzentyn, snow would begin to accumulate over the small streets and on the rooftops of the houses. Because there were no cars in town, there was no need for snow removal, so snow accumulated until soon the entire landscape was covered with a picturesque blanket of white.

One winter, I caught a bad cold and cough. For minor ailments, we would go to the local physician in town, Dr. Pabian, who resided on Kielce Street. For any illness perceived as potentially more serious, however, we would seek medical treatment in a larger city. When surgery was required, we would go to Warsaw. Once, Rachela was taken to Warsaw to have a growth removed from her nose. For my cough, it was decided I should be taken to Kielce. So Uncle Yank'l escorted me there by bus, and we stayed at the home of my aunt Brucheleh and uncle Pintche Greenbaum. My aunt and uncle were first cousins. They had two children, Moisheleh and K'silush, and were in a transportation enterprise, shipping export and import cargo for their entrepreneurial customers. I loved being there and playing with Cousins Moisheleh and K'silush. I was so impressed with the big city, its streets and cars, its buildings and stores, and especially the running water and flushing toilet in Auntie's house. Understandably, I was terribly disappointed when we had to leave for home after so short a visit. However, I became excited when Aunt Brucheleh said she might be coming with Moisheleh and K'silush to visit us in Bodzentyn during the coming summer.

A memorable winter occasion was the joyous eight-day celebration of Chanukah. Each of the eight nights began with the lighting of the Chanukah candles by Father: one candle on the first evening, two on the second evening, and so on until the eighth evening when all eight were lit. The special Chanukah delicacies were the sugar-coated potato pancakes, called *latkes*, that Mother made. I was served my *latkes* at "my" table, where I sat alone, or with one or two other children. One evening, Shloime, so absorbed in whatever he was reading, absentmindedly placed a latke in the pocket of a new jacket as he walked toward the desk in the boys' section of the bedroom. How exasperated Mother was when she discovered the oil spot on his new jacket!

Unlike the Sabbath and other Holy Days, the holiday of Chanukah had no restrictions on work activities. Moreover, we played games, sang songs, and received Chanukah *gelt,* gifts or coins, from adults. A lovely Chanukah song Mother used to sing was "O *Ihr Kleine Lichtelech*" (O, You Tiny Candles), which tenderly related the meaning of the candles to the historic event that the holiday celebrates, the miraculous victory of the Maccabees over the Syrian Greeks in the year 165 B.C.:

O ihr kleine lichtelech	O, you tiny candles,
Ihr dertzeilt geshichtelech	You do tell stories,
Meiselech un a tzul	Indeed countless tales.
Ihr dertzeilt fun blitigkeit,	You tell of bloodshed,
Beryeshaft in mitigkeit,	Heroism and courage,
Vinder fin a mul.	Miracles of days of yore.

I recall the Christmas lights and decorations of our Christian neighbors. They were so beautiful and festive looking. But what we Jews were always reminded of was the blind prejudice and hate the average Pole harbored inwardly against us, through his venomous catchphrase *"parszywy żyd,"* and through his continuous harassment, individually and in gangs, of Jewish children and adults.

We were always aware of the fact that this virulent prejudice was due in no small measure to the role attributed to Jews of the first century in the crucifixion of Christ, as told in the New Testament. It was no secret that this role was traditionally dramatized and taught to generations of Poles through church-inspired religious instruction, and that their hatred was vented against the contemporary Jews of their towns, cities, and country. For centuries, uneducated, illiterate Poles carried this bigotry in their hearts and in their homes, where it was nurtured and generally unabated despite modern public school education.

As a result, Christmas Eve to Jews was indeed an occasion to commemorate, but surely not one to celebrate. This evening, different from any other for Jews, was referred to as *Nit'l,* the night of protest against the anti-Semitic teachings of the Church. It was a night marked by the conscious avoidance of Jewish study, a night not to be sanctified by devoting oneself to sacred Jewish word and thought, but instead to be spent playing cards.

A chief source of fun for the children of our family in winter was skating or sledding. My brothers and sisters loved to skate over the accumulated snow, especially downhill and across the frozen Psarka River near the castle remains at the western edge of town. I, too, would have loved to skate, but Father and Mother considered ice skating too hazardous for me, and therefore did not allow it. Instead, I used to sled along the sidewalk in front of our courtyard in Żwirki Plaza sloping downhill northeastward. Best of all, however, was a marvelous winter ride Father devised for us. He attached runners to an unwheeled wagon that we normally used to transport grains and hitched a horse to it. He then sat us in the makeshift sled, mounted the horse, and away we went over the snow-covered ground. Father, an expert horseback rider, was in complete control at all times.

These rides were thrilling, and at times a bit scary, even more so when Father led the sleigh downhill. We would laugh and scream as we held on desperately to each other. Our cheeks became reddened from the cold air, and steamlike air flowed from our mouths as we exhaled. It was so much fun, we never seemed to have enough. What a letdown it was when one of those rides ended; we could hardly wait until Father would take us on another one.

Father was often away from home—out of town, visiting Polish gentry and landowners, negotiating or consummating sales of grains, at times as far as Warsaw or Gdynia. He would load a wagon with sacks of grains and travel out on the road. During the winter he would dress heavily, in tall boots, fur hat, and coat, before venturing out into the rough elements of winter. It was, to be sure, somewhat hazardous for Father to travel alone, especially at night with a wagon filled with sacks of grain. He was therefore licensed to own and carry a gun for protection. The gun was always kept under lock and key when Father was home, and none of us children ever knew where he kept the key.

Winter evenings at home were warm and cozy and filled with shared family experiences. Often we would sit around our tiled parlor heating stove. The stove had an opening beneath the heating surface, into which we tossed first a few pieces of treated wood that ignited easily, and then a few pieces of ordinary wood and much coal. On evenings when Father would be expected back home from one of his many business trips, Mother would keep his supper in the opening above the middle of the stove so it would stay heated. Mother would often be sewing or knitting. Whenever she worked on a garment she happened to be wearing, she would always keep a piece of thread in her mouth.

"Why do you do that?" I asked once.

"In order to prevent my brains from getting sewn up in the process," she replied.

Rachela also enjoyed sewing. Often she would make clothes for her dolls out of scraps of materials she collected from Aunt Gitteleh and Uncle Froyim Biderman's yard goods stores. She and I had endless fun playing dolls together. On occasion we would make potato chips. We would peel potatoes, cut them into slices as thin as possible, and place them over a red-hot burner on our kitchen stove. In a minute the slices would brown and we would turn them over. In another minute, the slices would begin to curl. I remember still the crisp and delicious hot chips.

We children often sat around, reading or doing homework for public school. I would usually do my writing or arithmetic homework at my table. Father would often help Irka. Once a geography assignment called for the drawing of a map, one that Moishe had already completed masterfully but that seemed an insurmountable undertaking for Irka. Father took Moishe's map, connected an electrical light bulb to a wire whose energy was generated by our mill, placed the lit bulb into a dishpan, then placed a piece of glass over the pan and proceeded to trace Moishe's map for Irka. Many evenings after supper, Irka went back to the Bet Yaakov Hebrew School where rehearsals for plays were taking place, because she often had solo singing parts. The rehearsals lasted till late evening, when some of the older children would escort Irka home.

Since our parlor stove was our primary heating source during the winter, its chimney frequently needed to be cleaned. It was not at all uncommon for fire to billow out from it and create an immediate fire scare. Once when this happened, Mother became terrified and ordered us all to hurry out of the house. Everyone seemed to be in a rush to comply, except Shloime, who was so absorbed in his reading that he remained practically oblivious to what was happening. He began walking half-heartedly, reading as he was walking, until Moishe finally pulled the book out of his hands and shouted, "Don't just stand there like a *leimerner goilem* [clay dummy]—move!" Shloime's surprised expression revealed how stunned he was, as if woken suddenly from a daze. After considerable commotion and several buckets of water, the fire was successfully brought under control.

Toward bedtime, we children would take turns pressing our feather quilts against the tile-covered stove. Then we would quickly run into our cold beds and cover ourselves with the heated quilts. It felt so good with our warm beds and quilts protecting us from the cold, wintry night.

SPRING

By the middle or end of March, as spring made its way once again to Bodzentyn, rising temperatures began to melt the snow. Soon, we could not cross the street without passing through streams of cold water everywhere, and people could be seen chopping away large, thick chunks of thawing ice from the front walks of their residence-stores. From that time until well into April, we had to wear rubber boots to keep our feet dry. The severe winter weather had forced us to discontinue those marvelous strolls into the fields and forest; now, the beauty of foliage and blossoming flowers once again filled the air with renewed freshness and fragrance.

Early one Sunday morning at about 6 A.M., I woke up to Mother's and Father's hushed, tiptoeing movements. They were setting out on the first nature stroll of the season. I quickly sprang out of bed and insisted I be allowed to go with them. We walked far into the fields and meadows, where we strolled for some two hours. The spring air and reawakened nature were ever so invigorating.

Another reminder of the coming of spring was the feast of *Purim,* the holiday that commemorates the late fifth/early fourth century B.C.E. plot by the Persian viceroy Haman to destroy all the Jews that was foiled and averted by the counterplotting of young Queen Esther and her clever cousin Mordechai. Purim plays and skits dramatizing this story were an annual activity of the Bet Yaakov and other religious organizations in town. Older children, and even adults, would appear in costumes and made-up or masked faces portraying the main characters of the drama. They would go to houses of family and friends, knock on the doors, bring baskets of goodies to the poor, and jovially greet them, to the amusement and merriment of all. The traditional delicacies of this holiday were three-cornered, fruit-filled or poppy-seed-filled cookies called *Hamantashen,* which means Haman pockets.

By the time Purim was over, only four weeks remained before the major Jewish spring festival of *Pesach,* or Passover, the eight-day festival commemorating the deliverance of the Jewish people from slavery in Ancient Egypt. During this holiday, Jews are prohibited from eating leavened foods like bread and are required to eat instead a waferlike, unleavened form of bread called *matzah.* This and other religious ordinances recall the hasty exodus of the Israelites from Egypt, before even their baking breads had time to leaven. I recall the weeks-long elaborate preparations amid continuous activity and commotion. New clothes and shoes were ordered and fitted; the house underwent a more thorough cleaning than usual; the curtains were taken down, washed or replaced, and hung back up; extra washing was taken outside to dry. All sufficiently durable objects, including even some pieces of furniture, were taken outdoors to be thoroughly scrubbed and scrubbed again with soap and water until the wood was white clean. They were then left outdoors to dry in the sun before being brought back into the house, fully readied for the holiday. Finally our year-round dishes and silverware were replaced, in accordance with Jewish Law, by our special Passover silver and utensils. Large pots and pans, however, which were used during the year but which were needed for the holiday, could be used only if put through a procedure called *Kasher'n* (ritual cleansing). This was the domain of Grandfather Nus'n. In his courtyard outside the kitchen, he would set a couple of huge kettles over columns of built-up bricks, leaving spaces for small pieces of wood to be placed under the kettles. He would ignite the wood, fill the kettles with water, and bring the water to a boil. He would then clasp a separate brick with a pair of tongs, place it into the fire under the kettles until it grew red hot, and put it into the utensil; with a pitcher he would quickly take boiling water from one of the kettles and pour it over the brick, filling the utensil to overflowing. This caused a swift, sizzling column of steam to rise. This is how he ritually cleansed the pots and pans that were needed. Mother would bring her cookware and Aunt Gitteleh hers, and we children stood by, intrigued as we observed Grandfather repeat this procedure.

The special matzahs for Passover were baked in Grandfather Meier's ovens, specially cleansed for the holiday. The matzahs were made into average plate-size round shapes, perforated by parallel rows of tiny holes, with a small wheel. After they were baked, they were placed into huge white sheets, whose four corners were tied together into a knot; the matzah-filled sheets then formed huge bundles that were hung over large hooks along a wall in our house.

The day of Passover Eve was especially busy at home. Mother was pre-occupied the entire day, cooking for the festive *Seder* ceremony-suppers to take place on the eves of the first two nights. The atmosphere was much like Fridays in preparation for the Sabbath, but it was somehow more intense and more festive, and it had a special feeling. The food, for instance, was made without flour or leavening ingredients, and so it had a different texture and flavor.

Although we dressed in festive attire and set the table accordingly in honor of every Sabbath day, on Passover we put on our new clothes for the first time. The same lit candles and white tablecloth that we used for the Sabbath bedecked our parlor room table, but the dishes and silver were the special Passover ones; for the Passover Eve Seder, a wine cup was set up for each member of the family. The special Seder plate containing the six prescribed ceremonial foods gave the table its unique Passover ambience. In place of the chalah at Father's head place, which characterized the Sabbath and every other festival table, there was a special plate containing the three ceremonial slabs of matzah, which were placed in a beautiful, ornamented matzah cover. Copies of the Passover *Hagadah,* the special service booklet that tells the story of the Exodus, were set at the place of each family member.

Father was dressed in a white prayer robe for the Seder, and he sat on an extra cushion placed on his chair because the Seder was a time to relax and be comfortable. The Seder was a long service-ceremony that was interrupted midway by the festive holiday meal. Singing of special Hagadah songs and hymns added a musical dimension of beauty to the service, especially toward the end.

The first two and last two days of Passover, being major festival days, were sanctified by the avoidance of work and mundane activities, much like the Sabbath. However, the four intermediary days, termed *Chol Hamoed,* were designated by Jewish law as semisacred days, and so general weekday activities were allowed. These days were particularly exciting because each year at this time our aunt Feigeleh and uncle Y'shia Ehrlich and their three daughters—our cousins Chantche, Rivtche, and Ruchtcheleh—came from Szydłowiec to visit with us. We children had so much fun just being together. Unfortunately, these visits were short because Chantche and Rivtche had to be back in time for school. Uncle Y'shia, a pious and learned Jew, who wore a long beard, was the town *shoichet* and could also not be away from home for too long.

After the Passover holiday, we looked forward to one more holiday seven weeks later, the two-day festival of *Shavuot* (Pentecost), and then the coming of summer and summer vacation. The last major event of the school year was often an outdoor music festival on the Castle grounds. Rehearsals took place there, and children looked forward to the gala event with much enthusiasm, as it signaled the culmination of the school year and the long-awaited beginning of summer vacation. The festival featured songs, skits, and colorfully costumed folk dancers. Student performers were selected on the basis of ability. One year, Irka was one of those chosen to participate. Being the only Jewish child among the performers, she was disliked and harassed by the other performing schoolmates. Irka began to feel unwanted and unhappy in the group, and she and Mother decided she should withdraw from the festival. At the very next rehearsal, it became apparent that the quality of the singing group deteriorated significantly without Irka's voice, and the singing teacher pleaded with Irka to reconsider her decision. Irka complied with his wishes and rejoined the singing group only, and did take part in the grand music festival that year.

SUMMER

Of all the seasons of the year, summer was by far the most enjoyable and the most memorable. Even our regular family strolls seemed fresher and newer than at all other times of the year. The air had an exhilarating feeling—cool but not cold in the mornings and early evenings, warm but not uncomfortably hot later in the day and in the afternoons—so we always were able to dress lightly. In the summer air outdoors I felt free.

By 6 A.M. the sun was already beginning to appear, and on Sunday mornings Father and Mother would rise early to take in the summer sunrise. My brothers and sisters were still sound asleep, but I couldn't wait to jump out of bed and get dressed quickly so I could join Father and Mother, walking through the fields and meadows. We often picked *shchav*, little green leaves that were smaller and lighter in color than spinach, which Mother would later cook into a borscht. During our after-supper and Sabbath afternoon promenades, Rachela also used to come along.

The confectionery stores were open from morning until late evening. There we would see people of all ages munching on ice cream or chocolate bars. Even for the young adults who had been going there to sit and socialize throughout the year, summertime brought a fresh new phase to the life cycle of the year. No longer was it necessary to lug coal or wood into our houses to heat the stoves, or be concerned with keeping residence-stores warm; no longer was it desirable to remain indoors because of the cold air outdoors. The spirit of summer brought with it feelings of renewed buoyancy and optimism as people could once again promenade, meet, and socialize freely in the warm, open air.

The coming of summer always brought visits to and from our aunts, uncles, and many cousins. I could hardly wait for those visits. Several summers we traveled in Father's horse and buggy to see my aunt Dineleh and uncle Yoss'l Schreibman in Starachowice. I loved playing there with my cousin Irka. She was named after our late maternal grandmother just as my sister Irka was, but Cousin Irka was nicknamed "Lalunya" (Little Doll). Lalunya was about three years younger than me. She had a still younger brother, our little cousin Moisheniu.

Once Lalunya was sent to spend a couple of weeks in Bodzentyn, where Uncle Yank'l looked after her at Grandfather Nus'n's house. In the excitement of play one day, I accidentally pulled her arm too forcefully and she began to cry. Uncle Yank'l, generally as mild a person as anyone could imagine, spontaneously ran up to me and spanked me, and reprimanded me for getting so carried away in play. I ran home, frightened that I had caused serious damage to Lalunya's arm and hoping that nothing would develop from the incident. As the day wore on and I heard nothing more about it, I realized all was presumably well with her.

Quite often during the summer, Aunt Brucheleh Greenbaum came to visit from Kielce with Cousins Moisheleh and K'silush. Sometimes Uncle Pintche came with them. They, too, always used to stay at Grandfather Nus'n's house. Some of our uncles—that is to say, Grandfather Nus'n's sons—would rent a room at the Jakubowski estate next door in order to relinquish their beds to our out-of-town relatives. The weather was typically warm and sunny, so we would often walk out far, to a sloping meadow area. There we children would roam about and play, while Mother and Aunt Brucheleh sat and talked. They seemed always to have so much to discuss and derived immeasurable joy from being together. We didn't understand what they were talking about, nor did it really matter to us. Cousin Moisheleh was about Rachela's age. His hair was straight and as light blond as anyone could imagine. He was freckled and had light blue eyes. His younger brother K'silush was about my age. He was slender like I was and had blond curly hair similar to mine. People said we looked like twins. At times Auntie or the children would tease us, saying I would one day be his bride. I didn't really mind because I liked him very much.

Aunt Brucheleh used to enjoy teasing me. Once when I was lying on the ground, my attention diverted by the smell of a flower, she placed a small twig between my toes and tickled me. I liked her very much and particularly admired the way she dressed and used cosmetics, so she used to give me the empty jars and boxes of creams and powders. I adored smelling them and playing with them.

I used to love to lie down at the top of a grassy hill in a meadow and roll myself down the slope. Cousin K'silush would follow me and roll himself down. Mother urged Rachela to roll down, but she was rather plump and felt disinclined to try. Aunt Brucheleh encouraged Cousin Moisheleh, but he too was unwilling. K'silush and I, however, ran up and tumbled down, ran up and tumbled down, again and again, until we became exhausted. Sometimes we would pick flowers, especially blue cornflowers. We would then braid them for garland headbands, although not on the Sabbath, as it is then forbidden to pluck flowers.

Almost every summer at least once, Cousins Chantche, Rivtche, and Ruchtchele from Szydłowiec would come to visit with us for several weeks. Rivtche would get homesick after three weeks and would return home with little Ruchtchele. Chantche, on the other hand, loved Bodzentyn so much that she would often come immediately after the last day of school in June and remain until a day or so before school resumed in September. While in Bodzentyn, our cousins always stayed at Grandfather Nus'n's house. Often, our family and the Biderman family would gather there for dinner in his parlor room. In addition, the girls often ate and slept at our house.

One feature of summertime in our house was the strips of flypaper that hung from our ceiling, speckled with trapped flies. But we did not spend much time indoors. The outdoors was much too alluring. We used to love wandering together past the mill, then Grandfather Nus'n's entire vast backyard, past the huge double-door gate that led to Bodzentyn's town limits and beyond. There I often roamed by myself or with our immediate family. It was much more fun with all our cousins, as we went out to pick flowers and vegetables, sit on the meadow peaks, and run about and play.

A favorite place we used to go together was the site of the castle remains and its surrounding grounds near the river toward the western edge of town. Chantche was near my sister Irka's age, Rivtche near my sister Rachela's, and Ruchtchele was about fifteen months younger than me. All six of us would stroll there together. Sometimes Mother also went along. The landscape there was scenic and beautiful, a mountainous area surrounded by meadows and valleys. At the foot of a hilly meadow was the still, blue Psarka River. The grounds were an ideal recreational area where many people came to spend their leisurely hours. A photographer who lived nearby had his cameras set up on the grounds and took numerous pictures.

On one occasion there, we met Irka's friend, Ruchtche Barainska, and her mother. It was said that I was an unusually beautiful child. Ruchtche's mother, who admired me and was very kind, remarked to me, "Goldeleh, you look just like your father; your high cheekbones are exactly like his." Another time, Ruchtche told Irka that a medieval King Bodzenta, after whom she said Bodzentyn was named, used to live in the castle. I, for one, never stepped into the castle because of the many legends that were attached to it: that it was haunted, that ghosts came out at night, that if one entered it with a lit candle the light would become extinguished. Children and even many adults were afraid to tempt the castle's spirits. But not Father. According to one family story, Father once made a bet that he could enter the castle with a lit candle and that it would still be burning when he came out. I am certain that he entered and came out, but I don't know if the candle was still burning. Because Cousin Ruchtchele and I were close in age, we made wonderful playmates. Once when we all came to the castle grounds, we found a huge pile of straw and hay. I climbed to the top of it, and Ruchtchele followed me, and then we slid down together. We climbed up and slid down again, up again, and down again all afternoon. How much fun we had. Chantche and Rivtche kept a cautious eye on both of us.

When we would be sitting and resting, Rivtche, who had a natural motherly inclination, would braid her sister Ruchtchele's hair and select a matching ribbon to tie up the end of each braid. I was envious of Ruchtchele's hair because mine was too fine to form thick braids. Mother had to place a ribbon inside my hair in order to give it sufficient body for braiding.

During the summer, when Father would go out of town on business trips, he would occasionally take some of the children along. When his trips extended as far as Warsaw, he would often return with items that were unavailable in Bodzentyn, such as a special hide for making a particular color or quality of shoes or boots, or special fabric from which a particular suit or dress could be made. He might also bring home an unusual gift for Mother or the children.

On one occasion, Shloime wanted to go along. For some reason unknown to me, Father did not allow any of the children to accompany him on that particular trip. Shloime, however, was determined to go along. So he hid himself at the last moment under a pile of straw in the rear of the wagon, just as Father was mounting the driver's seat in front. Father proceeded on his journey, unaware that he had a passenger. Only after some thirty kilometers did Shloime suddenly jump up and jubilantly announce, "Papa! Look who's here!" Father was generally a gentle, warm, and loving parent, but on occasions such as these he would display the iron-willed, if not intemperate, side of his character. Although taken aback for the moment, he almost instantly and resolutely announced, "We're going right back home." Despite Shloime's urgent pleas and bitter disappointment, Father turned the horse and buggy around and proceeded all the way back home to drop Shloime off before resuming his journey.

Once, several summers earlier, when Cousin Rivtche was visiting with us, Father traveled by train to Warsaw. For one quarter *zloty* or twenty-five *groschen* per child, an adult could take as many as four children, so Father took Irka and Rachela and Cousin Rivtche. As the train approached Rivtche's hometown of Szydłowiec, she suddenly experienced an intense feeling of homesickness. She pleaded with Father, "I want to get off and go home. Please, Uncle, let me off!" Father reasoned with her as persuasively as he could, "You must realize, my dear Rivtcheleh, that the train station is five long kilometers from your house. How will you be able to get home?" But young Rivtche was totally overcome with her strong longing to return home, and she insisted, "Everyone at the station knows me, and I know them. They will take me home. Please, Uncle, let me off." Father, realizing how determined she was, took Rivtche off the train, put her in a *dorożka,* a horse and buggy taxi service that would take her home from the train station, paid the driver, and instructed him to bring Rivtche to the address of Aunt Feigeleh and Uncle Y'shia. He kissed little Rivtche good-bye and returned to the train.

The highlight of our summers was our yearly family vacation. The preparations, the anticipation, and the trip itself conjured up thrilling memories of previous summer vacations. These, in turn, only stimulated my imagination and impatient desire to already be at the site of the coming vacation, and to already be experiencing its continuous moments of delight. Once, before embarking on one of our annual summer trips, I felt I should go over to say good-bye to Great grandfather Alter. As I entered his residence, I greeted him and told him I had come to say good-bye because we would soon be leaving for our summer vacation. Smiling, he gestured for me to come toward him. He stuck his right hand in his pocket, took out a half-złoty, and gave it to me as a going-away gift. Whereupon I replied, "No, Grandfather, it is I who is going away. I should be giving you a *letzt-gelt* [going away] gift," which was indeed the custom among Polish Jews. His old bearded face beamed in a beautiful paternal smile, as he drew me toward him and kissed me good-bye. He replied warmly, "Go with Godspeed and good health, my child."

There were three vacation sites where we used to go. One was the tiny farm village of Celiny, a popular, secluded vacation spot within walking distance, some two or three kilometers from Bodzentyn. There we used to rent two rooms with cooking facilities in the Bartkiewicz peasant house. At first the entire family went, Mother and Father, all the children, and a maid. Father would then leave on business trips and, as a rule, return for dinner and the evening every other day. However, if his business took him to more distant places, he would return on Friday and remain through the Sabbath and Sunday. (Our mill operated on the Sabbath, but Father never went in there on that day.)

When the younger children were small, Celiny was an ideal place to vacation, since it was so close to home. Our maid could walk back to town to purchase groceries, although at times she would get a ride by horse and buggy. At Celiny we would always meet a cousin of Father's, Chayim Leibish Wandersman, who would be sitting in the grass field eating hard-boiled eggs and sandwiches from home. We children had immeasurable fun roaming about and playing here in this completely rustic environment, seemingly worlds away from home.

A second place where we used to go on vacation was Czarniecka Góra (Black Mountain), some fifty kilometers from Bodzentyn. To get there, we used to charter a minibus that transported us, our maid, and our belongings.

Our third and favorite summer vacation site was Berezów, a village on the outskirts of Suchedniów, some fifteen kilometers from Bodzentyn. We rode there in a horse and buggy from the stable in Grandfather Nus'n's estate. In Berezów we rented a small white cottage in the middle of a forest. Father and Mother used to go on very long strolls, past a meadow to a river. I never missed a chance to go with them. Hours seemed to pass by unnoticed. At times we would take along a *leżak,* a reclining lounge chair, deep into the forest, for relaxation. Or, we would attach a hammock between two adequately spaced trees and stretch out. How relaxing. The air was exhilarating here amid the tall, dense, fragrant pine trees. Mother wanted all the children to have a grand time, but she was particularly anxious for me to enjoy the air and work up an appetite, since I was so slender and generally such a poor eater. She always brought along plenty of food, including hard-boiled eggs and sandwiches. Mother knew that in the open, airy outdoors, I would eat: I used to love picnics. We children would also play games—ball games, checkers, or chess—as well as free play.

Although our hometown of Bodzentyn was essentially rural, our vacation sites were even more rural, so we children had much more room to run and play. Moishe and Shloime used to bring their bicycles to the cottage in the forest. When it rained, the thunder and downpour seemed heavier than in Bodzentyn. Since bike riding in the thunder was considered unsafe, they would keep their bicycles in the cottage until after the rain stopped.

In the depth of the forest we would meet friends. Among the people we would encounter was a young, obese woman, who seemed somewhat unbalanced mentally and who walked with a cane. She would always stop us and ask us for food. Mother always gladly shared some of our picnics with her. But regardless how much food Mother gave her, her appetite seemed insatiable, and she always had one ready comment, "You have given me enough food to satisfy exactly a half of one tooth!" As I recall the wonderful summers of childhood, one Sabbath afternoon stands out in particular, when Father took me through the forest, past the clearing where there were no more trees. It was the only time Father and I went there alone. The meadow leading down to the river formed a beautiful view, and the air was as refreshing as it can only be in the midst of these wide, free, open expanses of God's nature.

But the most exciting part of our summer vacations occurred when my aunts and their children came to join us. From Szydłowiec, from Kielce, from Starachowice, as well as from Bodzentyn, at least three aunts of the five sisters were together with their children most of the time. Each rented an apartment a kilometer or so from the small cottage where we stayed.

The men came only on Fridays, toward late afternoon, remained over the Sabbath, and returned home on Sundays to tend to their businesses. Father had a business route near Suchedniów, so on Sunday he would often leave our cottage to visit customers and collect outstanding bills. Rachela usually went with him. She loved and looked forward to those trips. They would leave about 9 A.M. and travel by horse and buggy. They rode past huge expanses of open, green farm areas and sparsely spaced cottages under blue, sunny skies. From time to time, approaching horses and buggies would cross paths with Father's. On unpaved roads, the sound of the hoofbeats gradually grew louder as the horses drew near. On the newer asphalt-paved roads, however, at the moment the horses got very close, the trotting suddenly sounded overwhelming and frightened Rachela. Father would patiently explain to her why the loud noise of the horses' hoofs came on suddenly, and she would no longer be frightened— until the next time. No matter how many times Father repeated his explanation, she never failed to panic the next time.

Father would return about one or two in the afternoon to bring back Rachela. He would remain for the rest of the afternoon, then continue on home alone to Bodzentyn in the evening. Our cottage was in a heavily wooded area, while the others were near a clearing or meadow a kilometer away. We used to love walking through the forest to be with the other family members. Around their cottages we had much more room to roam about. We would go together to the water pump or into the forest with our mothers. We would run about in the woods, except for Rachela who didn't like doing that, despite Mother's urgings. We played catch or volleyball, or just bounced a ball back and forth to each other. We played together in sandboxes, building castles, squashing them down, and building them up again. We took long walks together, ate outdoors, played hide-and-seek, sang Hebrew songs, and danced a Hora, which the older girls had learned at the Bet Yaakov.

At times we younger children rode on scooters while the older ones rode on bikes. Often the older children refused to play with us, but they were not allowed to tease us. Whenever they did, we would complain to our mother or our aunts, and our antagonists would be decisively reprimanded. Often the older children went swimming in a deep lake nearby; we younger ones were not allowed to join them there. At other times, they walked to a railroad depot some two kilometers in one direction to watch the passengers coming and going, or to a sawmill in Bogaj, some two kilometers in another direction, where wood was cut and transferred to and from huge wagons. On occasion, the whole family would eat in the woods at the Sherman Hotel, which was owned by a Jewish family from Kielce.

Time seemed to pass by so quickly, almost unnoticeably. Once as we were returning from a long walk, Aunt Brucheleh remarked how none of us seemed to realize how far we had apparently walked. Being together and playing together brought so much joy that the end of a day came almost as a disappointment—but one that was easily and quickly overcome by the onset of the morrow.

These blissful summer days were interrupted for Mother and me for a few weeks. This hiatus, however, provided yet other wonderful experiences for me. For a few years in the late 1930s, when my brothers and sisters were old enough to be left alone, Mother would leave our vacation sites for a four-week visit to an *Uzdrowisko,* a health spa and resort, named Krynica. Krynica was located south of us, in beautiful surroundings in the Carpathian Mountains, near the Czechoslovakian border. There she received mineral water baths, treatments, and diet supervision for gall bladder ailments and arthritis. She used to bring along our maid, who looked after me when Mother was undergoing the treatments. A temporary maid was hired for the rest of the family during the period we were in Krynica until 1938, when Mother began taking only me along unassisted by a maid.

I remember the long overnight train ride to Krynica. Toward morning, as the train passed by Tarnów and then Nowy Sącz, I knew we were getting close to our destination. My heart would beat faster from the excitement of knowing that soon we would be arriving at that wonderful health resort once again.

In Krynica, I was deeply impressed by the elegant stores, with their colorful, elaborate advertising displays that made Bodzentyn seem so provincial by comparison. Mother used to take me to a square at the foot of a lovely stone stairway, the site of a fountain that was set within a circular stone structure with imaginative stone carvings about its circumference, and whose waters were lit with color in the evenings. Benches along the walk lined the perimeter of the fountain area. Here people sat down to relax and converse, as many others wandered about.

At the spa, two silver stairs led to a forest where many fenced-in gardens were cultivated, each with different-colored beds of flowers. Plucking any flowers there was strictly prohibited, but they were so beautiful that one time I became entranced and picked a gorgeous flower here, and another of divine fragrance there, bringing them up to my nose, swallowing the wonderful smell. Suddenly, a young man rushed up to us and sternly informed Mother that touching any of the plants was strictly prohibited. When he fined Mother for the flowers I plucked, she was left no choice but to pay.

In the evenings at Krynica, the forest was crowded with elegantly dressed people promenading about. Every evening, I would see there groups of bearded and earlocked pious Jews, *Chasidim*, dressed in caftanlike coats and black hats, standing together, meditatively swaying, as they intoned their Mincha-Maariv, their late afternoon and evening service prayers.

I used to enjoy when Mother would take me into one of the restaurants for tea. On one occasion, however, a big fly flew onto our table and rested itself there. Perceiving the place as unsanitary I indignantly stood up and announced to Mother, "Oh, I am leaving! I cannot drink tea together with flies! This place is simply not clean enough! Please, Mother, let's go!" Mother, somewhat startled, shrugged her shoulders while smiling sympathetically, but she did not attempt to persuade me to stay, and we left.

Once toward the end of the four-week period, I began feeling lonely and longed to be back with the rest of the family. Mother pleaded with me, "My dear Goldeleh, how can you be lonely here with so many people all around?"

"But Mother," I answered, "to me all these people are like bunches of little ants. I want to go home."

No, Mother explained, I would simply have to wait patiently for another few weeks until her therapy sessions were concluded.

During the times Mother was scheduled for treatments, she used to leave me at a playground where wealthy families, for a fee, could leave children to be supervised and cared for while we played on swings, slides, and other recreational facilities. By now, however, I no longer wished to be left there, and I insisted that Mother take me along wherever she went. Finally, Mother prevailed on the authorities to let me join her in one of her arthritic health baths. I loved watching Mother seated in an indoor tub of bubbling water; she usually remained for about a half-hour. Then she was treated, dried, and dressed, after which she met with a doctor for a consultation.

Once, however, when Mother had an appointment with one of her doctors, she asked me to wait for her in the waiting room. Instead of sitting and waiting, I decided to walk around and enjoy the grounds and scenery. I slowly began a little tour of my own, continuing a bit further, and just a little further again, until finally I realized I did not know my way back to the doctor's office. Frightened, I began asking people how to get back. But where to? to whom? and how? Only after what seemed like an interminable period of uncertainty and anguish did these good people succeed in bringing me back to the doctor's office. There Mother was waiting for me, terribly concerned—and understandably exasperated by my whimsical excursion.

When the four-week period of treatments ended, Mother was probably more eager than I was to return to our vacation site and be back together with our family. Before returning, though, Mother would always buy some souvenirs to take home for the children. The mountain people around Krynica used to make lovely hand-carved canes. They also used to rear sheep. In due time they would shear the sheep, leave the leather, suedelike texture of the sheep hide on the outside, and line them with fur on the inside to make jackets. Then the mountaineers would hand embroider the jackets, which were made in a variety of colors and were very impressive looking. With these souvenirs in hand, we would be ready for our return journey to our summer site, where we would spend the remainder of our vacation once again with our family, before returning home for the fall season and the beginning of another year.

In this environment I spent the early years of my childhood. These years were filled with boundless joy, pleasure, and fun. I experienced consummate happiness and was always conscious of that happiness. I enjoyed the love showered upon me by grandfathers, parents, brothers, sisters, uncles, aunts, and cousins. Ours was such a close, intimate relationship. The wonderful times we spent being together and playing conjure up precious memories. How I loved nature and the rural atmosphere in and around Bodzentyn, as I roamed past the huge wooden gates at the far end of Grandfather Nus'n's estate, past fields and meadows, and more fields and more meadows. How could I ever forget the fragrance of the freshly cut hay, the flowers, and the streams, and the still greater, invigorating smell of the forest. How could I ever forget the horse-led sleigh rides in the winter; or the wonderful summer strolls with Mother and Father; or the exciting summer visits from out-of-town cousins, aunts, and uncles; or the thrilling summer vacations with Mother and Father, Moishe and Shloime, and Irka and Rachela. Mine was a life of earthly bliss. I believed it would never be different; that it would continue forever, without end. If only it could have.

II

WAR COMES
TO POLAND

8

The Approach of War

FROM THE TIME I was an infant of sixteen months, events began to take place in Poland's neighboring country to the west, Germany, that increasingly sent ominous and menacing signals to Poland, to Europe, to the world in general, and to the Jewish people in particular. The world had as yet not known an evil force so powerful and thorough, so determined to carry out its plans, or so deliberately deceptive in its operations, as Adolph Hitler and his Nazi Party. As a result, the nations of the world, great and small, long failed to recognize the hideous dangers that lurked behind the seemingly idealistic pronouncements of Hitler's spellbinding oratory.

From the moment the Nazis rose to power in Germany, the Jewish people began to taste their terror and fury, which increased with such boldness, efficiency, and savagery that, by the mid-1930s, anti-Semites in Poland became inspired and emboldened to step up their own anti-Jewish activities. Meanwhile, the continuously mounting danger of war portended infinitely greater danger for the Jews of Poland than for any other ethnic group—if and when Nazi Germany were to vent its fury and power eastward and strike out against Poland and its defenseless Jews.

Awareness of these realities came slowly, but unmistakably, to the Jews of Poland. Through newspapers and radio, Hitler's virulent speeches were communicated to the world, along with news of militant statements and actions by his Nazi government. Other reports told of the ceaseless, raging anti-Semitic assertions and of the anti-Jewish violence being perpetrated almost daily in the Nazi state. Moreover, as German Jews began fleeing to Poland, Polish Jews learned firsthand of the terrors suffered by their fellow Jews in Nazi Germany and became convinced of the potential danger to themselves as well.

The militant mood of Nazi Germany was trumpeted by the bellicose slogans of the Nazi Party from the earliest days of the regime, even before its rise to power: *Deutschland über alles* (Germany over all), and *Heute*

Deutschland, morgen die Welt (Today Germany, tomorrow the world). By 1935, Germany had begun a full program of militarization: full conscription and all-out production of tanks and other armaments, full-scale development of ground, naval, and air forces. In March 1936, Hitler defied the world by sending in troops to occupy the Rhineland, which had been demilitarized since the end of World War I. Two years later, Germany annexed Austria into what was now called "Greater" Germany.

The Nazi Party's fury against Jews began to be unleashed even before its ascent to power. Nazi propaganda blamed the Jews for the defeat of Germany in World War I and for the current raging economic crisis in Germany. Slogans and songs gave expression to such horrifying sentiments as *Juda Verrecke* (Death to the Jew) and *Und wenn das Judenblut vom Messer spritzt, dann geht's nochmal so gut* (When Jewish blood splatters from the knife, then things go twice as well [for us]). From the start, inflammatory headlines screamed across the front pages of the official Nazi Party newspaper *Der Völkischer Beobachter* (The National Observer): *Wir warnen das Judentum* ("We warn the Jews"—3/27/33); *Boycottiert die Juden* ("Boycott the Jews"—3/28/33); *Schlagt den Weltfeind* ("Strike the world fiend"—3/31/33); and *Der Abwehrkampf hat begonnen* ("The defense battle [against the Jews] has begun"—4/1/33).

During the first months of the Nazi regime, laws were enacted that excluded Jews from the medical and legal professions and from civil servant jobs, causing the victims to lose previously granted tenure and pension privileges. Jews were also legally excluded from journalism, from the arts, and from the right to ownership of land. Even the citizenship of naturalized Eastern European Jews living in Germany was revoked.

At the local level, social contact between Jews and non-Jews was forbidden and punishable by imprisonment. Jews were expelled from theaters, concert halls, museums, and parks, and storm troopers made frequent surprise raids on shops, cafes, theaters, and parks in search of Jews. Signs appeared everywhere: "Jews unwanted here"; "Forbidden to buy in this Jewish establishment." On office doors of Jewish doctors or lawyers, signs read: "Beware! A Jew! Visits prohibited." Trespassers were beaten, imprisoned, or deprived of employment. Eastern European Jewish pedestrians along the streets of Berlin were assaulted by gangs of Nazis, while police frequently seized bypassing Jews and forced them to clean the streets.

By a legal edict of 1934, Eastern European Jews residing in Germany began being deported to their countries of origin. The next year produced edicts expelling Jewish children from the schools of Germany and excluding Jews from service in the armed forces of Germany. The infamous Nuremberg Laws of November 15, 1935, defined a Jew as one having more than one Jewish grandparent, and all legally defined Jews were stripped of their German citizenship and reduced to "subjects." In the speech in which Adolph Hitler proclaimed these new laws to the world, he made the portentous assertion that the purpose of the new laws was to provide a tolerable solution of the Jewish problem. But should this solution prove to fail in its objective, then "the problem will have to be handed over by law to the Nazi Party for a *final solution.*" Thus, for the first time the world listened to and heard the euphemistic phrase that at the time implied the expulsion of the entire Jewish population of Germany to the island of Madagascar, but that six to seven years later was to mean the planned genocide of the entire Jewish nation.

A 1937 speech by Hitler contained the following incredible assertion: "Only . . . he who knows the joys of cruelty can be historically effective today. . . . The bases of my program are blood and fire. . . . I hate all that is spirit and humanity." By 1938, signs reading "Jews not admitted" were seen throughout Germany in front of hotels, grocery stores, butcher shops, bakeries, and dairies. Milk was unavailable even for Jewish infants. Medicine and drugs were likewise no longer sold to Jews. The year 1938 also witnessed decrees excluding Jews from industrial enterprises and forcing the transfer of Jewish businesses to non-Jews, as well as decrees requiring the registration of all Jewish property and the carrying of special identification cards stamped with a big black *J*.

Anti-Semitism in Poland had a long history. However, the depth and intensity of anti-Jewish propaganda, edicts, and violence inundating Germany served to embolden and encourage anti-Semitic feeling and activity in Poland. Masses of Poles had long noted and resented Jewish enterprising initiative and skill, but now, by the mid-1930s, their displeasure was becoming increasingly manifest. Jewish residence-stores in the center of town, as well as Jewish dominance in enterprises providing vital services or commodities to the local economy and community, were more openly being viewed with envy and hostility.

The resentful glances were being accompanied more and more by actions. In a statement in 1936, Cardinal Hland, Archbishop of Poland, accused Jews of practicing fraudulence and usury and advised his countrymen that "one does well to prefer his own in commercial dealings, and to avoid Jewish stores and Jewish stalls in the markets." Poles were quick to follow the archbishop's advice. In Bodzentyn, tailors, hat and cap makers, and makers of the upper parts of shoes had been for the most part Jewish craftsmen. Similarly, food enterprises had been primarily in Jewish hands. Now, non-Jewish Poles began entering these trades and enterprises, in an outspoken effort to displace Bodzentyn Jews. Boycotts of existing Jewish establishments were openly encouraged. On the weekly Monday market days, once-friendly Poles began standing in front of Jewish stalls in Żwirki Plaza with picket signs reading, "Don't buy from Jews." Others stood at store entrances attempting to block fellow Poles from entering the premises and photographing those customers ignoring their attempts.

During this time, an anti-Jewish pogrom erupted in Przytyk, a small town near Radom. This pogrom initiated a new wave of anti-Semitism across Poland and sent a chilling fear deep into the heart of every Jew in the country. In Bodzentyn, signs were seen on buildings, fences, and benches that read: "Poland without Jews," "Jews go to Palestine," "Don't trade with Jews."

On Langiewicza Street, an anti-Jewish incident erupted in the grocery and grains store of Y'chiel Grossman, who used to have his grain seed ground at our family mill. A non-Jewish neighbor of the Grossmans would come periodically to their store to borrow a scale, which Mr. Grossman, as a rule, gladly lent him. One Saturday afternoon, the neighbor came in to borrow the scale once again. Being the Sabbath day, the store was closed. Since religiously observant Jews desist on the Sabbath from handling any items relating to mundane occupational activities, Mr. Grossman refused to lend his neighbor the scale that day.

Two days later, the tall, muscular neighbor, in a visibly irritable mood, entered the store. He approached Y'chiel Grossman, grabbed hold of his beard, pulled him over the counter, and ranted at the top of his lungs, as his face reddened with rage and hatred: "Why in hell didn't you give me your Goddamned scale, you filthy Jew?" Mr. Grossman, in pain and bleeding, cried out desperately, as his beard remained tightly clasped within the strong grip of his powerful neighbor. Quickly, his son Nuter picked up an iron weight, rushed up to his father's tormentor, and struck him with a heavy blow over the head. Blood flowing from the top of the man's head forced him to release his hold on Mr. Grossman.

Within minutes, the incident drew the attention of practically the entire community. The neighbor, bleeding and smarting from the wound on his head, but feeling more intoxicated from hate than intimidated from pain, ran home. Shortly, he came strutting back into the store, this time with a billy club in hand, cursing and in a rage, and began chasing Mr. Grossman around the store. Quickly, Mr. Grossman's older son Alter grabbed a weight and began charging after their implacable neighbor. In the excitement and in flight, Mr. Grossman fell to the floor, hurt, as Alter continued pursuing the attacker until he finally succeeded in striking him down with another severe blow to the head. Having subdued the vengeful neighbor, the Grossman boys thundered a warning to him that, should he make himself the cause of such unprovoked trouble in the future, they would not hesitate to kill him. However, lending moral support to their defeated fellow native were some of the non-Jewish Polish spectators, who countered, "Hitler will come soon and get you Jews out of here. He will know how to take care of you."

In this increasingly anti-Jewish climate, Father began entertaining thoughts of abandoning our deep roots in Poland and moving to Palestine or Canada. This was actually not the first time Father had thought along these lines. As far back as 1920, even before he married Mother, he had considered moving to Canada but, because Mother was unwilling to leave the family, Father abandoned the idea. Now, however, he began corresponding with a brother of Uncle Froyim Biderman, who resided in Palestine, and with a cousin living in Canada. In Palestine, he learned, living conditions left much to be desired. Numerous items, services, and conveniences were either unavailable, difficult to acquire, or exorbitantly expensive. Moreover, the threat of Arab attacks was ever-present. Correspondence from Canada indicated that farmland was readily available, but that land in the larger cities was costly.

Mother, being accustomed to a life of relative luxury in Poland, would not hear of moving to Palestine. As far as Canada was concerned, she argued that she would not be happy living in a farmland area of Canada, where almost no Jews resided and where the children, therefore, would probably lose touch with their Jewish identities. Because we were not being directly affected by events a hundred or even two kilometers away, she rationalized that conditions in Poland were not so bad as to warrant an expensive move to a strange country. She preferred to leave well enough alone and allow events to unfold as they may in Poland. Moreover, she very much wanted Father to remodel the large storage building adjacent to our house and convert it into a new home for our family, as originally intended. Father gave in to her desire to remain in Bodzentyn. However, he opposed and rejected her remodeling idea. He considered the political situation in Europe and the social environment in Poland far too volatile and tenuous to allow for any such major investment of a permanent nature.

Nonetheless, day-to-day life proceeded in an atmosphere of relative normalcy. During the spring of 1938, a building was constructed on the far south side of the mill which consisted of several rooms that were used for administering the business of the mill. In it, Uncle Leib'l built an office for himself, where he kept records of machinery-related purchases and transactions.

That summer, we spent one of our most enjoyable family vacations at Berezów, on the outskirts of Suchedniów. The wonderful air and flowers and foliage were as inspiring and invigorating as ever, and the gorgeous summer skies seemed to belie the gathering political clouds. Mother took me for her annual four-week visit to Krynica in the Carpathian Mountains, where beauty in nature seemed as alluring and tranquil as can be imagined. In the fall of 1938, I entered the first grade in school, as Shloime and Rachela entered the fifth grade and Moishe and Irka entered the seventh and final grade of elementary school in Bodzentyn.

The main family event of the year, meanwhile, was the marriage of Uncle Moishe to a young woman from Kraków named Chava Gitler. I recall the bustle and excitement at home as Mother prepared for the wedding. She undertook a couple of trips to Kielce to have her special wedding clothes fitted and made by a well-known, exceptionally fine tailor. I was particularly impressed by her beautiful, rich-looking fur coat and hat. From our immediate family, only Mother and Irka went to the wedding. Naturally, Grandfather Nus'n and Uncles Froyim, Yank'l, and Leib'l attended, as did Aunt Brucheleh and Uncle Pintche Greenbaum from Kielce and Uncle Y'shia Ehrlich and Cousin Chantche from Szydłowiec. I recall Mother bringing me a large red ball as a souvenir when she and Irka returned home from the festivities. I enjoyed playing catch with it with my girlfriends. After the wedding, Uncle Moishe and his new wife moved to Kielce, where they opened an ironware store similar to Grandfather Nus'n's, which Uncle Moishe had managed up to the time of his marriage.

As normal life continued in Poland, a quick sequence of actions by Germany brought Europe to the brink of war. In early September 1938, Hitler demanded that the Sudetenland area of Czechoslovakia be ceded to Germany, under the pretext of bringing "freedom" to the "persecuted" Sudeten Germans. On September 12, he threatened war to bring about their "liberation." Cowering before his brazen threat, the heads of state of

England, France, and Italy met with him in Munich on September 29 and succumbed to his ultimatum. Two weeks later, on October 11, German troops moved in unopposed and occupied the Sudetenland.

On October 28, 1938, over fifteen thousand Jews, former Polish citizens, were arrested by the Gestapo, herded together, and shipped to Zbąszyń, a small border town along the Polish-German frontier. From there they were driven across the border into a no-man's-land by German police and SS guards. One of these unfortunate Jews, whom we knew from Bodzentyn, related to us firsthand the colossal tragedy and humiliation that had befallen the Jewish communities of Germany. In this most recent deportation experience alone, he said, many of our brethren had perished from blows and exhaustion during the journey.

On November 7, in Paris, France, Herschel Grynspan, the seventeen-year-old son of one of those unfortunate Jewish couples who had been deported back to Poland, avenged his parents' maltreatment by shooting and killing an official of the embassy of Nazi Germany in Paris. Using this incident as a pretext to intensify its rabid Jew-baiting program, Nazi authorities in Germany unleashed a nationwide pogrom. From that evening of November 9, the date that became known as *Kristallnacht* (The Night of Broken Glass), through November 10, the Germans destroyed 76 synagogues, set ablaze or severely damaged 191 others, and vandalized or burned 7,500 Jewish shops, homes, and businesses. Thirty-six Jews were left dead, another 36 were severely injured, and 30,000 more were arrested and sent to concentration camps in Buchenwald, Sachsenhausen, and Dachau. As a crowning irony of the tragedy, Nazi authorities fined the German Jewish community one billion marks as reparation for the damages.

On November 15, a new decree allowed the Nazi government to confiscate all gold and valuables heretofore owned by Jews. Two months later, in January 1939, Hitler sardonically declared, "Today, I wish to be a prophet once more." Should international Jewry once again plunge the nations of the world into war, he predicted, the result would bring "the annihilation of the Jewish race in Europe."

On March 14, 1939, this time with no pretext, Hitler ordered troops in to occupy all of Czechoslovakia. Exactly one week later, German forces seized the bordering Lithuanian port city of Memel and at once demanded of Poland the free city of Danzig and the right to build a road across the Polish corridor. The Polish government immediately rejected the demands and appealed for support from the governments of England and France.

Both governments responded by publicly guaranteeing the integrity of Poland's borders, pledging in effect that they would go to war against Germany in the event of a Nazi attack against Poland. Six weeks later, in a speech delivered on April 28, Hitler responded by repudiating an earlier nonaggression treaty between Germany and Poland.

Despite the mounting political tension, particularly between Germany and Poland, daily routines of our rural life in Bodzentyn proceeded in an air of relative normalcy. By the end of June, we had all completed our school year without interruption. Still, adults were in varying degrees apprehensive of the dangers of a possible war. Because of Father's own concerns, the summer of 1939 was spent at home. For the first time in recent years, Mother did not go to Krynica. Cousins Chantche and Rivtche from Szydłowiec did come to visit with us, though, and we children greatly enjoyed spending the summer in Bodzentyn. As usual, Rivtche left for home after three weeks, while Chantche remained with us throughout the school vacation period.

Our summer was unfortunately marred by the sudden passing of Great grandfather Alter. He had lived a long and fulfilled life, but his death nevertheless deeply saddened the family. Along with his death, however, came two joyous and auspicious family events: Uncle Froyim became engaged to a young woman from out of town, and Uncle Moishe and Aunt Chavtche, now living in Kielce, had a blond-haired baby boy, whom they named Samush.

News during the summer continuously told of negotiations being carried on between the British-French alliance and Russia, and warnings came from Russia about the possibility of renewed negotiations between it and Germany. In Poland, the threatening clouds of war seemed more ominous than ever as August drew to a close. One of Father's business trips took him to Katowice, near the German border, where he sold clover seed to a German client who subsequently shipped the cargo to Germany. While he was in Katowice, Father talked politics with his business client. From him, Father heard a frightening assessment of current events from the German point of view. Father's client was certain that war would break out any day and that Poland was totally unprepared to engage the modern, mechanized army of Germany in battle. Any attempted defensive battle by Poland, he believed, would be futile and crushed within a matter of days.

When Father returned home, he related his client's predictions and expressed grave concern as to what might happen to us Jews in the event they proved to be correct. Mother reminded him that we had lived through war and terrible times before and had managed to survive. As a matter of fact, she continued, during World War I, when the Germans had occupied Bodzentyn, their occupational administrations were very reasonable and considerate. It was the Russian and Ukrainian Cossacks we had to fear. In the meantime, she suggested, we are here, there is no war, and there are no Germans here.

Suddenly on August 23, the radio and newspapers reported the official signing of a nonaggression pact between Germany and Russia. It took little imagination to realize that if Germany attacked Poland, then England and France could no longer count on Russia to join them in guaranteeing the integrity of Poland's borders. In Bodzentyn, war fever began to spread everywhere. I recall people standing in groups in Żwirki Plaza anxiously discussing the political situation. Although I did not understand the discussions themselves, I could feel the excitement, the expectation of something momentous about to happen. Never having experienced war, I could not imagine what it might be like. Might it be something good? Something bad? The intensity of discussion created within me a feeling of almost eager anticipation.

I heard some people saying that bombs might fall from the air. One man was saying that if war came he would run to Warsaw. When Father asked him, "Why Warsaw?" the man replied that in 1917, during the world war, as the Austrians were retreating from the advancing Russians, Bodzentyn was burned to the ground, while Warsaw completely escaped the ravages of battle. Father countered, "But there is an important difference this time. Now there is a Hitler in Germany, and from all indications he will not spare big cities of foreign countries in order to preserve their beauty or national historical sites." The man replied, "Though you may be right, I have the feeling I will be safer in Warsaw than in Bodzentyn."

On August 29, the newspapers and radio reported that Germany had called for full mobilization of its armed forces. War was now imminent.

9

The Outbreak of War

At DAWN on the morning of Friday, September 1, 1939, the armies of Nazi Germany stormed across the Polish border. Fully mobilized with the most modern military tanks and equipment, seventy divisions of the best-trained army of that time in Europe drove deep into Poland from seven different points. At the same time, an equally well-prepared air force dropped bombs from warplanes over countless cities and villages, spreading destruction and terror throughout the country. England and France immediately responded by declaring war against Germany, and the world reeled from the sudden realization that World War II had begun. Unfortunately, neither England nor France was in a geographical position to render Poland any direct assistance, nor were they prepared to attack Germany from the west and thereby offer even indirect military aid. Thus Poland remained, in effect, without allies, left to absorb the full thrust of the German onslaught alone.

Poland began its mobilization on Thursday, August 31, only hours before the German invasion began. The Polish army of some 350,000 men consisted primarily of infantry, a few tanks, some 800 warplanes, and little heavy artillery. Its main mobile force was a large but completely outmoded and ineffective cavalry. By the end of the first day, the German armies had already plunged deep into Poland. By Saturday, the still-grounded Polish air force was bombed out and destroyed from the air. The Polish military staff had planned to withdraw and form a defense line at the Vistula River. The German forces, however, with unprecedented speed, which soon came to be designated as *Blitzkrieg* or lightning warfare, swept beyond and around Polish armies, enveloping them and isolating them into small units that were easy to defeat.

In Bodzentyn, the grim war news instantly began to spread feelings of fear and desperation. At home, immediate concerns were many. Uncle Leib'l had been drafted into the Polish army in 1938; now that war had broken out and Polish resistance seemed to be so ineffective and disorganized, who knew what dangers he might be in.

Grandfather Nus'n had gone to see a doctor in Kielce several days earlier. After hearing a radio broadcast that said Kielce had been heavily bombed, we were terribly worried. He did not arrive home until evening, having braved the hazardous journey. Cousin Chantche was vacationing with us; getting her back home to Szydłowiec was surely no priority against the sudden and extreme risk factor. The most imminent considerations focused on planning for the now likely event of bombs falling over Bodzentyn or of German units battling in the town and capturing it. Father began attaching green strips of paper to our windows, designed to prevent them from vibrating to the breaking point in the event of air bombardment. He also placed a large sum of United States paper currency in a bottle, dug an opening into a wall of our kitchen, and hid the bottle in the wall to be kept safe for emergency situations.

Meanwhile, throughout Bodzentyn, mobs of people, Jewish and non-Jewish, began running aimlessly, not knowing in which direction to turn. Those people owning a horse and buggy drove away. Others ran on foot. Many headed toward Russia. Already on Saturday, September 2, word was spreading in town to the effect that Jews in particular would be wise to flee Bodzentyn. The rumor had probably been initiated by anti-Semitic German sympathizers among the Polish peasantry. Nonetheless, it compounded the already enflamed panic situation.

Our family was not prepared to flee the city quickly. Since there were young children in our family, Father realized we were perhaps not as mobile as some other families. Nonetheless, he felt that we should make every effort to get to our powerful neighboring country to the east. Mother, however, felt terribly insecure about going to a strange country where conditions were thought to be dubious at best. "We are completely unprepared for the severe Russian winters," she argued. "Our clothing is inadequate and we could freeze to death there. We would probably have no more to eat than bread and oil, if that. And what if we become entangled with the retreating Polish army, or get caught up in an area of battle? I am afraid to go to Russia."

Nevertheless, when faced with the alternative of remaining in Bodzentyn in the path of the advancing German army, and then under Nazi occupation, Father concluded that we must abandon Bodzentyn and head toward the Russian border. Specifically, he decided we should travel to Koprzywnica, a town some eighty-five kilometers southeast of Bodzentyn, where an affluent Polish landowner and business client of Father's resided on his own large estate. There, Father hoped we could stay for a few days and have an opportunity to think, free of pressure, and weigh all possibilities before proceeding further.

Thus, plans became crystallized. We would leave for Koprzywnica the very next day. Father arranged for the services of a Polish peasant to drive one of the two wagons we would be using for the journey and instructed him to prepare for an early morning departure. Events, however, moved faster than Father had anticipated.

We were abruptly awakened about 4 A.M. the next morning by a frenzied rapping on the door. It was Uncle Froyim, who had come to inform us that a general panic had erupted in town. "Everyone seems to be fleeing," he announced. "Yank'l and I are starting out immediately for Russia." Then he added, "Do whatever you can, but hurry. There is no time to lose." I recall the rushing, the excitement and commotion, as we hurried to leave Bodzentyn. Father hitched horses to the two wagons, as originally planned, and rushed to get the Polish peasant he had engaged the day before. In a state of near panic, we all assisted in quickly loading one of the wagons with food, clothing, and numerous other items Mother felt we might be needing along the way.

In our haste, Father accidentally dropped the bottle he had filled with money, and the American dollars scattered across the kitchen floor. Visibly upset, he remarked impetuously, "Oh, we have enough money without it. Let's just go." Without taking the time even to collect the money, we rushed from the house and downstairs to the wagons that were now standing ready in our courtyard.

The Polish peasant was already outside waiting for us. He stepped up to the driver's seat on the wagon containing our possessions, as our entire immediate family—Mother, Moishe, Shloime, Irka, Rachela, and I—hurriedly boarded the empty wagon, and Father mounted up to the driver's seat. Away we rode, following roads that were densely cluttered with panic-stricken people, some riding, some walking, all seeking refuge, but none knowing where it could be found.

Our journey was long, although we were fortunate in having a sunny day for traveling. Nonetheless, the fact that our future was so uncertain and traffic was so heavy and noisy made the trip seem more wearing than it would have been under normal circumstances. Father was reasonably optimistic that his client would welcome and accommodate us. Father had been selling him large amounts of grains and seeds on credit for quite some time, and he happened to owe Father for a number of recent purchases. In addition, he and Father maintained a cordial personal relationship, and the wealthy landowner seemed to have deep respect for Father as an individual.

By midday, weary from the long journey, we arrived at the estate. Father approached his trusted business client and explained our predicament to him. We were relieved to learn that he responded warmly and graciously offered us his servants' quarters as a lodging. It felt so good to dismount from the wagon and unload our possessions, even in a temporary lodging such as this. The landowner had food brought to us, and we were made to feel comfortable. The following morning we were served breakfast. As we ate, we looked forward to enjoying a day of rest and relative relaxation.

Father, meanwhile, was anxious to learn of the latest war developments so he could contemplate carefully our next moves. Upon his shoulders lay the responsibility of choosing a course of action whose consequences were of life-and-death magnitude. If we undertook the journey to Russia, we had neither family nor friends there to assist us. Who could tell what risks might be involved in attempting to cross the border, especially with five children aged seven to fifteen, who would only decrease mobility and increase the risk factor in an emergency situation. In a strange Communist country, where would we stay, and would Father have the same freedom of movement as in non-Communist Poland, where money and bribery could go a long way? Would food, clothing, and shelter always be available, even for purchase?

On the other hand, if we remained in Poland under Nazi occupation, perhaps we could hope to survive if the Germans governed as they did when they occupied Poland in World War I. Judging, however, by the public utterances of Hitler and by the persecutions already experienced by the Jews of Germany, who could tell how badly Jews might be treated in a Nazi-occupied Poland? Father knew that daring risks loomed before us regardless of which course of action he chose, so he hoped he could think in relative peace for several days before deciding.

After breakfast, however, we sensed a less than friendly attitude on the part of the landowner's wife, and a notably less cordial demeanor on the part of the landowner himself compared to his warm acceptance of the preceding day. In a family chat, we surmised that his wife felt uneasy giving shelter to such a large group of Jews, particularly one with so many possessions. Father decided that he should confront the landowner directly to find out whether we had indeed already overstayed our welcome.

Father approached him and was invited into the house, where they conferred for a considerable length of time. When Father returned, he told us what had happened.

According to Father, the landowner had admitted that our mere presence on his estate was creating an atmosphere of restlessness and panic among his servants. They realized, he explained, that we were obviously fleeing from something, and so they were assuming that the Germans must be quickly approaching in this direction and that their arrival could be imminent. In addition, both he and his wife felt uneasy over the possibility of being caught sheltering Jews. Furthermore, he added, he was of the considered opinion that it would be even more dangerous for us than for him if the Germans found us on his property. He did not, however, directly ask that we leave. Nonetheless, Father realized clearly that we were no longer welcome. He also began to fear the servants might even kill us. However, he replied to our host simply that he understood his point of view, and that we would remain only until the following morning.

Early the following morning, on Tuesday, we again loaded the one wagon with our possessions and boarded the other. Then we set out wandering on the road. This time, however, Father was disappointed and discouraged. If this was what could be expected of people in Poland, and if not even money could buy security, he wondered how much greater would be the risk of going to Russia. Father would not make any hasty decisions on such life-and-death matters before having had the chance to think calmly and clearly for several days, so he decided we should travel to the home of a Mr. Langer, a wealthy Jewish grains merchant and longtime trusted friend and customer. Mr. Langer lived with his family in Waśniów (called Vushnyev in Yiddish), a small town some sixty kilometers northwest of Koprzywnica and some twenty-six kilometers southeast of Bodzentyn. This move brought us about two-thirds of the way back to Bodzentyn, but Father believed he would have the opportunity to hear opinions and thoughts of other Jews here that would help his own inclinations to crystallize and take shape. He felt certain that we would be completely welcome and could stay as long as necessary with Mr. Langer and his family.

By early afternoon, we arrived in Waśniów, and Father proceeded to the house of his business associate. After speaking to him for merely a few moments, it became apparent that indeed we would be made to feel comfortable here for as long as necessary. Completely sympathetic to the plight of fellow Jews, and entirely in the spirit of the ancient Jewish tradition of *Hachnasat Orchim* (hospitality to wayfarers), the Langer family greeted us warmly and most graciously invited us into their home. For the next three days, they shared everything they had with us, as if we were family. In fact, Mr. and Mrs. Langer and their three children could not have treated us more cordially and courteously. They went out of their way to make us feel welcome and managed to find places for all of us to sleep in their house. Our peasant driver slept in one of our wagons and looked after our horses, wagons, and possessions.

During these three days, Father met with other Jewish friends and families, and our next moves became clear to him. The consensus was that, if we could get there, we would be safer in Russia. Although the risks were great indeed, the risk of remaining under the occupation of a force that was so openly and blatantly anti-Semitic would be decidedly greater. Hence Father's plan was, finally, to attempt to get to Russia. If, however, circumstances along the way should preclude that possibility, he would then take us back toward Bodzentyn and let events unfold as they may, while we hoped for the best.

In any event, he clearly foresaw grave perils lying ahead that could easily claim the lives of at least some members of our family. He made it a point, while still in Waśniów, to prepare us children mentally and psychologically for these possibilities. He advised us, as only a loving father could, how to cope with the seemingly certain dark days ahead. He exhorted us, in the most serious tone of voice I ever heard him speak, that if and when we found ourselves in a life-threatening situation, each of us must think only of his or her own safety.

"Do not look back," he said. "Do not concern yourself with any other member of the family. Run to save your own life. It is very possible that the family may be separated. It is possible that neither Mother nor I will survive; and if you try to help anyone else, you will only endanger your own life, without being able to help the others." We children began to cry, but Father insisted with frightening severity that each of us must put forth the greatest effort and concentrate only on fighting for and saving his or her *own* life.

Thursday, the third day of our stay in Waśniów, Father decided that we should be on our way. He reasoned it was wiser to travel at night than by day so as not to be recognized as Jews on the run, so he informed Mr. Langer that we would be leaving toward evening that day. As the sun began to set and dusk gradually descended, we once again prepared our wagons for the next leg of our journey. Before leaving, we bade the

Langers a warm farewell and expressed to them our heartfelt gratitude for their exemplary hospitality. We extended to each other our emotional wishes for Godspeed and divine salvation.

Then we mounted our wagons and headed east toward the Russian frontier. We followed the crowded roads in a cautiously optimistic frame of mind. We traveled for several hours, with hardly any change in the routine pattern of the scenery. We passed by open fields, then a farm with grazing livestock, then another interval of open space, and another farm with grazing livestock. As we rode, we hardly noticed the time passing by, until twilight finally darkened into night. Still, we continued riding into the night, following throngs of people, some walking with packs on their backs, others on horseback, still others in horse-led wagons. Suddenly, from afar, we began hearing thundering sounds of artillery shells and bursting bombs. Crisscrossing rocketlike fires could be seen blazing across the distant sky. Soon we realized we had crossed paths with a retreating Polish army unit. Many of the soldiers came lunging toward any civilian horses within reach, in an effort to snatch them for the army effort.

Father paused for a brief moment to ask a soldier what was happening. The soldier informed Father that innumerable horses had been killed or injured in battle and that the army was planning to reorganize and re- group in order to confront the enemy with an effective defense line before Warsaw. Horses and wagons were desperately needed by the army, he added, and he cautioned Father we had better get off the main road or we might lose our horses to the war effort. No sooner had Father proceeded toward a side road when one soldier, and then another, came charging at the horse that was pulling our wagon. Father, who was an experienced and skillful horseman, succeeded—but with great difficulty, to be sure— in fending off their assaults. He realized, however, that within minutes all horses and wagons would be seized by the desperate army and that we had to abandon this route as quickly as possible.

As fast as possible, Father drove off the main road to the first accessible side road. He immediately concluded that conditions were by now much too hazardous for us to continue on toward Russia, so he decided to fol- low his alternative plan, namely to head back toward Bodzentyn. Instead of returning straight to the city, though, Father reasoned that we would be safer near a forest area, where an invading enemy force would not likely venture. An ideal place, he decided, would be Celiny, one of our former summer vacation sites. The roads leading there were narrow and bumpy; but it was adjacent to a thickly wooded area, and it was no more than three kilometers from Bodzentyn.

Father led us onto a road that he was almost certain should lead to Celiny. However, he soon realized that he had been mistaken. In a flash, he remembered that he did know the way to the residence of a Polish peasant acquaintance named Piórczyk, whom he liked and trusted, and who would undoubtedly know how to direct us to Celiny. Quickly, Father changed course and took another road, leading to the village where Piórczyk lived.

After riding a considerable distance, we finally approached Piórczyk's residence. Father halted the horse and went up to the door and rapped. How relieved we felt when the peasant came to the door with a lit kerosene lamp. Father explained our situation to Piórczyk and asked him if he could direct us to Celiny. Having been well treated by Father over the years, Piórczyk readily answered in the affirmative, asking only for a few moments to ready himself. Shortly, he came out, hopped up onto our wagon, and began leading the way. What a stroke of good fortune.

To avoid paths likely to be taken by the retreating army, Piórczyk led us over secondary and very inferior, rough dirt roads that, in the pitch black of night, required all the experience he had and more. We children, half-asleep and exhausted both emotionally and physically, were shaken awake several times when our wagons were accidentally led into a ditch. We all had to disembark from the wagon to help lift it back up onto the road before we could continue. The journey seemed interminable. At irregular intervals, Father would pause to talk to and glean information from people along the road, and he would then turn around and tell something to Mother. The long, tiring ride was traumatic—traveling on and on, not knowing where we were going or what hazards lay in our path.

At last, in early morning, and with one of our wagons almost completely damaged, we arrived safely at the gate of the Bartkiewicz farm in Celiny. After such a harrowing experience, it was a relief to have found a familiar site near the forest, where the idyllic quiet had brought us so much joy in summers past, and which now could possibly offer us at least temporary refuge.

Father approached the door and rapped on it. Soon Mr. Bartkiewicz responded with a lit kerosene lamp in hand, looking somewhat startled. But when Father explained our situation to him, Mr. Bartkiewicz immediately and very graciously agreed to set us up in his barn. Although we would have been more comfortable in our old summer cottage, we realized we would be safer in the barn. Mr. Bartkiewicz was pleasant to us and made us feel welcome and comfortable. The barn was surrounded by vines of cone-shaped hop flowers that were used for flavoring beer. The scent of the hop vines and the freshness of the early fall air in the rural environs near the forest brought back memories of the wonderful summers spent here. They also gave us a feeling of temporary tranquillity and respite from the storms of war, which for the moment seemed infinitely far away. Our nostalgia, however, was shaken by the reality that we were now indeed fortunate to have been given a stack of straw and hay on which to rest—for the time being at least.

We rested peacefully in the barn for the remainder of the night. In the morning, we had a relaxed breakfast. After breakfast, Father was anxious to learn of the latest war developments. What he discovered was that the Germans were moving at lightning speed on all fronts and meeting only feeble resistance. The one bright note for us in the otherwise grim war news was the fact that the road that Father had initially rushed onto when fleeing the retreating Polish army the day before, and which he had hoped would lead us to Celiny, had been bombed. Indeed, the very fact that Father had strayed and had abandoned that road when he did may well have saved our lives. Hopefully, this would prove to be a good omen.

During our stay at the Bartkiewicz farm, our host saw to it that food was brought to us regularly. On one or two occasions, he even invited us into his house. We enjoyed a feeling of relative security in our familiar, one-time summer vacation surroundings and so we remained there for three days, biding our time, waiting to see how the military situation would unfold. Realizing, however, that we had no recourse but to remain in Poland under seemingly inevitable Nazi occupation, Father again spoke to us, repeating his earlier stern advice. He added that at the first opportunity he would have money sewn into our clothes and sealed into our shoes. This money was to be spent for emergencies, for food, or for bribing someone in order to save a life. Our sole priority must be survival.

After several days, on the following Tuesday, a radio announcement from the local police informed us that our entire area was now in German hands and that the situation had become stabilized. The local population was kindly requested to cooperate with the new government and to return home and proceed with the routines of daily life as before the commencement of hostilities. The police emphatically assured local inhabitants that the change in political status should cause no concern to any law-abiding citizen.

That afternoon, Father and Mother and we five children set out for Bodzentyn, this time by foot. It was a balmy and beautiful sunny day in early fall, and the crowds were already much smaller than in those ten or so panic-filled early days of war. With the approval of our hosts, we stored our horses and badly abused wagons as well as our possessions in the barn and joined the other Jews and non-Jews along the three-kilometer route to Bodzentyn, proceeding leisurely, homeward bound.

As we approached Bodzentyn, we were anxious to see what had happened there since we had left over a week before. We could hardly wait to reach our courtyard. We rushed into our house, up the stairs, and into our residence. How amazed we were to see that everything was exactly the way we had left it. Even the loose American dollar bills we had left strewn about on our kitchen floor, in our frenzy to flee Bodzentyn, remained untouched. Also the green strips of paper, which Father had attached to our windows to minimize their vibration in the event of a bombing, were totally intact. Nowhere throughout our house were there signs of disturbances or intrusions of any kind, nor any indications that a war had ever taken place.

We proceeded to collect the dollar bills and put them back into the bottle and into the kitchen wall. We took out our linens and bedding and made up our beds. We were back home, together, safe and sound. Perhaps it was the right decision to return home. Perhaps things would be no worse than during the German occupation of World War I. Perhaps things would work out for the best. Perhaps.

10

The Beginning of the Occupation under the Nazis

AFTER SETTLING back at home, we had many thoughts and immediate concerns. Uppermost in our minds, of course, were the question of our future as subjects in Nazi-occupied Poland and our hope that the occupation would not last indefinitely. We were also deeply concerned about Uncle Leib'l. Had his army unit engaged in battle? Had he been, God forbid, a casualty? Where might he be now? And we naturally thought of Uncles Froyim and Yank'l. Had they made it to Russia safely? Where could they be now, and how might they be faring?

We were elated to learn that all was well with our family in Bodzentyn, with Grandfather Meier, his wife, and her sister; with Grandfather Nus'n and Cousin Chantche, who had remained with Grandfather in Bodzentyn; and with Aunt Gitteleh, Uncle Froyim Biderman, and Cousins Moishe, Itche, and Shloime.

We were, however, saddened and shocked to learn that the Germans, as they were entering Bodzentyn the preceding week, had shot a number of innocent people in cold blood. We were also informed that a curfew had been imposed and that it was strictly forbidden to be outdoors from 7 P.M. until morning. In fact, a German army unit appeared in Bodzentyn daily, toward evening, to enforce the curfew.

We were also concerned about the well-being of our other family members in Szydłowiec, in Kielce, and in Starachowice. Where had they been during the hostilities? Had their cities or homes been bombed? Where and how were they now?

In the meantime, the day after we returned home was the eve of Rosh Hashana, and we had almost no time left to prepare for this great Jewish holy day. Fortunately, with the cooperation of the entire family, Mother managed to prepare meals that compared admirably with those of past years.

It was always customary for Jews to greet and extend pious and heartfelt wishes to each other for the coming New Year as they crossed paths during the day of the eve of Rosh Hashana, but this year was different. Żwirki Plaza was, as usual, buzzing with Jews doing their last-minute shopping for the holiday, but the manner in which they encountered friends and fellow townspeople was much more tearful and emotional. One could not help sensing that this year's traditional New Year's Eve wishes had infinitely deeper intensity and feelings of apprehension than had any other in anyone's memory. As always, the air was charged with a mixture of fear and hope, but this year the anxiety and the urgency of prayerful hope were perceived and transmitted as never before.

Thoughts expressed in the High Holiday prayers permeated the minds and fibre of every Jewish soul in Poland. On Rosh Hashana, one's destiny for the coming year is inscribed, we believe, and on Yom Kippur it is sealed, and the decision is made by God "who shall live and who shall die . . . who shall perish by fire and who by water . . . who by the sword and who by beast." "But repentance, prayer, and charity cancel the evil decree," we read during the services. These thoughts were keenly felt this Rosh Hashana Eve, just after the opening days of the war and during these first days under the occupation of a foreign government that was already notorious for its anti-Semitic words and deeds. I was too young to comprehend the full impact of the situation or the deep fears in the minds of the adult Jews around me, but I was nevertheless overcome by their tense expressions and serious tones of voice.

Toward evening we heard approaching motorcycles. Sheepishly and fearfully, we walked up to the windows of our parlor room and peeked out into Żwirki Plaza. There we saw, for the first time, some twenty-five to thirty uniformed German soldiers, goose-step marching and parading about, apparently intending to intimidate and terrify the local population. Indeed, their presence and ostentatious display of military force and authority were frightening reminders that we were now under the domination of a cruel foreign power.

We Jews considered it unwise, and perhaps even life threatening, to hold High Holiday services in the synagogue this year. Instead, we locked the gates of our courtyards and arranged *minyanim*, public prayer quorums constituted by the participation of at least ten Jewish men, in private homes throughout Bodzentyn. Our family went for services to the private home of a distant relative who lived two courtyards east of ours. Rather than venture into Żwirki Plaza, we walked there through the backyards of the two courtyards, partially breaking down one of the fences, in order to avoid being seen by any German soldiers who happened to appear in town and become tempted to harass us.

As the services were in progress inside the home, we children sat outside, in front of the house. We would get up from time to time and peak through a fence to see if soldiers were around. The streets were empty and quiet, as if deserted, except for Polish police who were apparently stationed all about to discourage Jews from venturing out to the synagogue. The stillness of the streets was abnormal and frightening, the atmosphere somber and disquieting.

Events during the ten-day period from Rosh Hashana through Yom Kippur led to the total collapse of Polish army resistance and the virtual end of the war in Poland. By the second day of Rosh Hashana, Friday, September 15, the Germans had reached Warsaw. Two days later, the Russian army invaded Poland from the east and swept through virtually unopposed as far as the German lines. Thus, by September 20, Poland lay conquered and divided by its two powerful neighbors, with Germany occupying its western half and Russia its eastern half.

On Wednesday, September 27, the eve of the first day of Sukkot, Poland surrendered officially. To the extent possible under the circumstances of foreign occupation, life proceeded normally. We prepared and decorated our sukkah for the holiday, and Mother prepared the special festive meals as always; we enjoyed sitting and eating in the sukkah area throughout the seven-day holiday. Except for the fact that no effort was made to hold services at the synagogue, the holiday took place peacefully and relatively joyously, as in years past.

One day during the Sukkot festival, we were sitting in the parlor of Grandfather Nus'n's residence enjoying a leisurely visit, reminiscent of prewar days. Suddenly we were jolted by a crashing sound in the room. We looked in the direction of the noise and noticed an empty spot on the wall where a framed picture of Uncle Leib'l had been hanging. It had mysteriously, for no apparent reason, dropped to the floor. The glass from the frame was broken and splattered about. Mother spontaneously exclaimed, "This is a sign of *mazel* [good fortune]. I know now that the boys, Leib'l, Froyim, and Yank'l, have met. They are together, and all is well with them. I am no longer worried. Thank God."

Without attempting to dampen her enthusiastic optimism, we all questioned her. How could she be so sure that all was well, just because a picture fell from the wall? Mother insisted, however, "Don't tell me. There is no question about it. What you all do not know is that last night my mother, your Grandmother Irka, came to me in a dream and told me that the boys have met and are safe. That alone was enough for me. But, in addition, the glass on Leib'l's picture has broken into pieces, and broken glass is a sign of mazel. The boys are together and safe. There is no question about it. Remember my words. You may write down the date, and when they come home you will see that I was right." It goes without saying that we hoped Mother was right. But what was for her convincing proof was hardly that for anyone else. Nonetheless, we made a note of the date—and hoped.

As the war in Poland came to an end, the local population had no choice but to adapt to the living conditions under the German government of occupation. The main routines of daily life resumed at a more normal pace. Stores, service trades, and businesses operated once again at near-prewar levels of activity. The Monday market days were held again and proceeded with their usual bustling, bargaining, and trading.

One day, Father happened to encounter the acquaintance who had run to Warsaw, where the gentleman reasoned he would be safer than in Bodzentyn. Father had cautioned him that with Hitler at the helm in Germany, all such assumptions were baseless. Now, this gentleman reminded Father of their discussions and sadly acknowledged, "How right you were, Sir Y'chiel. If only I had listened to you. Warsaw was bombed mercilessly and completely destroyed by those bastards, while Bodzentyn was hardly touched. As things turned out, I am lucky to be alive."

We were elated to receive word at last from our family members in Kielce and Szydłowiec, and to learn that they had all survived the hostilities and were well. It was decided that Cousin Chantche should remain in Bodzentyn with Grandfather Nus'n, at least until the safety of a trip to Szydłowiec could be more clearly ascertained.

Rachela and Shloime resumed school, entering the sixth grade in the upper grades elementary school building in Żwirki Plaza near the well, and I began attending second grade in the lower grades elementary school building in the Upper Plaza. Since Irka and Moishe had completed the seventh and highest grade of public school education available in Bodzentyn during the preceding school year, under ordinary circumstances they would have been sent out of town, probably to Kielce, for further schooling. Because of the war, however, they remained home with no plans for the foreseeable future.

In the meantime, the German authorities began instituting governing agencies in Bodzentyn that were to be charged with various responsibilities in carrying out the policies of the occupational government. The German gendarmerie in charge of the area that included Bodzentyn was located in Bieliny, a small village some twenty kilometers south of Bodzentyn. Whereas in the early days of the occupation the Germans made daily appearances in Bodzentyn, gradually they began coming into town less frequently. They would generally motor in on Monday market days, but the times of their appearances were unpredictable. Most administrative responsibilities in carrying out the policies and orders of the German gendarmerie were charged to the local Polish police, who carried out their duties unflinchingly.

For centuries throughout Poland, and throughout remembered history in Bodzentyn, the Jewish community had had its own elected self-governing committee that cared for the needs of the community and represented it in any dealings with the local government. This committee was traditionally referred to by Jews as the *Yidishe Gemeinde* (the Jewish Community Organization) or the *Yidishe Komittet* (the Jewish Committee). The German authorities chose now to make use of this communal organization to carry out its policies against the Jewish communities of Poland. Through a decree issued by the Governor General of German-occupied Poland on November 28, 1939, each Jewish community was ordered to select a local committee, called a *Judenrat* or Jewish Council, which "would be required to carry out, through a president or vice-president, the demands of the German authorities" and which "would be responsible for the strict fulfillment of those demands to the smallest detail." According to the decree, "the orders issued by this Judenrat for the purpose of fulfilling German demands must be obeyed by all Jewish men and women."

The old Jewish Communal Organization had at various times been headed by Grandfather Nus'n, as well as by other respected elders of the community. At this time, Grandfather Nus'n remained head of the Committee, so at periodic intervals he would be visited by the German gendarmerie, who would come to impose new demands for large sums of money and gold and endless other items, particularly yard goods and coffee.

The presence of the oppressive army of occupation made itself felt through recurring actions that terrified the community. I can never forget the first bestial act of theirs that I witnessed. In the last days of September and in early October, the weather was warm and beautiful; when the army unit rode into town near the curfew hour of 7 P.M. it was still broad daylight outdoors. Often, German soldiers would be seen washing themselves at the well. One evening, I was standing on our balcony, looking down into Żwirki Plaza, when I saw a girl whom I knew walking leisurely near the well. I could not understand the movement of a German soldier when he took out a gun from a holster and slowly and deliberately followed her with his eyes while aiming his gun at the girl—and shot her dead. I was shocked beyond words. I quickly ran into the house to tell what I had seen. The family had already heard of similar acts of horror. What I had just witnessed merely served to corroborate the terrifying fact that, clearly, it was now mortally dangerous to be outside when the Germans were in town.

Another time, I was in the hallway of our building sitting at the foot of the stairway leading up to our residence. Through a small crack in the wall, I peeked into the backyard of a house opposite ours in the courtyard, where I saw one of our distant cousins working at something. Out of nowhere, two German soldiers entered his backyard and walked up to him. They bullied him toward a wall and began amusing themselves as they teasingly pulled hairs out of his beard. As he groaned out in pain, they beat him and continued to torture him mercilessly, until their sadistic urge had been sufficiently satiated. It was painful to witness the suffering of innocent victims of such untamed brutality.

Friends told of other Jews being assaulted by soldiers and forced to sit as the soldiers cut off part or all of their beards or sidelocks with scissors. Other reports told of Germans seeking out religiously observant Jews during morning prayer services, then scornfully harassing, mocking, torturing, and sometimes shooting these pious, unsuspecting, defenseless people.

More horrifying was an incident that served as a precedent for incalculable repetitions of the same atrocity. There was a Jew in Bodzentyn who used to commemorate the anniversary of the death of his parents by visiting their grave at the Jewish Cemetery down Kielce Street and by reciting the memorial prayer there. One day, as he was standing in front of the tombstone intoning his prayer, the German gendarmerie happened to pass by the cemetery on its way into Bodzentyn. Apparently, a German caught sight of this Jew in the cemetery, and the head of the gendarmerie, Herr Dumker, halted the advancing group. The Jew was probably questioned and then ordered to go along with the Germans to a lot adjoining the property of the synagogue. There, Herr Dumker was seen taking out a revolver and shooting the guiltless Jew in cold blood. He photographed his slain victim before ordering him buried in this lot. From this point on, the gendarmerie chief periodically sought out victims for his new Jewish cemetery in Bodzentyn, wherever and whenever the spirit so moved him. Each burial was enacted only after his murdered victim had been photographed.

The Germans undoubtedly realized that their atrocities would offend the sensibilities of every thoughtful person of any religion. In order to minimize the possibilities of renewed resistance against their domination, the gendarmerie arrested many of the intelligentsia of the community, Jews and non-Jews reputed to be cultured and of liberal inclination. They were taken from their homes, herded off to unknown destinations, and never heard from again.

With such brutalities occurring regularly, it would seem impossible that life could proceed with any semblance of normality. However, because these incidents seemed to occur only sporadically—maybe once every few days—in between life did seem to resume its routines and flow of activities. We somehow slowly became almost shock-resistant and therefore capable of absorbing the emotional residues of terrifying experiences.

As early as October 1939, general announcements as well as new anti-Jewish decrees began to be issued from the Governor General of German-occupied Poland. These were often posted on kiosks in Żwirki Plaza and the Upper Plaza. One of the first announced that all Polish territories that had belonged to Germany before World War I, in addition to the Lodz area of Poland, had been annexed to the Third Reich. The rest of Poland, which of course included our town, was designated as occupied territory. In those territories, all Jews were now classified as second-class citizens.

Before the end of October, a number of other legal decrees were issued that were explicitly directed against the Jewish population:

1. All Jews from age six were required to wear a white armband with a blue, six-pointed Jewish star, when in public
2. Ritual slaughter of animals, a cardinal requirement of Jewish law, was forbidden
3. The curfew, from 7 P.M. until morning, was extended indefinitely
4. Jews were no longer allowed to own radios. Jews were ordered to deposit their radios at the local police station.

Wherever possible, Jews attempted to evade the cruel decrees, although at grave risk. In Bodzentyn, for example, we took chickens or other fowl to the shoichet when the Germans were not in town. Similarly, we gave away our large parlor room radio, but Father kept a small radio hidden away. In larger cities, however, where the German presence was more pervasive, Jews were not as fortunate.

In the midst of this darkening climate, scores of native, non-Jewish Poles sensed the opportunity to subdue us as never before. Picketing Jewish stores became more prevalent than at any other time, and the sight of Poles standing in front of Jewish stores, blocking the entrances from would-be customers, became an increasingly common scene.

One day in October, an announcement was made by all teachers in the Bodzentyn public school system, which I heard in my class in the lower elementary grades building in the Upper Plaza and which Rachela and Shloime heard in their class in the upper elementary grades building in Żwirki Plaza: "As of tomorrow, Jewish children will no longer be permitted to attend public school." Just like that, through a single announcement, we found ourselves expelled from school. For the crime of being Jewish, we were no longer entitled to receive public school education.

Because our own family had the good fortune of being wealthy, expulsion from public school did not pose as great a problem as for those less fortunate. Private tutoring was arranged with professional teachers in the community, not only for Rachela, Shloime, and me, but for Irka and Moishe as well. I was taken for regular instruction to a Mme Nawrotowa, a former public school teacher of Irka and Moishe who was now married to a violinist and music teacher. Together with their small child, they lived in the Bielawski building near the bus stop on Kielce Street. Other teachers came to our house for reading, writing, English, and Hebrew. One Roma Saksówna, a former teacher of English at the British Consulate in Warsaw, taught English to Irka and Rachela. It was considered unsafe, however, to keep textbooks and notebooks out in the open, so when they weren't in use, we kept them hidden under our wooden flower pots on the stone sill outside our kitchen window.

11

1940:
New Edicts and the Influx of Refugees
into Bodzentyn

IN JANUARY of 1940, a new edict prohibited Jewish public worship. This decree actually made but slight impact on the Jewish community, because the moment the Nazi army had moved into Bodzentyn the week preceding Rosh Hashana, Jews had realized that using the synagogue for public worship would be potentially life threatening. As an alternative, minyanim had been organized in private homes for Rosh Hashana services. These minyanim continued on a daily basis. Similarly, official cheder attendance was discontinued from the moment the Germans took over Bodzentyn. Instead, Jewish children were taught their Jewish lessons in private homes.

The Nazi yoke continued to be felt through unabated persecution. One day a Jew would be assaulted; on another day a member of the Polish intelligentsia would be sought out. One day a home would be raided; another day a store would be looted. Once a friend came running to tell us that only moments before some Germans had stalked into Aunt Gitteleh and Uncle Froyim Biderman's yard goods store, apparently to help themselves to some fine fabrics—and that Aunt Gitteleh had fainted.

Our hearts went out to her. If only we could help. But what could we accomplish by running over there? We might only endanger ourselves and possibly Aunt Gitteleh and her family also. All we could do was wait, hope, and pray. We lived through agony that entire day until the Germans left town and we were able to go over and discover that our aunt and her family had survived the terrifying ordeal. But who could know what the morrow might bring?

In the meantime, worsening conditions in Kielce began to take their toll on many Jewish households. Uncle Pintche Greenbaum had earned his livelihood through transporting merchandise for entrepreneurs to various cities across Poland, but business had deteriorated so much by now that he was almost totally idle. At the same time, Grandfather Nus'n was in need of help at home in Bodzentyn. Uncles Froyim, Leib'l, and Yank'l had not been heard from since the war had begun, and their long absence was becoming a cause of increasing anxiety with each passing day. Moreover, Grandfather Nus'n's maid had become pregnant and could no longer continue to perform her household chores for him. It was therefore decided that Aunt Brucheleh, Uncle Pintche, and our cousins Moisheheleh and K'silush should move in with Grandfather Nus'n. Aunt Brucheleh also brought her maid to work in the house, and so the new arrangement was to the advantage of all concerned.

During this time, in the late winter and early spring of 1940, the pace of events seemed to settle down. For a while, the border stringency between Germany and Russia became somewhat relaxed, and movement from one side of the border to the other began to take place. On one fine day, we all were elated—but especially Grandfather Nus'n—when Uncles Froyim, Leib'l, and Yank'l returned home. Now, thanks to God, we were all back home together again. Mother lost no opportunity to remind us that she had known all along the boys were safe and together, and that they would return home. We were all curious—but Mother was especially anxious—to hear how the boys had found each other in that vast expanse known as Russia.

Then Uncle Leib'l told his story. He said that as the Polish army was nearing the point of collapse, he decided it would be wisest to desert and escape to Russia. His unit was stationed near the newly forming Russo-German frontier, so he knew he could make it across. He realized, however, that he could not be mobile in a Polish army uniform so, at a propitious moment when no one was in sight, he dashed behind a barn, hurriedly removed his civilian clothes from his knapsack, and changed clothes. No sooner had he begun stuffing his uniform into his knapsack than he was seen by a Polish peasant, who ran instantly to inform the local police, as well as everyone around. Realizing escape was now hopeless, Uncle Leib'l did not resist arrest and was jailed.

While in jail, he was tried and sentenced to be executed. On the night preceding the date set for the execution, a guard came to Uncle Leib'l's cell with some food. As the guard was unlocking the cell door, he heard his name being called from the front office. Apparently assuming he would be gone but a few seconds, he left the cell door unlocked while he ran up to the front desk. Seizing this miraculous opportunity, Uncle Leib'l sneaked out and fled for his life into the night. He succeeded in reaching the border and crossing into Russia. The next day, toward evening, Uncle Leib'l made his way to a border town where food was being served to people standing in long breadlines. Hungry and weary from the harrowing experience of the day and preceding night, he joined the line. While waiting, he thought he saw, he was almost sure he saw—yes indeed, he did see—his brothers Froyim and Yank'l!

Mother could hardly wait. She had to interject, "When did you meet? Do you remember the date? You must remember."

Uncle Leib'l asked, "What difference does it make? Why is the exact date all that important?"

Mother insisted, "Never mind. Just tell me the date you met Froyim and Yank'l if you can remember it." Uncle Leib'l thought for a moment, and was able to mentally place events in perspective and recall the date—the very date Mother had insisted they had met! Jubilantly, Mother repeated, "I told you that our Mother had come to me in a dream and told me that the boys had met. Oh, thank God!"

After the excitement over the return of our uncles had settled down, we began to concentrate on finding a new residence for Aunt Brucheleh and her family. Grandfather Nus'n's living quarters were simply not large enough to house him, his three unmarried sons, and the four members of the Greenbaum family. Hence an apartment was found for the Greenbaums on Synagogue Street. Uncle Pintche, now totally idle, spent his days there reading the Chumash and the Talmud. He would interrupt his studies only to join the family for meals.

While conditions remained relatively quiet, Grandfather Nus'n felt that this was an opportune time to send Cousin Chantche home to her parents and sisters in Szydłowiec. She had been staying with Grandfather since early summer in 1939 and longed to be with her family once again. Needless to say, they could hardly wait to have her back home. Escorted by Uncle Yank'l, Chantche was driven back home safely by horse and buggy.

Meanwhile, Irka needed some dental work done, and it was decided that this also was as good a time as any for her to be sent to Kielce to be treated by a competent dentist. She traveled to Kielce and back by bus and stayed with Uncle Moishe and Aunt Chavtche Szachter while she was there. The apartment of Uncle Moishe and Aunt Chavtche was extremely overcrowded, because wartime exigencies necessitated that two other families live with them, so Irka helped out by cleaning house and tending to the children. During her first night there, the entire household was awakened by the cry of one of the children. As the adults were slowly rising, they suddenly realized how groggy everyone was. Frantically, they all ran to open every window and door; were it not for the cry of the child, they all would have been asphyxiated by the carbon monoxide leaking from the space heater in the main room of the apartment. Following this exciting episode, all went smoothly, and within a few days Irka was back home safe and sound.

While the pace of events was more relaxed in Bodzentyn, anti-Jewish Nazi brutality in other places, especially in larger cities, was in high gear. Many of our unfortunate brethren from these cities, who had some family in Bodzentyn, moved into our town at this time. The communities hardest hit were those in the territories that had been directly annexed to the Third Reich. There, the savagery was unprecedented.

In Łódź, for instance, a ghetto was erected for the Jews as early as February 1940. Jews with homes outside the ghetto area were forced to leave their homes and to take with them only what they could carry on their backs. Many of these people fled to Kielce, and some came to Bodzentyn. In Kalisz, Jews were herded into the synagogue, then taken to a nearby forest and shot. Some Kalisz Jews managed to escape to other cities, including Bodzentyn. In Sosnowiec, the synagogue had been burned in the early days of Nazi rule. Shortly before Passover 1940, when the entire Jewish community of nearby Oświęcim (the future site of the infamous Auschwitz concentration camp) was expelled from that town, the Jewish community of Sosnowiec took upon itself the nearly impossible task of inviting all five thousand of them to celebrate Passover with them.

Among the Jewish residents of Sosnowiec was our old family friend, Shmiel Weintraub. Shmiel had moved there at the time of his marriage some five years earlier. Now he moved back to Bodzentyn to be with his parents and family. He had two children, the oldest of whom was a few years younger than me. I recall playing with them on our outdoor balcony.

Through contacts made between Jews traveling to and from Bodzentyn, it was learned that even outside the annexed territories, Nazi bestiality surfaced in all its fury from the beginning of the occupation. In Kraków, for instance, Nazi raiding and looting of Jewish homes and stores was rampant and unbridled. During one killing spree, Jews sitting out on their balconies were shot at random, while on another occasion, Jews were called out in front of their homes and simply murdered. By mid-1940, many Kraków Jews were deported to Kielce, where the Jewish community was confronted with the awesome task of providing shelter and food for the helpless victims.

Soon the mounting pressure and hardships were felt deeply among the Jews of Kielce, and a considerable number of them who had families in

Bodzentyn began moving into our city. Among them was a poor, distant relative of ours, a brother of Uncle Pintche Greenbaum. Similar to his brother's predicament, Ich'l Greenbaum's prewar import-export business collapsed as a result of the war. He was married and had two young children, a boy and a girl. His wife, however, was seriously ill from depression and was unable to function. Mother was fond of Ich'l and empathized with his tragic situation, so she saw to it that the children came to our house for their daily meals.

Uncle Moishe and Aunt Chavtche also decided to leave Kielce at this time with their son, Samush, who was by now about ten months old. They returned to Bodzentyn to live in the grain storage building behind Grandfather Nus'n's residence, where a room was finished for them. Aunt Chavtche's younger sister, Pola, also moved in with them.

Among the many refugees moving into Bodzentyn was a girl from Łódź named Elżunia. Elżunia came from a wealthy family that had owned a soap factory in Łódź. She was freckled, rather plump, had short, thick red hair, and often wore knee socks. Elżunia and I had a great deal in common, and I became very fond of her. In addition, I admired her manner of dress and demeanor, which were very cosmopolitan. She introduced me to children's books written in Polish and illustrated with colored pictures and to some unusual plastic toys, the likes of which I had never known or seen. Unavailable in Bodzentyn, these modern big-city products made a striking impression on me. I especially enjoyed reading the books she lent me. She would sometimes go with me to my private teacher, Mme Nawrotowa, or come to our house, where we would sit in front of our parlor stove or play in our courtyard.

As the Bodzentyn Jewish community began to swell through the continuous influx of refugees, and as ever-new pressures on the community from the German gendarmerie continued to mount, Grandfather Nus'n began to feel he could no longer bear the responsibilities of heading the Jewish Community Organization. He called a meeting of the members and asked to be relieved of his duties. Under the circumstances, as they now existed and as they loomed for the foreseeable future, the town elders deemed it wise to select, in his place, a younger man who would be better suited to cope with the expected difficult demands of the cruel occupation government. The committee saw fit to place its trust in Uncle Froyim.

Uncle Froyim was a deeply pious man, and yet he was clean shaven. He was tall and blue-eyed, sedentary by nature, astute, and witty. At twenty-eight years of age, he was already an extraordinarily sagacious man. As head of the Jewish Community Organization, Uncle Froyim employed every device his brilliant mind could devise to placate the German gendarmerie, in its constant demands upon our community. He actually succeeded in establishing an almost friendly relationship with the Germans, who appeared to enjoy themselves during their frequent visits to Grandfather Nus'n's home, where Uncle Froyim lived. They would sit in the dining room and engage in jovial conversation, as Uncle Froyim wined and dined them. Before leaving, Uncle Froyim would escort them to the Sewerynski tavern, where he would treat them liberally to drinks of hard liquor.

Always striving to minimize the frequency of Nazi raids on Jewish homes and businesses, and always trying to mitigate their harsh demands on the Jewish community for more and more gold and valuables, he maintained a surface cordiality with the German authorities. The gendarmerie once even surprised Uncle Froyim by presenting him with a box of oranges.

In the fall of 1940, however, a new crisis befell the Jewish community of Bodzentyn. Earlier in the year, the Nazi government had begun deporting Jews from cities within the annexed territories to cities in Occupied Poland, allowing them to take with them no more than they could carry on their backs. During the month of October, some 200 impoverished Jews from the city of Płock thus arrived in Bodzentyn, and overnight the approximately 300 Jewish resident families were faced with the responsibility of absorbing all of them into our already-crowded community.

The Bodzentyn Jewish Committee under the leadership of Uncle Froyim arranged hospitality for some of these unfortunate refugees in as many Jewish homes as possible. Many other refugees were housed in the synagogue, while still others had to be crowded into empty stores. A mother of two girls from Płock was taken in by a grocer whose residence-store was located across the plaza from our house. Unfortunately, the grocer felt that he could not house the girls as well, so our family agreed to take them into our home. The older girl, Adella, was a year or two older than my sister Irka, and her younger sister, whose name was Lilli but whom we addressed as Lilka, was approximately the same age as Irka. Through this arrangement, Adella and Lilka were able to see their mother often. Our mother, however, had thus taken upon herself the responsibility of preparing meals for these two girls from Płock and the two children of Ich'l Greenbaum, as well as the five children of our immediate family, Father, and herself.

Whereas older children from Płock were taken into families' homes, the Jewish Community Organization set up an orphanage to shelter the younger children. The orphanage housed about seventy children and was located in the back of a residence-store two courtyards east of ours, the former location of one of Bodzentyn's four cheders (Hebrew schools). This was also the place we attended Rosh Hashana and Yom Kippur services when we returned to Bodzentyn in September 1939. The orphanage was headed by Hirsch Wolf Weinrib, a self-educated, civic-minded young man who also had been among the organizers and regular board members of the Bet Yaakov school for girls in Bodzentyn.

In addition to housing the poor Płock victims, the Jewish Community Organization formed a volunteer committee in charge of baking bread and cooking potatoes or soup in the synagogue for the hungry masses. The depth of poverty was painful to witness. I was shocked when, for the first time, I saw a Płock Jew drinking the water in which potatoes had been cooked. Many of the Płock refugees were totally idle, impoverished, and starving, and a considerable number of them died within the first few weeks, including the Płock spiritual leader, Rabbi Ashkenazi, and his wife.

Shortly after the orphanage had been set up, Sir Weinrib approached some former students of the Bet Yaakov school and asked them to form a committee to be responsible for entertaining the young children of the orphanage. Irka was totally preoccupied with helping Mother in these terribly trying times. Rachela, however, did join and even assumed a leadership role in the group of eight girls, which included my friend and playmate, Shprintzeleh, and Rachela's schoolmate, Reiz'l Winograd. Although not originally part of the group, through Rachela's involvement, I too participated in the activities. We collected children's books and clothes and received money from the Jewish Community Organization to provide refreshments for the boys and girls. The group went to the orphanage almost every day. Some girls would read books to the children and some would sing songs they had learned at Bet Yaakov. Others would prepare little plays to be performed by the youngsters. When the weather permitted, they would go outdoors to play in the street in Żwirki Plaza or in nearby courtyards.

With so many children in the orphanage, birthday celebrations were frequent. On these occasions, tables were set up and cake or cup cakes would be served with milk and chocolate candy. It was the committee's responsibility to collect the remaining food and clean up before leaving.

With these activities, the girls on the committee raised the spirits of the young children and occupied themselves in a meaningful way during these tragic times.

We were fortunate to have among the refugees in town a number of professional teachers. It was obviously mutually advantageous for them to become our private tutors. We needed the education they had to offer and they welcomed the opportunity of some employment and income. And so they were invited to come to our house as our new teachers.

One of the teachers was a petite young woman with medium blond hair and brown eyes. Her name was Miss Goldberg. She used to come up to our residence to teach Rachela and me. I recall how she struggled to teach me to tell time on the tall grandfather clock in the corner of our parlor room near the balcony. A gentleman from Kalisz came over to teach the older children Hebrew. Still another teacher was a woman from Płock who taught English to Moishe and Irka. In between lessons, Moishe and Irka would compete with each other as they studied in their respective parts of the wide, divided bedroom. "How many new words did you learn?" they would challenge each other. "Can you spell them? Guess how many I learned." In this manner, we were able to continue to some extent with the education that our Nazi tormentors had denied us.

We all felt deeply indebted to our teachers, but no one appreciated their efforts more than Mother. Knowing of their plight only too well, Mother often made it a point to serve them liberal portions of tasty and nourishing snacks. I recall one occasion when Mother treated them to some of her truly wonderful homebaked pastry. They delighted in partaking of the savory delicacy.

Our two adopted young guests from Płock, Adella and Lilka, meanwhile, were generally personable and amiable. Lilka, the younger of the two, once escorted me across Żwirki Plaza into the courtyard of Grandfather Nus'n's estate, where we seated ourselves in his yard. There, she patiently helped me practice the multiplication tables. The girls were not, however, very willing to assist in housework, despite the fact that their extra help would surely have been useful. Moreover, Lilka would at times appear cross, contrary, even bitter, undoubtedly a result of having to dwell with strangers and be dependent upon their charity.

The first year under Nazi occupation ended with countless incidents of brutality and heretofore unimaginable inconveniences, caused by premeditated cruel decrees, the likes of which were unprecedented in the experiences of any living Jew. Despite all, our family had survived. Like our ancestors, who had lived on hope in past periods of persecution, we now held on to the hope that the occupation would not endure for long and that we would somehow manage to survive.

12

1941:
The Confiscation of the Family Enterprises and the Arrest of Uncle Froyim

WHILE EVENTS in Bodzentyn were as yet relatively calm, an ominous harbinger of new anti-Jewish measures to come appeared across Żwirki Plaza in the courtyard of Grandfather Nus'n's estate. In the closing months of 1940, a minor German official moved into town and took up residence in an apartment within the Jakubowski estate, next door to Grandfather Nus'n. Actually, the official was a *Volksdeutsch*, a German living in Poland. Like many other native countrymen residing in Poland who were seen to be trusted Nazi sympathizers, he had been selected by the occupational government and elevated to the position of commissar. His function was ostensibly to administer and oversee large Jewish properties and business establishments. Inasmuch as our family enterprises were the largest in town, they were natural ones to be placed under his supervision.

The new commissar habitually greeted his neighbors cordially and consistently displayed a courteous and friendly disposition. At Christmas time, he and his wife invited our family to their residence to see their special holiday decorations and lit-up Christmas tree. They also asked us to join them the following Saturday afternoon for picture taking. Because Jews desist from all forms of mundane activity on the Sabbath day, including that of being photographed, Mother graciously declined their invitation.

Despite the outward friendliness displayed by the commissar and his wife, the commissar's authority over the mill gradually and steadily increased, as our family control of the business encountered ever-new restrictions. Before long, the German authorities placed a seal on the door of our mill, and the commissar apologetically informed Father that he had been instructed by his superiors to forbid the Jewish owners of the mill from entering the building henceforth. Our family mill had thus been confiscated by the occupation government and simply handed over to the commissar.

In the beginning, Father managed secretly to remove the seal at night and enter the mill for short periods of time, and then reattach the seal so skillfully that one could not recognize it had been tampered with. In this manner, he continued to conduct some business clandestinely for a while. He began to feel, though, that the entire procedure was much too hazardous, and resigned himself to the reality that the mill was indeed no longer ours.

Speaking to the family on the subject, he said, "We have plenty. I will undertake no more business; I will take no chances; I will keep my hands behind my back. In no way will I unnecessarily risk reprisals from the Germans or jeopardize the family's security in even the minutest way." We had rarely heard Father speak so emphatically. From this point on, no Jews worked in or were in charge of any aspect of the mill's operation, and we no longer had any direct access to flour or grains. Nonetheless, we were in no want of food; as long as there was ample money, and our family did possess it in abundance, food was continuously available in Bodzentyn.

With the mill now under the administration of the commissar, controlled specified amounts of flour and grains were distributed to storekeepers to be sold to bakers for making bread. In the beginning, the amounts distributed were in excess of the local need, and a number of storekeepers began selling the surplus flour and grains on the black market. This practice became widespread until it became known to the Nazi authorities. Suddenly one night, the German gendarmerie came into town with the intention of rounding up and arresting the black market racketeers. They came pounding aggressively on the doors of suspected agents of the illegal sales and found no more than perhaps ten at their homes. Apparently word had spread through town of the search under way, and many succeeded in being away from their homes when the Germans arrived. Unable to seize a considerable number of the suspected guilty parties, the gendarmerie canceled its search and released all those it had captured.

About a week later, the gendarmerie paid a visit to Uncle Froyim at Grandfather Nus'n's residence. They presented him, as head of the Judenrat, with a list of suspected black market peddlers of flour and grains and demanded information on their whereabouts. Among the names on the list was that of our friend Y'chiel Grossman, who used to have the grain for his grain store ground in our mill. Uncle Yank'l, in an adjacent room, overheard the names being read. When he heard his friend's name, he was terrified. Hurriedly but unobtrusively, he slipped out of the house and ran as quickly as he could to the Grossman residence-store on Langiewicza Street. He entered the premises, only to find Y'chiel already in bed for the night. Frantically, he explained to his friend the immediacy and severity of the danger lurking but a few meters away and urged him to run instantly for his life.

No sooner had Uncle Yank'l disappeared from the Grossman home than the German gendarmerie arrived. They beat barbarously at the door until Mrs. Grossman let them in. But when they demanded to see her husband, she told them that he was not at home and that his family was unaware of his whereabouts. The gendarmerie began peering about suspiciously. They walked up and down, searching the premises. Noting the bed was unmade, one German approached it and touched the bedding with his hand. Then he turned his head back so that he faced the Grossman family and, with a sardonic grin, uttered threateningly, "The bed is still warm; and you have no idea as to the whereabouts of Y'chiel Grossman? Very interesting." The German walked up to Mrs. Grossman and, standing tall and haughty with his hands gripping his hips, spoke down to her with intensifying venom: "So you have no idea where your husband is." With crescendoing fury, he began to shout, "The bed is still warm. He just left. He had to just leave. Where is he? Where is he?"

Nearly unconscious with fear, Mrs. Grossman pleaded and cried, "I don't know. I don't know."

Infuriated, the German ordered the gendarmerie to search every visible inch of the premises. But it was to no avail. They were unable to find Sir Y'chiel. All the while, he had been hiding in a small storage room behind stored-up materials, where there was hardly room even for a person to stand. Eventually realizing the futility of their search, the Germans stalked out, angry and suspicious.

One night about a week later, the gendarmerie paid an unannounced visit to Uncle Froyim. Unlike previous visits, when a veneer of cordiality covered the excessive demands of the occupational officials on the Judenrat, this time the head gendarme, without seating himself and with chilling formality, announced, "Mr. Szachter, you are wanted for questioning by the Gestapo in Kielce. You are to come with us immediately." In a moment, Uncle Froyim was gone, taken to face the dreaded Nazi secret state police for unspecified charges. Who could know the specific cause of the interrogation or how soon, if ever, Uncle Froyim would be released.

Almost immediately, the adults of the family gathered together in Grandfather Nus'n's parlor room to speculate as to the possible cause or causes of Uncle Froyim's apparent arrest. Focusing all their mental energies on possible ways to achieve his release, they decided that the most logical recourse was to work through the commissar. After all, he too was a German, like the arresting officers. If paid off sufficiently, perhaps he would exercise enough influence on our behalf to secure Uncle Froyim's release.

When the commissar was told of our plight, he appeared very sympathetic. He explained, however, that he could not simply intervene with his superiors on behalf of Uncle Froyim because the procedure was extremely complicated and dangerous. The implication was that he might extend some effort for the right price. Grandfather Nus'n handed the commissar a substantial "down payment," which he readily accepted. Then, he assured us he would find out what he could.

Day after day we waited in great apprehension and suspense, subconsciously fearing the worst, yet harboring some hope of salvation through the bribed efforts of the commissar. Finally, the commissar called on us to say that he had some news to share. With trembling hearts, we waited to hear his news. Prefacing his remarks with a description of all the difficulties he had to overcome, he finally revealed that he had learned Uncle Froyim was being detained in a jail in Kielce. Uncle Froyim was being charged with sabotage and with failing, as head of the Judenrat, to fulfill satisfactorily the demands of the German authorities. It had also been learned, the commissar told us, that from the beginning of the war until the spring of 1940 Uncle Froyim had been in Russia, and he was therefore suspected of being a Communist. The charges were quite serious, the commissar noted. He emphasized, however, that there definitely was cause for hope. He was again offered, and once again accepted, an exorbitant payment for his efforts. He assured us once again that he would do all in his power to help us and that he would let us know as soon as he learned of any further developments in the case.

The ordeal began exacting a terrible emotional toll on the entire family, but especially on Mother and Uncle Yank'l. Mother was completely beside herself; she was tense, restless, and abnormally preoccupied with her thoughts. Uncle Yank'l was heartsick and inconsolable. He developed such a severe case of hiccups that each contraction was accompanied by a long, deep, asthmalike gasp of breath. These unusual hiccups seemed to proceed as one continuous unrelenting seizure. The pressure on us all seemed unbearable. As the ensuing days and weeks passed, however, the commissar continued to report regularly that progress was being made.

He even went so far as to suggest that Uncle Froyim could be coming home within a matter of weeks. The commissar was given more money continually, and we began allowing ourselves an attitude of cautious optimism.

On June 22, 1941, Nazi Germany embarked on a full-scale war against Soviet Russia. At the same time, they stepped up their intensive campaign of anti-Jewish legislation and actions. Their first act was to issue a decree requiring every Jew to carry at all times a yellow *Kennkarte*, an identification card thirty millimeters long and five millimeters wide, with a big black *J* stamped on it.

Not long after that decree was issued, on one otherwise fine day, the commissar announced to Grandfather Nus'n, with regret, that he had been ordered by his superiors to serve Grandfather an eviction notice. Grandfather would have a limited amount of time to make other arrangements for living quarters, but eventually he would be required to relinquish his estate to the commissar. We found it difficult to imagine how events could get much worse than this. The Germans had already confiscated our family mill. Uncle Froyim had been arrested and was still awaiting an undetermined fate. And now they were placing their authoritarian arms on Grandfather Nus'n's estate. Was there no limit to the hardship and misery the Germans intended to inflict upon us? How much more could people endure?

Being unable to alter the turn of events, however, our thoughts turned to our newest emergency: finding an alternate residence for Grandfather Nus'n. It was decided that the storage building adjacent to the one housing Grandfather Meier and us would be remodeled for that purpose. This was the building Mother had wanted Father to develop into a new residence for us before the war, but which Father was unwilling to rebuild then. Now, converting it into a house had become an urgent necessity. Father and Uncle Leib'l immediately began planning its reconstruction.

As the fall of 1941 approached, the holidays of Rosh Hashana, Yom Kippur, and Sukkot came and went and were observed by our family for the last time in Bodzentyn. From this point on, living conditions deteriorated at an accelerating rate, as new and harsher edicts continued to come down. Even before the High Holiday season had ended, a new edict was issued that placed upon Jews the severest restriction of movement yet imposed by the Nazis. According to that edict, it was deemed a crime, punishable by death, for any Jew to leave his or her city of residence. Visits to and from out-of-town family members, business trips, out-of-town trips for dental or medical treatment or any vital purchases were now all outlawed and declared crimes of capital magnitude.

The seriousness of the new edict could not have been more grievously demonstrated than it was in an incident that occurred almost immediately after the edict was issued and which brought tragedy to friends of the family. The family Kornblum resided in an area on the outskirts of Bodzentyn. One of their sons was strolling leisurely near his home when he was spotted by a Nazi gendarme. Assuming the Jewish lad was a resident of Bodzentyn who had strayed beyond the city limits, the Nazi took out his revolver and killed the young man. News of the atrocity filled the heart of every Jew with benumbing anguish and fear.

Although it was still fall in Bodzentyn, severe winter weather had already set in along the Russo-German battle lines, deep inside Russia. The Russian winter was so extreme that all the clothing and supplies prepared for the Nazi armies were woefully inadequate to meet the needs of their freezing troops. In order to alleviate the emergency, the Nazis decreed that all furs and fur clothing owned by Jews were to be summarily turned in at the local police station, where they would be handed over to the government. Among the furs surrendered by our family was the beautiful fur-collared and fur-lined coat Mother had bought for me in the Krynica health resort, and which I loved so much. I truly hated to give it up.

Not all furs, however, were turned in. Some were hidden away by our family as well as by other Jews. Some gave their valuable furs to friendly Poles for safekeeping until better times, hopefully, would enable the furs to be reclaimed. Other valuables were entrusted to Poles also, or were hidden so that they would be safe from the carefree looting of marauding German gendarmes. Aunt Gitteleh and Uncle Froyim Biderman, for example, gave a large amount of the finest fabrics in their yard goods store to their trusted customer, Mme Surowjecka of Świętomarz.

To be sure, these measures were not undertaken without grave risk. Anticipating precisely this activity, the Germans made it a practice to raid houses randomly in search of hidden valuables. When they discovered a legally forbidden item, they would shoot the "guilty" owner on the spot, in an apparent attempt to make an example of him for the rest of the community. In this manner, the Nazi authorities spread terror throughout the community, discouraging the hopes and possible attempts of others to evade their brutish decrees.

In the meantime, construction by Father and Uncle Leib'l was under way for the rebuilding of our storage building for Grandfather Nus'n. It was considered prudent in times like these to provide a place where a sought-after family member could be hidden in the event of an emergency situation. So, as a special feature of the new residence, Father and Uncle Leib'l devised and built a secret attic room, concealed by a double wall, with an opening that was not recognizable to one unfamiliar with its precise location. Moreover, the opening was accessible by ladder only, and the ladder was at all times placed at a distance away from the entrance to the room. Behind the outer wall was the entrance door to the secret room.

The existence of the room was not made known to me or Rachela. It was, however, made known to the older children, as well as the adults of the family. Irka learned about it right after it was completed. Father was curious to test out its efficacy and pointed out to her the wall along which the entrance had been built. Then he said to her, "See if you can find the entrance." Irka tapped along the wall, to the right and to the left, once downward and once upward, once again here and once again there, but to no avail. Father hinted to her when she was "getting warm" and "getting cold," but she was still unable to pinpoint the entrance. It had indeed been well concealed.

Irka then asked Father, "With a room such as this, why should we have to give away our furs? Why not simply hide them here?"

Father replied, "No, my dear Irkeleh, this room was built not for things but for people: for the family, for us. The things will outlive us. This room must be reserved for saving lives—our lives."

Around this time, our commissar was suddenly replaced by a new commissar. Unlike his predecessor, who was at least outwardly cordial, the new commissar was cold, distant, official, and anything but friendly. Nevertheless, Father made overtures in an effort to placate and curry favor with him. Father removed the beautiful gray Persian lamb fur from Irka's coat and offered it as a gift to the commissar for his wife. Soon after this presentation, the commissar's wife was seen going about in a beautiful coat she had made for herself with that fur.

Similarly, no time was lost in working on the new commissar on Uncle Froyim's behalf. A large sum of money was now presented to him as a token of our appreciation for whatever efforts he could exert to secure Uncle Froyim's release. Like his predecessor, he accepted our gift and assured us he would endeavor to work toward the release of Uncle Froyim. One day, a week or so later, the commissar's wife called on Grandfather Nus'n. She was, of course, invited in and asked to join us in the parlor room. As soon as we were all seated around the table, she cheerfully informed us that she had just come from the Gestapo headquarters in Kielce and was able to relay to us the wonderful news that Uncle Froyim would almost certainly be released and should be returning home within a matter of days.

Our hopes now began to soar. After a week, and two weeks, and three weeks, however, those hopes no longer soared. Gradually, we became skeptical, and then pessimistic. The mood of the family was once again depressed, as we began another period of anxious waiting, hoping, fearing, and praying for Uncle Froyim's release.

To compensate for the loss of my sheepskin-leather coat, Father and Mother ordered a new coat for me. My new coat was to be made of a dark blue material with a pretty velvet collar and was to have a hat and purse to match. When it was ready, I was happy and proud to own it. I couldn't wait to begin wearing it, but Mother somehow could not bear concerning herself with new clothes for me when the family situation was so tenuous. She was totally rapt in thought, and the general atmosphere of the house was clouded heavily by the uncertainty of Uncle Froyim's fate, so she asked that I wait for things to settle down before wearing my new coat. I could sense the seriousness of the situation and realized I should not annoy her.

As the winter began to set in, the plight of the Płock Jews progressively deteriorated. There was much hunger and many began to shrink to skin and bones, often acquiring swollen features from the lack of food. Those individuals fortunate enough to have brought some jewelry from home in the bags they carried on their backs were now seen selling or bartering their valuables for bread. On one occasion at dinner, when discussion centered on the deepening tragedy befalling the Płock Jews, I told of overhearing playmates saying they wished their parents would buy some of the beautiful jewelry, which could probably be bought for little money. Father's reaction was despondent and pessimistic: "They may buy the jewelry, or they may not buy the jewelry. Your friends may have it, or they may not have it. With it or without it, one will eventually not be able to buy a piece of bread for all of it." And the subject ended.

Our hopes for the eventual release of Uncle Froyim were finally crushed and our greatest fears were realized, when one day the commissar came over to tell us the news that Uncle Froyim was no longer in the jail of the Gestapo in Kielce, but had been sent to a concentration camp at Auschwitz. He conceded that from there, he had no hope of being able to gain Uncle Froyim's release. Thus, at age twenty-nine, in the bloom of youth, Uncle Froyim had been plucked from life. Brilliant, witty, deeply pious, engaged to be married, but never having had the opportunity to meet his fiancée, he was taken away for the crime of being a Jew, for striving to retard the tempo and severity of the murderous oppression on his fellow Jews. With prospects for the brightest future before him, he was hauled away. Never again were we to see or hear from him. Stunned and broken from the news of this horrible tragedy, the family in more normal times would have needed some form of respite in order to adjust to the new reality. But with continuing persecutions and new emergencies always pursuing our entire community, we had no opportunity to dwell on the loss.

In Uncle Froyim's place, the Jewish Community Organization selected another young man, Shmiel Weintraub, as its head. Shmiel had been a lifelong friend of Uncle Froyim and the family. He was about a year older than Uncle Froyim, a cheder schoolmate, astute, learned, and a son of one of the most reputable and respected families in town. At age thirty, the yoke of dealing with the Nazi gendarmerie on behalf of the Jewish community was now placed on his young shoulders.

When the final touches on the storage building were completed, Grandfather Nus'n and Uncles Leib'l and Yank'l moved into their new residence. Uncle Moishe, Aunt Chavtche, Samush, and Aunt Chavtche's sister Pola abandoned their residential quarters in the storage building behind Grandfather Nus'n's old residence and moved into a separate apartment. I enjoyed going over to their new apartment and playing with little Samush, who was by now nearly two years old. He was an absolutely adorable baby, with light blond curly hair and blue eyes, and playing with him was like playing with a doll. He had so much charm and personality for a two-year-old baby. Aunt Chavtche was always nice to me, and I liked her very much. She once gave me a little three-in-one bracelet—one pink, one white, and one blue bracelet connected into one. I always looked forward to visiting their apartment.

With Grandfather Nus'n's estate now abandoned by our family, the commissar moved in and took up residence in Grandfather's old living quarters. He also took over the ironware store and the rest of the estate. Thus the main family properties and enterprises begun by Great great grandfather Shmiel Szachter—the only mill in town, the largest ironware store in town, the largest estate in town, handed down across three generations—were now all simply confiscated and handed over to the commissar by a decree of the Nazi government.

13

1942:
Father Is Sought for Questioning

ONE EVENING during the closing weeks of 1941, a Jewish baker in town was caught by a German gendarme transporting a concealed one-hundred-pound sack of flour. This was an unusually large amount of flour for anyone to be purchasing in Bodzentyn by this time. Moreover, no one in Bodzentyn had a legitimate source from which to purchase such an amount anymore. The German immediately demanded to know from whom the flour had been purchased. In an apparent desperate effort to divert attention from his own activities, or perhaps assuming that our family had sufficient financial resources to buy our way out of any predicament, the Jew alleged he had purchased the flour from Y'chiel Szachter.

Knowing Father's strong feelings concerning the dangers to the family in conducting illegal business, it seems doubtful that the accusation could have been true. However, the fact that Father had been accused of selling the flour, coupled with the fact that by now the mill had long been under the jurisdiction of the commissar, placed Father in a position of appearing to have committed a criminal act, at least according to the repressive laws imposed by the Nazi authorities. Undoubtedly, Father would now be sought for questioning.

A Polish policeman friendly to Father happened to be passing by and overheard the conversation between the German officer and the Jew. Realizing the imminent danger to Father, the Pole quickly made his way to our house to warn him. As soon as the man left, Father hurried over to Grandfather Nus'n's house and hid himself in the secret attic room. Only moments later, we heard loud, impatient rapping. It was already night, and Mother and all the children were home, but Mother would not think of sending any of us to the door. Instead, she opened the door herself.

Standing on the other side were two tall German gendarmes, who demanded to see Y'chiel Szachter. Although terror-stricken, we all managed to maintain a calm demeanor. Mother, who had learned to speak

German fluently during the several periods of occupation by the Central Powers in World War I, politely answered in perfect German that Father was not at home. The gendarmes then demanded to know where he was and when he would return home. When Mother replied that she did not know, the head gendarme coldly handed her an official summons for Father and ordered him to appear at the local police station immediately, without delay. And they left.

Knowing only too well that appearing for questioning at the police station in this situation meant certain arrest, deportation to a concentration camp, or execution, Father decided to defy the summons and not report to the police. A decision such as this, however, although the lesser of evils under the circumstances, placed Father in a situation of the gravest imaginable danger. He could now never allow himself to be home when the Germans appeared in town. He would have to be on constant guard for the gendarmerie coming into Bodzentyn and disappear to the home of a relative until they left. But this type of existence seemed far too precarious and hazardous for any extended period of time. Perhaps it might be better to flee to Kielce, we thought, where he could stay with relatives. But it was now a capital crime for a Jew to leave his town of residence. In addition, if Father, for whatever reason, were ever stopped and asked to present his identification card, he would be placed under arrest, if not immediately shot. Father therefore considered it wisest to remain in Bodzentyn just long enough to procure a false identification card and then move on to Kielce, perhaps to remain there in hiding indefinitely.

Thus Father arranged to have the false card produced. The procedure, however, proved to be extremely difficult. People were hesitant and disinclined, even for a high price, to become involved in so blatantly illegal and risky a process as this. Nevertheless, in the end Father succeeded in acquiring an identification card under the name Y'chiel Silberberg, who presumably agreed to risk selling his card for desperately needed money.

With the new card in hand, and disguised in entirely different attire, including eyeglasses, Father arranged for a reliable Pole to transport him by horse and buggy to Kielce, where he planned to stay with a cousin for as long as necessary. I was not told where he had gone. I knew that he had left town to hide in another city, but I sensed that Mother did not want to be asked anymore about it, and I actually preferred not knowing specific answers to such questions. What if I were caught by a German and questioned? If terrified or perhaps tortured, would I be able to withhold such information that might, God forbid, mean death for Father?

Life was, of course, difficult without Father. It is true that in normal times, before the war, he was also away from home for days on business, but we experienced this absence entirely differently. Continuous life-threatening but necessary risks had already become normal for him. Now, however, uncertainty of the future and constant fear of the unknown placed new stress on the whole family, especially Mother. Although she strove to shield the children from her adult concerns, the mood at home was decidedly more serious and unpleasantly somber. The older children, particularly Moishe and Irka, automatically sensed they had to pull together to support Mother. I was not required to help, but I still was keenly aware of the abnormality of Father's absence from home.

It was many weeks since Father had left town, and I never had any cause to suspect any change in that situation. One day, while playing outdoors, however, I noticed Mother carrying food next door to Grandfather Nus'n's new house. There was nothing unusual about that, but then I began to notice that she was carrying food there quite often. I started to wonder why, but somehow I could not bring myself to ask. Often I used to play in our courtyard. With the large red ball Mother had brought me from Uncle Moishe's wedding, I loved playing catch with one girlfriend or another. Once, Mother came out and asked me to stop playing and not to make so much noise. This request puzzled me. Mother had never asked that of me before. I became curious and began to suspect that Father must be hiding in Grandfather Nus'n's new house.

Late one Friday night, I drew up all the courage I could muster and slipped out of our residence unnoticed. Then, cautiously I walked up to the front entrance next door, recharged my courage, and knocked on the door. After a lengthy moment, I heard footsteps approaching the door. Next I saw the door open slightly, and Uncle Yank'l peered out from behind it.

"Can I come in?" I asked.

"Wait here a moment," he replied.

Then he closed the door and left. In a moment he returned and told me, "You can come in now." Seated around the parlor room table were Grandfather Nus'n, Uncle Leib'l—and Father! He looked terribly pale, gaunt, and distressed. But I was so happy to see him, as he was to see me. I ran over to him, and we kissed and embraced, and I sat myself on his lap. He asked if Mother had sent me, and I explained that she had not, but that I had suspected he might be hiding here and decided to come and see for myself. Father beamed a smile of satisfaction that betrayed his pride in me for having revealed such a level of understanding. We spoke for a while, but at no point did he as much as ask me to keep his whereabouts secret. He apparently knew that I could be fully trusted.

I considered it prudent to not stay too long and returned home. I later learned that Father, while in Kielce, had determined that it was more hazardous to remain there in seclusion than to be in hiding in Bodzentyn. Incognito he had returned to Bodzentyn after a few weeks and proceeded directly to Grandfather Nus'n's house, where he had been staying ever since in the secret room. I had no conception of the location of the secret room and preferred not to know. He was hiding out, of course, in the attic room behind the double wall that he and Uncle Leib'l had built for just such an emergency when the former storage building was being remodeled for Grandfather Nus'n.

I now understood why Mother had been carrying cooked food over there so often. I also realized why she had asked me not to play ball in the courtyard. Obviously the noise from the playing and the excitement of us children was annoying to Father, as he was sitting in solitary confinement, in hiding. I learned that the secret room was a small cubicle just large enough for one person to stand or sit and had but one small window from which Father could peek out and get a whiff of fresh air. Late at night, when the Germans were not in town and when it was quiet outdoors, Father would come down and take a short walk and mill about slightly, before returning to his secret room.

As Father continued to remain in hiding, the entire family—Father as well as the rest of us—felt enormous pressure. Mother had been suffering from gall bladder ailments and arthritis for a number of years. Now, experiencing unprecedented pressure and constant concern over Father, her arthritis affected her more than ever. In addition, she developed a case of sciatica that was so crippling that she could barely move about. During the last several prewar summers, she had been going to Krynica for special treatments, mineral baths, and consultations. All of this was now, of course, out of the question.

Grandfather Nus'n arranged for Dr. Poziomski, from nearby Suchedniów, to visit his house to examine Mother. During his visit, he suggested that perhaps boiled mud packs, specially prepared for and employed in a health resort in Busko-Zdrój (referred to in Yiddish as Busk), might help relieve the crippling sciatic pain. Father, from his place in hiding, arranged for the mud packs to be ordered by mail. They arrived in dried form, with instructions for their preparation, which Moishe followed. Then, with

Irka's help, he applied the boiled mud packs to Mother's left hip and thigh. These treatments brought temporary relief, and Mother was able to move around again; that is, until the next seizure occurred and the mud packs had to be applied again. From this point on, she found it necessary to lie in bed—indeed, for most of the eight-month period Father remained in hiding.

With Father in hiding and Mother in both emotional and physical distress, it was becoming increasingly difficult to keep Adella and Lilka, our heretofore permanent guests from Płock. Father considered the chance of their discovering his hiding place to be too great a risk, and Mother felt ill-at-ease over the fact that the older girl, Adella, was becoming increasingly fond of Moishe. The girls themselves longed to be with their mother. Lilka, in fact, directly asked that they be reunited. With the help of the Jewish Committee, her request was granted. A few weeks later, similar arrangements were made for Adella. Thus, that living problem was resolved to the satisfaction of all concerned.

The winter of 1941–42 proved to be much different from previous winters. During the evenings, as in years past, we sat around the parlor stove, each of us occupied with his or her own concerns. But this year, Father was in seclusion and Mother was laid up with sciatica and arthritic pain. Dr. Pabian, of Bodzentyn, was coming in regularly to give Mother injections to relieve her pain, so Irka and Rachela had to redouble their efforts in order to relieve Mother of her chores. From time to time, Aunt Gitteleh would come over to instruct the girls in various household matters or to help.

Irka would often carry food over to Grandfather Nus'n's house for Father. As one of the older children, she knew the precise location of the double wall and hidden door to the secret room. By nature, Irka feared heights. Nevertheless, she overcame her fear in order to climb the ladder to see Father, hand him his food or a newspaper, take back empty dishes, and be of whatever help she could. After shutting the secret door, she would descend the ladder and move it from the location of the double wall before returning home.

That winter also brought increasing hardships to all the Jewish inhabitants of Bodzentyn. While our family never experienced any difficulty in purchasing food, it was by now no longer plentiful. The Monday market days continued, but merchandise in stores was becoming scant and harder to come by. Hardest hit by the food shortages and deteriorating conditions were our unfortunate brethren, the poor refugees from Płock. Food rations allotted to Jews were but half those allowed to non-Jews and were far below subsistence levels. Only Jews with monetary resources were able to purchase food from unauthorized sources, but even they hardly had any food to spare. To the limited extent possible, those more fortunate helped the less fortunate.

But the needs far exceeded the availability of spare food. Płock Jews walked around town, literally swollen from hunger. Their unsightly feet were often bespeckled with ghastly open ulcers. Grossly underfed and living in conditions of filth and misery in unheated dwellings, these unfortunates were seen scouring through garbage cans searching for food. But there were no morsels to be found, since no family could allow itself the luxury of throwing out food.

Hunger and disease spread everywhere. When a typhus epidemic began to sweep the city, Płock Jews began dying in droves. Eight to ten frozen corpses were found daily on the streets. The synagogue was converted into a makeshift hospital and emergency center, but the overwhelming need and dismal conditions greatly outweighed the resources available for relief. As conditions worsened, people began assuming sardonic and fatalistic attitudes. As one doctor from Płock unwittingly uttered when made aware of a body on the ground that he had apparently overlooked, "Nu, a loch in him'l, a barg'l oif der erd!" (So, a hole's in heaven, a mound on the ground!).

In the midst of our compounding hardships and misery, one night a fire erupted at the makeshift hospital at the synagogue. The flames not only consumed the synagogue building but also swept across several adjacent houses, inflicting untold damage and havoc. Panic soon gripped the city, and there was fear that the Germans might burn the entire town to the ground, as the retreating Austrians had done during World War I. As the fire spread toward our house, Father came down from his secret room to help us pack bundles, anticipating the possible need to evacuate. He found us already downstairs. Fortunately, the fire was eventually contained. Father returned to his hiding place and the rest of us went upstairs for the remainder of the night.

The next day, several people said to us, "I thought I saw your father last night. I can't be sure, because there was no other light besides that coming from the flickering flames of the fire, but I could have sworn it was he." We naturally replied, "You have quite a vivid imagination. Our Father hasn't been in Bodzentyn for months. Didn't you know?" and the matter was laid to rest.

We soon learned that the fire that had consumed the synagogue had been ignited as an arson attack by a group of young Poles. As a result, many Płock Jews perished from burns and/or suffocation, and the few survivors were absorbed into homes. It was not clear whether the action had been motivated by anti-Semitism, ordered by the German authorities, or perpetrated as a plan to minimize the spreading typhus epidemic by destroying most of its carriers, who were housed in the synagogue. In any event, Aunt Brucheleh and Uncle Pintche, Moisheleh and K'silush, who had been living in an apartment on the street near the synagogue, decided to abandon their apartment. They transferred their few belongings and moved in with Grandfather Nus'n and Uncles Leib'l and Yank'l where they stayed for as long as we remained in Bodzentyn.

14

The Decision to Abandon Bodzentyn

FATHER remained in the secret attic room for eight months. During this period, he had much time to observe and ponder the quickly deteriorating conditions in Bodzentyn, as well as the current events affecting the Jews of Poland generally, and he placed them in the perspective of our immediate family's prospects for survival. He listened to the radio, read the daily newspapers, and remained acutely aware of what was befalling the Jewish people under the Nazi yoke in Poland. He observed the indescribable maltreatment of Jews in other communities, as told by the refugees who fled into Bodzentyn from those cities. He noted the deportation of a major segment of the Jewish community of Płock to Bodzentyn. He was aware of the Jewish ghetto erected in Kielce and of the horrors related by the Jewish refugees from Kraków who were sent there. People claimed to know of masses of Jews being taken to forests and shot. Others reported hearing of Jews being transported en masse to unknown destinations and never being seen again.

He reasoned that all these events were intertwined with the brutalities and atrocities occurring in Bodzentyn: the confiscation of Jewish properties and enterprises; the systematic impoverishment of Jews individually and as a community; the below-subsistence food rations allotted to Jews; and the starved, diseased, and dying Płock Jews on the streets of Bodzentyn. In addition, increasing numbers of reports told of mass "resettlement" programs (*Aussiedlung*) and liquidations of one Jewish community after another.

By mid-1942, Father had concluded that all this could only be part of a master plan aimed at the total destruction of Polish Jewry. He was convinced that it was but a matter of time—and little time at that—before the entire Jewish community of Bodzentyn would be liquidated. What could be done, if anything, to save the lives of our family? He tossed around in his mind all conceivable possibilities. He schemed and debated the relative strengths and weaknesses of each plan.

One night toward the end of the summer, when the Germans were not in town, Father came down from his secret room to Grandfather Nus'n's parlor to share with the family his fears, his thoughts, and his plan for our survival. He appeared pale and weary from the long months he had been deprived of fresh air. He looked shaken and sad from the enormous pressure. His tired shoulders bore the seeming impossible task of saving the lives of his family. He explained why he believed that remaining in Bodzentyn would amount to waiting for certain deportation and eventual death.

As he saw it, the only hope of avoiding that fate lay in our becoming part of a situation deemed vital to the interests of Nazi Germany. He informed us of the existence of a factory in Starachowice in which munitions were being produced and at which some Jews were already employed. Moreover, a native of Bodzentyn and one-time boyhood friend of his, named Shloime Ehnesman, who was a shoemaker for upper parts of shoes and boots and who now lived in Starachowice, was making boots for the Nazis in the munitions factory there. Shloime Ehnesman might therefore be in a position to offer the powers that were whatever would be required to "purchase" employment and a worker's identification card—as a worker in the factory—for each member of the family.

Therein, Father believed, lay our only hope to survive the impending catastrophe. Since Father himself was immobile because of being sought by the Germans, it became the task of Uncle Leib'l to make the necessary connections and arrangements with Shloime Ehnesman. In view of the age range of various members of the family, as well as the number of women and girls, the "purchases" for all of us could not be expected to be had cheaply—if at all. Uncle Leib'l immediately set out for Starachowice, where he stayed with Aunt Dineleh and Uncle Yoss'l Schreibman while working out the details of the plan devised and set forth by Father.

In the meantime, a Bodzentyn Jewish shoemaker for soles and heels named Yoss'l Shister was hired to come to our house for a very special job. He was instructed to remove the heels from shoes worn by members of the family, to insert Russian twenty-ruble gold coins between the soles and heels, and then to reattach the heels to the shoes. In this manner, each family member was supplied with an immediate monetary source with which to purchase any sudden and emergency ransom, security, food, or shelter. I was aware of what Yoss'l Shister was doing, and I understood why he was hiding our money within our shoes. His work made me realize all the more vividly what dangerous times loomed ahead for us.

Father also devised a plan to hide securely the large family surplus of gold and silver and pieces of jewelry. Instead of storing the total fortune in one single place, Father decided to store it in several specific locations within Grandfather Meier's fenced-in garden at the north end of our courtyard. He then drew up a map of those precise locations. Late one dark night, Father came out of hiding just long enough to bury the treasures himself.

Soon Uncle Leib'l returned from Starachowice and related to the family what he had been able to accomplish there. He had met with Shloime Ehnesman and succeeded basically in putting Father's plan into motion. First, he said, the family would have to be in Starachowice. Thereafter, procurement of identification cards could be worked out. Uncle Leib'l also succeeded, through Shloime Ehnesman and for a very high price, in arranging for the top-ranking German officer at the factory to come by truck personally to transport our entire family from Bodzentyn to Starachowice as a group of workers for his factory.

While preparing for the arrival of the truck, Father told Uncle Leib'l that he had buried our family fortune for safekeeping and advised him likewise to bury Grandfather Nus'n's fortune. Uncle Leib'l immediately proceeded clandestinely to bury their monies and jewels in another secluded area. He also buried a beautiful fur coat owned by Pola, the sister of Aunt Chavtche, of whom Uncle Leib'l seemed to be growing increasingly fond. She was a pretty woman, personable and bright, and Uncle Leib'l had been seen walking or spending time with her whenever an opportunity presented itself, ever since she had moved to Bodzentyn from Kielce.

With plans thus already laid out and enacted to shield us somewhat from the ominous and frightfully perilous times immediately before us, there was now also faint hope for salvation and renewed happiness and normalcy in the more distant future. And so the family waited with mixed emotions for the arrival of the truck that would take us from Bodzentyn to Starachowice. Our immediate anxieties were somewhat abated at the prospect of escaping a possible liquidation of the Bodzentyn Jewish community and enjoying the protection of being workers in an ammunition factory that was vital to the war effort of the occupational government. On the other hand, we were fleeing our home and town secretly, like hunted criminals. We were abandoning the place in which our entire family had been born, raised, lived, and died for generations. Robbed of our family mill, ironware store, property, and estate and denied our rights of earning a livelihood and freedom of action, we were fleeing in the narrow hope of escaping the hangman's noose, of cheating our marauding persecutors of the satisfaction of snuffing out our very lives.

Would we ever be able to return and reclaim all that was rightfully ours? Would we ever again be able to return and live normal lives, as we once did, enjoying our home, our family, our strolls, our Sabbaths, our holidays, our weddings, our very lives? Oh when, oh when? Evil had never prevailed indefinitely. We could hope only that there would one day be a brighter tomorrow after the deepening darkness of today. It must be so! It must be so!

III

FROM BODZENTYN TO THE LABOR CAMP AT STARACHOWICE

15

We Abandon Bodzentyn

ON ONE LATE afternoon in 1942, during the week following Rosh Ha-shana, the German head of personnel and staff of the Hermann Göring munitions factory in Starachowice, Kommandant Schwertner himself, arrived by truck in front of our courtyard to transport our entire family as his new crew of laborers. In two trips, all twenty-two members of our family were to be transported. Included in the first truckload were: the immediate family—Mother, Moishe, Shloime, Irka, Rachela, and me; and the Bidermans—Uncle Froyim, Aunt Gitteleh, and their three sons. Because Father was still being sought by the German gendarmerie, he considered it too dangerous for the entire family to leave on the truck with him in case he was discovered, so he made separate arrangements to travel clandestinely out of Bodzentyn alone.

The second truckload included the rest of our family: Grandfather Nus'n, Uncles Leib'l and Yank'l, Aunt Brucheleh and Uncle Pintche Greenbaum and their two young sons, and Uncle Moishe and Aunt Chavtche Szachter and Samush. Father had apparently made other arrangements for his own father, our Grandfather Meier, because he arrived at Starachowice separately from the rest of the family. His second wife and her sister were left in Bodzentyn. Apparently, Father had convinced Grandfather Meier that due to the abnormality of his sister-in-law, the women would have no chance of survival.

Father, of course, came out of hiding and saw to it that all last-minute details were completed. He paused only to remind the older children that money had been placed between the heels and soles of shoes and in the stay holders of girdles of all members of the family—to be used for whatever emergency might arise. Father also informed the older children of the whereabouts of the remainder of the family fortune, buried in Grandfather Meier's fenced-in garden at the rear of the courtyard. He then directed us quickly onto the truck.

Getting the Bidermans to board the truck, however, seemed to take an eternity. Cousin Moishe, who was about seventeen years old then, had apparently fallen in love with a girl from Płock and insisted adamantly that he could not leave without her. Aunt Gitteleh and Uncle Froyim entreated him to come along, pleading that they could not keep everyone waiting indefinitely, but he could not bear to part with his young sweetheart. At long last, he yielded and was torn away from her. Heartbroken, he mounted the truck together with his parents and his two younger brothers, and the first truckload was ready to depart.

Leaving our hometown was a traumatic experience for all of us. The emotional upheaval caused by our fear of remaining at home any longer affected Mother physically and resulted in an onslaught of diarrhea so severe that she felt impelled to take along a pot in case of emergency. We brought very few possessions, realizing only too well that as "workers" in a camp of a slave labor factory, we would have little use for many personal belongings and no place to store them anyhow.

With everyone now on the truck, Father went for the last time to our house, locked the door, hurried back, and directed the Kommandant to begin the journey. The Kommandant was instructed to drive only as far as a small village some five kilometers northeast of Bodzentyn and wait there for Father to rejoin us. Father then disappeared. We were seated in the open back of the truck. There, we were covered but not hidden from the view of pedestrians and other passing vehicles. The motor was started, the truck began to move, and we were on our way, headed for Starachowice—to unknown circumstances and to an unknown future. The sun was descending, and twilight was beginning to set in as our journey began. After about ten to fifteen minutes, our truck stopped at the designated meeting point, where we waited for a few minutes until Father appeared. The remaining fourteen kilometers of our journey were covered in a relatively short time. By early evening we arrived in Starachowice at the home of Aunt Dineleh and Uncle Yoss'l Schreibman.

Aunt Dineleh and Uncle Yoss'l Schreibman lived in a large apartment building that was considered to be the newest, most modern, and fashionable in town, on Kolejowa Street in Wierzbnik, twin city of Starachowice where most of the Jews resided. The main floor served as the premises for their ironware store, in which they sold sheet metal, nails, and other products similar to those sold by Grandfather Nus'n in his ironware store before it was confiscated by the Nazis. Beneath the ground level was a large empty basement with a cement floor, and the level above the store served as the residence of Aunt Dineleh and Uncle Yoss'l, Cousin Lalunya, who was about seven years old by now and some three years younger than me, and her younger brother Moisheniu.

On the ground floor of the opposite side of the building, Shloime Ehnesman had his shoe shop. There, he cut leather and made the upper parts of shoes and boots. His residence was also on the second level immediately above his shop. Another side of the building was occupied similarly, as a dental office on the ground level and as a residence on the second floor, by a Jewish dentist named Dr. Kurta. The building itself was owned by a Starachowice Jew named Y'shia Kozeh.

When we arrived at Aunt Dineleh and Uncle Yoss'l's, we were surprised to find Cousins Chantche and Rivtche Ehrlich there. We soon learned that conditions in Szydłowiec had left the entire Jewish population in a state of grave anxiety and restlessness. Jews from sixteen to sixty were being taken for slave labor, and people looked with envy at those families whose younger children were also taken as laborers: It was assumed that those people taken for slave labor and needed by the Germans would be relatively safe, while who knew what fate awaited those not taken as workers. Under these circumstances, Aunt Feigeleh and Uncle Y'shia Ehrlich bribed a German to transport Chantche and Rivtche—who were not taken as laborers—to Aunt Dineleh and Uncle Yoss'l's by truck. The girls had simply been told and had naively believed they were being sent to visit their aunt and uncle until conditions simmered down in Szydłowiec.

Uncle Y'shia had a brother in Lublin who had perished there with his family shortly after the fall of Poland in September 1939. As a result, Uncle Y'shia assumed a thoroughly pessimistic and fatalistic attitude and reasoned that a Jew was a Jew regardless of where he might be. "M'meint nisht bloiz mein Moishe," he insisted in bitter resignation (They don't have only my brother Moishe in mind). It therefore seemed immaterial to him whether he was in Szydłowiec or Starachowice or anywhere else, so he chose the path of least resistance, preferring to remain with Aunt Feigeleh in Szydłowiec and let events happen as they might. Inasmuch as Uncle Y'shia saw no hope of rescuing little Ruchtcheleh, since she was even younger than me, he decided not to send her along with Chantche and Rivtche but to keep her at home instead.

This situation tragically substantiated Father's decision to abandon Bodzentyn for the "privilege" of serving the Nazi cause as slave laborers when he did. Moreover, we had learned the week before Rosh Hashana that the entire Jewish community of Kielce had just been liquidated; that is to say that every Jewish man, woman, and child had been transported out of that major city to unknown destinations, leaving that city *Judenrein* (cleansed of Jews).

In this darkening and increasingly terrifying situation, we settled in at the home of Aunt and Uncle Schreibman. The twenty-two souls of our family from Bodzentyn had to be housed now, together with our aunt and uncle, their two children, and Chantche and Rivtche—twenty-eight people in all. Under these abnormal circumstances, Grandfather Nus'n, Uncles Leib'l and Yank'l, and Chantche and Rivtche slept in the residence on the second floor with Aunt and Uncle Schreibman and their two children. Our immediate family occupied the rear of the store premises, where we slept on the floor, crowded and uncomfortable. The Bidermans and the Greenbaums each rented a room within the same building, while Uncle Moishe and his family rented a room in an adjacent building.

Father and Mother went out regularly to shop for food and other necessities. Among the peasants in town selling dairy products, fruits, and vegetables from her farm in the village of Świętomarz near Bodzentyn was Mme Zofia Surowjecka. Mme Surowjecka was a former customer at the Biderman yard goods store. It was she to whom the Bidermans had entrusted a large stock of their finest material for safekeeping. Father had arranged for Mme Surowjecka to send foodstuffs to us at Aunt Dineleh's through her nephew, Ben Kazimierz. As a rule, he appeared regularly, but once a box of apples was brought by a young peasant farmhand worker of Mme Surowjecka's, named Juziek.

Our immediate preoccupation, however, was to procure the identification cards we needed to work as laborers in the munitions factory. The adults met frequently with Shloime Ehnesman while arranging the preparation of the cards. Cousin Rivtche happened to overhear one of the adult conferences. "How is it that Feigeleh and Y'shia are not here with us?" she heard Uncle Moishe ask Aunt Dineleh. "Are they not also a sister and brother? Chantcheleh and Rivtcheleh are the only two children here without parents?" The full adult conference agreed with Uncle Moishe's contention and decided that a Pole be hired to go to Szydłowiec and transport Aunt Feigeleh, Uncle Y'shia, and Cousin Ruchtcheleh Ehrlich to Starachowice, without delay. Uncle Yoss'l Schreibman immediately made arrangements.

The Pole left the next morning for Szydłowiec and returned shortly— but without the Ehrlichs. It was too late, he reported. The city was surrounded by Poles who were assisting the Germans in the liquidation of the Jewish community there. Wednesday, September 23, 1942, two days after Yom Kippur, that city too was declared Judenrein. Poor Chantcheleh and Rivtcheleh had not dreamed they would never again see their parents or younger sister, Ruchtcheleh, and now all hope for any such reunion was lost. The girls were, for all practical purposes, orphans.

With events occurring precisely as Father had foreseen, and with city after city being liquidated at an accelerating pace, people were now fleeing into Starachowice from cities throughout Poland. Included were old friends from Bodzentyn. All were flocking here in the hope of becoming workers in the munitions factory so they might be spared from otherwise almost certain deportation and death. Almost no entire families made it, but several members of the Y'chiel Grossman and Hersh'l Weintraub families were among those who did succeed. They rented single rooms, with all those members of their families present crowded into the one room.

Times were now more abnormal than ever. People were fleeing their homes and moving into temporary dwellings that were so overcrowded as to be hardly livable. They feared their unknown futures and their lives became burdened with anxiety that compounded their acute instability. The younger children managed to play and make acquaintances with children of other families living nearby, yet none of us could avoid sensing the gravity of events all about us. Nazis appeared periodically on the streets and would often raid houses or stores. They would frequently seize people, sometimes quite young ones, and kidnap them, often to work at camps in Poland and Germany. This danger loomed greater for the older children, who would be likely prospects for slave maids in addition to camp workers. Thus, when Nazis were seen coming, all children would flee in terror. The children of our family would run to Aunt Dineleh's basement to hide. Few customers were coming into their store now; when they did, we children quickly disappeared from the premises. Life was terribly frightening and unpredictable, and our primary concern was hiding safely from the Nazi terror raids.

In the meantime, Father learned from Shloime Ehnesman that identification cards were being prepared for all the members of our family—over age twelve. However, he would not be able to issue cards for any members who were younger than that. This situation, of course, presented a new and most serious problem: What should be done with the younger children of the family—Cousins Moisheleh and K'silush Greenbaum, Cousins Lalunya and Moisheniu Schreibman, little Samush, and me?

Only one possibility existed: that we be temporarily adopted by Polish families. But which families? Could we trust them? How could we contact them? Time was undoubtedly running short. The adults huddled in conference and discussed Polish families they knew who might be agreeable to taking in one or more of the children. Uncle Froyim Biderman strongly felt that his former customer, Mme Surowjecka of Świętomarz, could be trusted and might very likely be willing to take in a child. He had the greatest confidence in her decency, honesty, and fine character. Piórczyk, the Polish peasant who drove us to the Bartkiewicz barn in Celiny at the beginning of the war, was also considered, as were several others. Contacts and negotiations were initiated, and plans were begun for all the younger children to be taken in by friendly Polish families.

Father decided to approach Mme Surowjecka with the proposition of taking me into her home and caring for me for the duration of the Nazi domination. He explained to her the extreme danger that hung over every single Jew, even children, and the fact that taking in a Jewish child at this time was therefore tantamount to saving the child's very life. Imploring her to seriously consider the proposition, Father offered Mme Surowjecka 50 percent of the earnings of our flour mill should he survive the war, if only she would agree to house and take care of his youngest child at this most perilous of times. Without responding directly to Father's huge, compensatory offer, she replied that she was decidedly sympathetic and favorably inclined to do what she could to spare the life of an innocent child, but in view of the obvious dangers to all concerned, she would need some time to consider the matter carefully before making any definite commitment. She promised to reply to us within a few days.

In the meantime, Father made preliminary arrangements with another, rather wealthy Polish family to take in my sister Rachela. Despite the fact that Rachela was already thirteen years old, Father felt she looked immature and would be safer with a Polish family than in the labor camp.

Soon Mme Surowjecka made her promised reply to Father; it was in the affirmative. The family, with mixed feelings to be sure, felt a sense of relief. After all, there was hope now that I might survive. Second, the rest of our immediate family would surely be in a considerably less perilous situation in camp without the constant presence of a ten-year-old child. The next hurdle was for Father to inform his youngest child that she would have to be sent away from the rest of the family, alone.

Father mustered the courage, approached me, and sat me down next to him. He patiently explained to me that the entire family was attaching all its hopes of surviving the war to the possibility of working in the munitions factory in town. Unfortunately, an identification card as a laborer could not be obtained for me because I was simply too young. Father continued to explain that he had made arrangements with a fine, honest Polish family to take me in and care for me for as long as necessary. He told me that the people's name was Surowjecki and that they lived in a small village, only five kilometers from Bodzentyn, called Świętomarz. They were not total strangers, he added, because they had been fine customers of Uncle Froyim, and Uncle had assured Father that these people could be fully trusted.

Despite Uncle Froyim's assurances, I was terribly unhappy at the thought of having to go away from the family to be in some strange Polish household. On the other hand, I realized that it would not be fair for me to remain and thereby endanger the lives of the rest of the family. Although Father had not quite put it to me that way, I understood that the entire family could perish because of me; if the family remained in Starachowice as an undivided group, and I was unacceptable as a worker, then the entire family could be rejected as workers. Moreover, I was fairly certain that if I refused to go, Father would undoubtedly give me up against my will, because he would not risk sacrificing the entire family for me. And even if Father thought I might have to perish in the process, he would still not act differently. Had he not repeatedly exhorted us, "If a brother or sister is shot, do not look back and get shot, too. Just keep running"? So I decided that in actuality, only one option existed for me: to go to the Surowjeckis' in Świętomarz.

One evening, as I was walking up the stairs to Aunt Dineleh's residence, I overheard the adults discussing arrangements being made to send away my little cousin Lalunya. I ran up to Father and pleaded with him, "Oh, Father, you know I am willing to go to the Surowjeckis. But why can't Lalunya go together with me? Please? Please?" Father knew, of course, the impracticality of my urgent desire. Undoubtedly, he thought to himself how fortunate we were that Mme Surowjecka had consented to take me in and care for me. How could he as much as entertain the thought of imperiling that arrangement by placing a new burden on an already tenuous and risky situation? Father simply replied, "No, Lalunya cannot go with you."

The two cogent questions facing the family at this point were: When should the family take up places in the munitions factory and when should the younger children be sent to their newly designated foster homes?

Obviously, no one wanted to begin their slave labor any sooner than absolutely necessary; and it was surely loathsome to send away the young children any sooner than necessary. On the other hand, it most assuredly made no sense to risk waiting until it might be too late.

Father therefore made it a point to stroll about, particularly during evenings, to learn whatever he could of impending German plans. He would speak to Shloime Ehnesman, he would eavesdrop on conversations heard while passing open windows of residences, he would acquire bits of information by overhearing people conversing on the streets as he walked past them nonchalantly. Although there was no indication of any imminently scheduled Nazi order to liquidate Starachowice, Father learned that Nazi actions typically were executed in advance of rumored timetables. It was therefore decided that we should begin our new lives as soon as possible.

The couple that was to take in Rachela was immediately contacted. However, when they arrived at Aunt Dineleh's and were introduced to Rachela, second thoughts began plaguing their minds. A change of heart seemed to overtake them as they began commenting on how typically Jewish Rachela looked. If only Rachela had not appeared so characteristically Jewish, they explained, they would have been willing to risk taking her into their home. But because her appearance would immediately betray her Jewish identity to the Germans, both her life and theirs would undoubtedly be placed in grave jeopardy. Thus, the entire plan no longer made sense and was discarded. Instead, it was decided that since an identification card actually could be obtained for Rachela, perhaps she would pass as a laborer in the factory. There was no other choice.

Father then contacted Mme Surowjecka and asked her to come for me at her earliest convenience. She replied that she would send her nephew, Ben Kazimierz, on either the following Tuesday or the following Thursday in the late afternoon. As the time for the actual parting drew near, Mother began to grow increasingly apprehensive. As her thoughts crystallized, she concluded, "Only if the young man arrives on Tuesday will I allow Goldeleh to go, because Tuesday is a lucky day. If, however, he fails to come on Tuesday and comes instead on Thursday, Goldeleh is not going. I will not let her go." Fortunately, fate brought Ben Kazimierz on the designated Tuesday, September 29, during one of the intermediary days of Sukkot, and the time came when I had to be separated, for the first time in my life, from my parents, my sisters and brothers, and my entire family.

Parting was painful for me, and perhaps more painful for the family. But we all held up bravely. I realized fully that I had no other choice and was therefore actually ready and willing to be on my way. The family also was relieved at the thought that I would be safer elsewhere, and that they would at the same time have greater mobility and freedom of action without a ten-year-old around to endanger their status as workers in the factory. Mother gave me a bag with a few belongings that she had prepared for me to take along. We then kissed and embraced, one by one. As I waved good-bye to the family, and they to me, Ben took me by the hand and led me away.

16

To the Surowjecki Farm in Świętomarz

THE SUN was beginning to set on that late Tuesday afternoon as Ben Kazimierz escorted me from Aunt Dineleh's home to the outskirts of town where he had parked his horse and buggy. It was, of course, dangerous for him to be seen leaving Starachowice with a Jewish child whom people might recognize, due to the capital crime status placed by the Nazi authorities on Jewish intercity travel. And so we strolled along on what seemed like a very, very long walk toward the outskirts of town.

We had gone only a short distance when we were noticed by Tevel Szachter, a first cousin of Father and Grandfather Nus'n. He walked up to us, bent down to give me a kiss on my forehead, and, without saying a word, walked on. He seemed to understand thoroughly the circumstances under which I was being escorted away. His eyes, demeanor, and actions conveyed the feelings of his heart to mine more cogently than any words could have expressed. As we continued to walk, I was overcome with loneliness and anxiety. I was too frightened to think clearly; my thoughts were paralyzed from fear. I only knew that I had to keep on walking. Daylight slowly waned, and by the time we reached Ben's horse and buggy, the sun had begun to redden in the gradually darkening sky. As we mounted the buggy, again I encountered such gnawing feelings of isolation and fear. I felt bewildered, but somehow gathered up all the bravery I could find. I knew I had to persevere; I had to persevere.

On the way, Ben took out a couple of sandwiches he had brought along for the journey, one for himself and one for me, and offered me one. I was shocked when I saw and smelled the pork in the sandwiches. I shuddered at the thought of bringing it to my mouth. All my life, I had been reared in a strictly observant Jewish home and community, where our dietary laws, ordained in our Scriptures, explicitly forbade us from consuming any cut of pig meat. Therefore, the mere thought of my young system swallowing and trying to digest his pork loomed in my mind as a loathsome, physically impossible feat. I politely thanked Ben, claiming I was not hungry.

By the time our horse and buggy arrived at the farm, it was already night. Ben drove the buggy up to the wooden entrance gate and was stepping down to open it when I suddenly became terrified by the loud, powerful bark of an approaching dog. It somehow compounded the strange feeling of being away from the family with a strange man here in totally dark, unknown surroundings.

When finally we entered the farm house, I felt exhausted from the long walk, from fear, and from the journey. I was relieved when Ben showed me the room where I was to sleep. He removed the pretty crocheted maroon bedspread from the bed and warmly bade me good night. I changed clothes into a nightgown Mother had included in the bag she had prepared for me, and I went to bed. I was soon asleep, and I slept peacefully through the night. I was awakened by the light the following morning and by the sounds of activity from the early-rising farm household. Soon, Mme Surowjecka appeared in my room. She introduced herself and warmly welcomed me, and invited me to come in for breakfast as soon as I made myself ready.

Shortly I was in the kitchen, where she introduced me to her household as Halinka Bertusówna, her niece from Kraków. The fact is that she indeed had a niece by that name in Kraków, whom no one at the farm had ever seen or met. She thus concealed my Jewish identity from the rest of her household, including her own husband, and foresaw no problems in presenting me to the residents of the village as well. In this way, I, "Halinka Bertusówna," was introduced to the man of the house, Sir Józef Surowjecki, and to the two teenage-girl permanent farmhands, named Marysia and Juzia.

Ben Kazimierz, the nephew of Mme Surowjecka, was of course fully aware of my true identity. He was a bright and liberal-minded young man in his early thirties. Somewhat under six feet tall and of medium build, blond, and intelligent-looking because of the glasses he wore, he was respected and admired by all the village residents. As a zealous advocate of social justice and equality, he was a leader among the local underground Communist activists battling the Nazi occupation. An intellectual, particularly by village standards, he was the main support for his aunt when the question arose as to whether they should consent to shelter a Jewish child. When Father had initially approached her on my behalf, and she replied she would need time to consider the proposal, she probably felt she needed to consult with her educated nephew about the wisdom of such an undertaking. And Ben Kazimierz, whom Mme Surowjecka loved and trusted as if he were her adopted son, was of the strong conviction that it was the only proper and humane thing to do, despite the risks, inconveniences, and potential sacrifices.

Seated at the breakfast table, all were served a bowl of beet borscht and potatoes. This was a common breakfast dish in Polish peasant households, but I had never eaten beet borscht and potatoes for breakfast in my life and felt simply unable to bring a spoonful of that dish to my mouth so early in the morning. Mme Surowjecka, observing that I was not eating and apparently realizing I was not accustomed to this type of breakfast, kindly prepared some eggs, bread and butter, and chocolate milk for me. These foods were much closer to what I might have eaten at home, and I was able to enjoy the meal.

Particularly in my first days at the Surowjecki farm, I had frequent onslaughts of longing, loneliness, and fear. I knew, of course, that I must not complain. I found some comfort in two belongings I had brought along with me: a small picture of Father and a single page from a Siddur that contained the opening daily morning prayer:

Modeh ani l'fanecha	I am thankful to Thee
Melech chai v'kayam	Living and everlasting King
Shehechezarta bi nishmati	For having restored my soul
B'chemla raba	With great mercy
Emunatecha.	In accordance with Thy faithfulness.

I was actually unaware of the fact that I had taken this page of the prayer book with me. But when I discovered it, I clung to it and cherished it. It served as a poignant reminder of my heritage and gave me the spiritual strength to carry on.

Mme Surowjecka would look in on me several times a day to observe how I was adjusting to my new "home" and environment. She was easily able to see how sad and lonely I felt being separated from the family, and that I would at times be sitting alone in my room crying. With extraordinary sensitivity, she strove to cheer me and boost my spirits. She suggested I write a letter to the family and promised that it would get to them.

And so I did. Writing the letter brought me a great measure of solace because it was a way I could actually communicate, even if indirectly, with my family. I looked forward to writing a letter home every day. I recall writing in one letter:

Roses are red
And violets are blue
If only you knew
How I miss you!
    Signed,
    Halinka Bertusówna

When either Mme Surowjecka or Ben went into Starachowice on business, they would deliver my letters to the family and report to them on my
well-being, as well as on my progress in becoming acclimated to my new
environment. Upon returning, they would bring me regards from the
family and deliver mail from them to me. I recall one occasion when I
received a letter from each and every member of the family—from Father
and Mother, from Moishe and Shloime, and from Irka and Rachela. How
good that made me feel. In different ways, each one exhorted me to hold
on and be brave, and to be a good girl.

I knew I must strive to do exactly that, to hold on and be brave, but I
could not avoid moments of melancholy and severe pangs of loneliness.
When Mme Surowjecka would see me sitting in deep thought, saddened
and at times in tears, she exhibited supreme empathy and compassion. She
would urge me to take a walk with her into the wonderful rural surroundings, where the early autumn air felt refreshing and invigorating. We
would stroll some distance up to the village cemetery and back, and I felt
much better.

Mme Surowjecka also obtained some Polish children's storybooks and
would sit me down from time to time and read them with me. I recall one
story in particular, entitled *The Cat in the Shoes*. Mme Surowjecka was
extremely thoughtful. Whenever she served meats to the household that
she knew Jews were not allowed to eat and which would be repulsive to
me, she would extend herself and prepare alternate foods for me. To the
rest of the household, she would explain that her "niece Halinka," being a
big city girl, was unaccustomed to village-style foods and cookery.

I gradually became accustomed to the strange surroundings, only to
learn one day that mail could no longer be delivered to the family. Mme
Surowjecka was about to leave for Starachowice that morning when I
approached her with a letter I had just written. Taking the letter from me,
she said, "Halinka, sit down a moment. There is something I must tell you.
I have no choice but to inform you that the city of Starachowice has been
liquidated, and that all Jews from there have been taken away." Then she

added, "And at the moment, I have no idea as to whether any members of your family have survived."

I was too numb to react, but even before I could begin to ponder what I had just heard, Mme Surowjecka continued, "Halinka, you should know that Jews are disappearing from every city and village in Poland. But I want you to know that should it happen that there are no Jews left anywhere, you are welcome to remain here as one of us, and in time you could even become an heir to what you see here. Have no fear, you are not alone. You are not lost."

I felt saddened, but I did not feel crushed, or even lost. Somehow I was unable to admit to myself that the entire family might have perished. I simply could not accept such an assumption as fact; not yet, at least. As I sat lost in thought, Mme Surowjecka left and proceeded on her way to the market stalls at Starachowice. It was by now approximately four weeks since Ben Kazimierz had brought me to the Surowjecki farm. During these few weeks much had taken place—dreadful events of horrifying magnitude—in Starachowice and in Bodzentyn.

17

The Liquidation of Bodzentyn

FROM THE TIME our family left Bodzentyn, Jewish life and trade activity continued to deteriorate there, as poverty, deprivations, and hunger took the lives of more and more Jews.* Although Jews still participated in the Monday market days, conditions gradually worsened to the extent that they bartered goods because they no longer had currency with which to purchase necessities. Similarly, Jewish stores suffered from progressively dwindling volumes of merchandise until there was practically none at all and meaningful trade was impossible. Jews continued to seek out various ways of subsisting through work or by selling services. Meanwhile, news of the many liquidations reached the Jewish community and terrorized them as they anticipated the day that they too might be liquidated.

When it became known in town that the Szachters had fled to Starachowice to seek work in the German munitions factory, other Bodzentyn Jewish families considered doing likewise. However, relatively few had the means or the initiative to do so, and hardly any entire families arrived in Starachowice other than the Szachters. Instead, almost the entire Bodzentyn Jewish community remained in town to await its destiny.

By the time of the High Holidays of fall 1942, most Jews had long since considered it hazardous to venture out to a place of worship. Nonetheless, a small minority defied the risk by convening in a few private homes to honor the Days of Awe, the most sacred days of the Jewish calendar year, and to commune with and pour their hearts out to their Creator with a never-before-experienced depth of petition and quest for Divine Mercy. On Yom Kippur, Monday, September 21, one of the services took place in the home of Hersh'l Weintraub, the town's recognized honorary public Torah Reader. Some sixty to seventy Jews crowded into his parlor room,

*The material in this chapter was described to me by Shmiel Weintraub and Moniek Grossman in preparation for this book. To my knowledge, Shmiel is the only surviving Jew to have witnessed the liquidation.

where his son Shmiel served as the primary lay cantor for the day-long service. This Day of Atonement, the principal fast day and most sacred day for Jews, was observed in an atmosphere filled with premonitions that this might be the last Yom Kippur for any Jew in Bodzentyn.

By the afternoon, the community was shaken by the arrival of a Jew from nearby Suchedniów, who had fled by foot and was winded, exhausted, and terrified. He reported that the Jewish community there was in the process of being liquidated, and that by now probably not a single Jew was left in the entire town. The Jews of Bodzentyn then realized that, barring a miracle, they were in all probability the next victims on the Nazi agenda for liquidation. Toward late afternoon, the German gendarmerie made its appearance and stalked into the home where the family of Y'chiel Grossman was attending the Yom Kippur services, in order to observe the goings-on at the makeshift synagogue. At one point, one of the Nazi gendarmerie taunted, "Pray, Jews! Pray! Pray! Pray all you want. All the prayers in the world are not going to help you." And with haughty, jeering laughter, they turned and left.

Under these grim circumstances, some Jews stepped out from the services and began discussing alternatives and possibilities of escaping from the tightening net of their barbarous conquerors. Where might they go? What, if anything, could be done? A few, but only a few, opted for escaping to Starachowice as the Szachters had done, so they might also work their way into the munitions factory. The rest felt unable to undertake such a move. Some felt they could not in good conscience abandon wives, children, babies, or old parents and grandparents, while still others felt that the dangers involved would make such a plan far too forbidding, with or without the young and the old. Still others were skeptical as to their futures even if they succeeded in getting as far as Starachowice.

The time had come for the concluding prayers of the N'ilo (Conclusion) Service. Tradition defines this service as the one that accompanies the closing of the portals of Heaven, as the great season of petition and atonement draws to a close in the final hours of Yom Kippur. This service ends with a final blast of the Shofar and the final congregational response, "L'shana habaa birushalayim" (Next year in Jerusalem), which signals the official conclusion of the High Holiday season. This service has always been characterized by a depth of solemnity and contrition that exceeds any other section of any other service of the Jewish year. Many are the passages within it that have traditionally evoked tears of prayer and repentance. Some of the most poignant of these are:

Hashem, Hashem	The Lord, the Lord
Kel rachum v'chanun	is a merciful God
Erech apayim v'rav	Slow to anger and abounding
chesed ve'emet . . .	in kindness and truth . . .
V'salachta laavonenu	Do pardon Thou our iniquity
U'lchatotenu unchaltanu.	and our sin, and make us thine own.
Y'hi ratzon mil'fanecha	May it be thy will
Shomea kol bichyot . . .	Thou who hearest the voice of weeping . . .
V'tatzilenu mikol	To deliver us from all
G'zerot achzariyot	Cruel decrees
Ki l'cha l'vad enenu t'luyot.	For to thee alone are our eyes clung (for salvation).

As Shmiel Weintraub walked up to the makeshift pulpit to lead the congregation this day, sobs of heartbreaking prayer and fear filled the parlor prayer chapel. As he intoned the many poignant prayers, the very floor of the room became drenched from tears that poured from the eyes of the Bodzentyn Jews praying in desperation for miraculous deliverance from the portending imminent calamity.

Four days after Yom Kippur, the festival of Sukkot came and ran its seven-day course relatively uneventfully.

The long-feared, dreaded day began in the predawn hours shortly before 5 A.M. on the morning of *Sh'mini Atzeret* (Eighth Day of Solemn Assembly), Saturday—our Sabbath—October 3, 1942. The German gendarmerie motored into town and this time knocked on the doors of Jewish homes, shouting "Juden, 'raus!" (Jews, out!). They were assisted by the local Polish police, who came calling at every Jewish house in the city, summoning each man, woman, and child to appear immediately in Żwirki Plaza. The police informed the Jews they were being taken for resettlement to an unknown destination and would be allowed to take along only as much as could be carried by hand. Our unfortunate brethren, for centuries, time and again, had been thrust into the position of having to sustain life through hope. Thus, they now allowed themselves to be deluded into thinking and hoping that perhaps they were not being sent to their deaths, but merely to some unknown place to be "re-settled." And indeed, most came with packages and packs on their backs, in preparation for the promised resettlement, offering no challenge or resistance to the orders of the Nazi gendarmerie or their Polish police puppets. Żwirki Plaza quickly became crowded as the entire local Jewish community swarmed into it.

A sizable crew of Polish peasants had been organized in advance by the local Polish police. They now appeared with their horse-led wagons. The Jews were ordered to get in, one by one, until as many as six to eight were crowded into each small wagon. The entire operation was executed with typical German efficiency and impeccable order; there was no shouting, no beating, and no shooting. All rolled smoothly according to plan. Wagon by wagon, the Jews were driven to the nearby Suchedniów railroad station, where they were unloaded from the wagons, herded and jam-packed into cattle cars, and transported away. The wagons were then driven back to Żwirki Plaza, reloaded, and driven again to the Suchedniów railroad station to be unloaded of their human cargo—back and forth, again and again, all morning—until about noon. By that time nearly all the Jews of Bodzentyn had been shipped away. How many? And to what destination? According to Herr Dumker, Kommandant of the Nazi gendarmerie, "from Bodzentyn and surrounding areas, approximately 3,850 Jews had been transported—to Treblinka." To the Treblinka Death Camp! All the Jews of the town of Bodzentyn, all but thirty-two, to be exact, had been sent to their deaths.

The thirty-two left included Shmiel Weintraub, head of the Jewish Community; twenty-nine Jewish men and women, mostly from the Płock refugees, who were assigned under Shmiel to assist the local Polish police in cleaning and tidying up the city after the mass uprooting operation; and two Jews, one adult and one child, who were unable to fit into the last, crowded wagons. A Nazi gendarme then drew a pistol from his holster, took aim at the one remaining adult Jew, and killed him. Another Nazi then grabbed the last Jewish child of Bodzentyn and shoved him against a wall, where he was used as the object of target practice for a group of jeering Nazi sharpshooters. All that remained to be done in order to leave Bodzentyn orderly enough to meet the standards of German cleanliness and discipline was to sweep and clear the streets of refuse and debris.

The remaining Jews were ordered to be housed—stuffed rather—in the Weintraub home and placed under the charge of Shmiel, whose responsibility was now to carry out the task of thoroughly cleansing the newly purged town. Actually, the charge extended beyond that of cleanliness. Each abandoned home was to be carefully rummaged in search of valuables such as gold, silver, jewelry, and furs, which were to be deposited without fail at the Bodzentyn police station.

As the cleansing and rummaging operation was under way, it became clear to Shmiel how delighted the rank-and-file Polish peasants were that the Jews had been ejected from their midst. For, in the aftermath of the operation, the Poles were permitted to help themselves to practically all that was left—towels, linens, clothes, old furniture, utensils, notions, and the like. Not only did they no longer have Jewish business competition to contend with, but they were now heirs to their former neighbors' possessions. Their eagerness to take possession of the myriad unclaimed objects was visible in their behavior and facial expressions. Never had they been able to manage so well as with Nazi assistance.

In the process of perusing the abandoned homes of his martyred fellow Jews, Shmiel came across thousands of volumes of the sacred literature, prayer books, copies of the Bible and its commentaries, tomes of the Talmud, and more—left orphaned in the deserted homes. It was heart-breaking for him to behold the treasured volumes of the victims, who under normal circumstances would have observed traditional burial procedures for the holy books. Not only were the sacred books denied the honor of proper Jewish burial, so also were their owners!

Early one evening, after some ten days and when the assigned task had been completed, Shmiel was suddenly visited at his home by the Nazi gendarmerie, who ordered him to go with them to the police station. On the way, one elderly member of the gendarmerie looked at Shmiel and remarked, "It's no good. It's no good," and did not elaborate. Once in the police station, however, Herr Kommandant Dumker coldly and officially addressed Shmiel, saying, "Herr Weintraub, you have done your share and now I must do my share. I shall have to shoot you."

Effectively concealing his emotion, Shmiel calmly asked that he be allowed to return home in order to bid a final farewell to his friends and coworkers. Obligingly, Kommandant Dumker personally escorted Shmiel back home. As they approached the Weintraub residence, Shmiel went toward the side door entrance via an alley. He opened the door and gestured to the Kommandant to enter first. At the very instant the Kommandant entered the doorway, Shmiel frantically slammed the door and ran feverishly for his life down the alley. Within seconds, he turned the corner onto another alley and fled to a place of refuge in an abandoned Jewish home a short distance away.

As he was running, Shmiel noticed a Polish peasant woman, who had caught sight of him as he entered the empty house. In the house, he remained hiding, but intensely alert as to the movement of the Germans and local Polish police who were searching for him, particularly because he had been seen by the Polish woman. He was able to overhear the searchers as they asked individuals whether they had seen him. He was heartened to overhear the woman who had actually seen him reply to a searcher that she had seen absolutely nothing. The search continued for hours, well into the night.

When all seemed quiet, and Shmiel felt reasonably certain that the Germans were no longer in town, he fled by foot through the darkness of night—to Starachowice. The remaining twenty-nine Jews, left in the former Weintraub home, are believed to have been sent to Auschwitz. They were never heard from again.

Thus ended the Jewish community of Bodzentyn.

May the Father of Mercy, who dwelleth on high, in His mighty compassion, remember the pious, the righteous, and the guiltless of the sainted communities who laid down their lives for the sanctification of the Divine Name. May He avenge before our eyes the blood of the innocent, and may He speedily render divine retribution to the perpetrators of the mass bloodletting of His servants.

18

The Liquidation of Starachowice

AFTER I was sent away to the Surowjecki farm in Świętomarz, Father felt that the time had come for the family to begin working at the munitions factory. He had regularly been in contact with Shloime Ehnesman and continued periodically to wander about and eavesdrop from below open windows along the backs of apartments of those engaged in making boots and clothing for the German military staff. From listening to and observing the movements of those in contact with the Nazi camp Kommandant Schwertner, he thus had at least indirect knowledge of projected German plans of action and learned that those supposedly "in the know" had already begun sending their families to work in the factory. Father therefore assumed that the time had come for him to do likewise. He also surmised that the day of liquidation could not be far in coming.

Moreover, Father either learned or reasoned that liquidations of cities began before daylight and that, in Starachowice, because of the presence of the munitions factory in the area, a selection would be made in which only the most able-bodied would be chosen for work. Desperate struggles would undoubtedly ensue as the strongest, most aggressive individuals forced their way into the group selected as laborers. In a situation such as this, surely neither Mother nor Irka and Rachela, to say nothing of our grandfathers or the other women in the family, would have the slightest chance of survival. Father therefore arranged through Shloime Ehnesman for our entire immediate family and our two grandfathers to be placed on the night shift at the factory so that when the liquidation came, presumably before daylight, our family would all be in the factory working and thereby escape witnessing or experiencing the horrors and fierce, hopeless struggles certain to take place at the liquidation.

With identification cards now ready and in hand, and assigned to the night shift, our immediate family and grandfathers began working at the factory daily from 11 P.M. until 7 A.M., at which time they returned to sleep during the day. For the children, having never worked before, this change in schedule was difficult enough to adjust to, but now the time was filled with fear and suspense as well. Surely, sinister events of horrifying magnitude were impending, and so the ensuing days constituted the most traumatic period of waiting. All Jews were plagued with the unavoidable thoughts: Exactly what was going to happen? Who would survive? Who would perish? Under what circumstances? How soon?

As the leader of our family, Father never panicked. He was at all times a pillar of strength. His astute, penetrating mind was continuously observing and analyzing every new move and occurrence, and he repeatedly spoke to the family about the struggle to survive. "Money is for one purpose," he would emphasize, "to save lives." The family, in turn, maintained its composure, adults and children alike. At no point was there cursing or shouting. All maintained a strong, quiet, and determined front, with no one demanding anything from or blaming anyone else. No one would allow himself or herself to depress or demoralize the others.

During these grim days, knowing that the liquidation of Starachowice could be expected at any moment, Jews would encounter one another and speculate on what they could do to save themselves. On one such day, a Jew from Suchedniów had just arrived in Starachowice after escaping from the Majdanek Concentration Camp. He spoke of experiences more horrifying than had ever been heard of before. He told of Jews being starved and worked to death; and of severe beatings, clubbings, and torture. Most revealing and shocking, however, was the news that Jews were being herded regularly from the camp in large masses to a nearby open field, where they were ordered at gunpoint to dig their own graves. When the graves were ready, he said, the Jews were routinely machine-gunned into those same graves and then covered with soil by their Nazi murderers—even before some had totally expired.

Knowledge of such savage atrocities stimulated a number of Jews to consider the possibilities of escape to some forest, in the hope of surviving there for the duration of the war. Father was approached by the young sons of Y'chiel Grossman, Nuter and Moniek, and together they discussed a plan of escape for Father, the elder Grossman, and his two sons. Father was evidently curious to hear the reasoning and tentative plans of long-time townsmen and friends, but he obviously could not bring himself actually to abandon the family.

In the meantime, Father once again hired the Jewish shoemaker from Bodzentyn, Yoss'l Shister, who had managed to reach Starachowice. In

Bodzentyn, Yoss'l had been asked to insert money into shoes. At this time, Father felt that money should be placed into boots instead, in case we might have to walk or run long distances in flight or in search of food. In situations such as these, boots would prove more sturdy and durable than shoes. Once again, Yoss'l removed the heels, inserted Russian twenty-ruble gold pieces between the heels and soles of the boots, then reattached the heels to the boots. Similarly, money was sewn into clothes. Still stays were removed from women's girdles and were replaced with American dollar bills. Then Father once again gathered together the immediate family—Mother, Moishe, Irka, Shloime, and Rachela—and told them what Yoss'l had done. He also reminded them that the family fortune had been buried in Grandfather Meier's backyard garden and described the specific locations of the interred valuables. Once again, Father exhorted each member of the family to be constantly vigilant and to strive for his or her own survival, in the face of the worsening conditions looming ahead.

Then he packed several knapsacks with a few of the most necessary items of clothing, plus bottles for both water and paper currency. Feeling certain that liquidation was absolutely inevitable and probably imminent, he felt it was wise to have these items handy, ready to grab at a moment's notice.

As each day passed, it was becoming increasingly more dangerous for the young children of the family to be kept home and not be sent to the Polish families who had so humanely agreed to take them in. However, Aunt Brucheleh and Uncle Pintche Greenbaum, Aunt Dineleh and Uncle Yoss'l Schreibman, and Uncle Moishe and Aunt Chavtche Szachter found themselves incapable of parting with their precious young offspring. Each passing day that did not bring the liquidation encouraged them to hope for one more day, and another day, and perhaps one other day. When the slightest indication of the impending liquidation became evident, they thought, they would then act with dispatch. But maybe some unexpected event would cause the Germans not to carry out a liquidation at Starachowice altogether. They decided to judge the situation from day to day, subconsciously hoping for a miracle to prevent what was generally assumed to be inevitable.

By the evening of Tuesday, October 27, there was as yet not the slightest hint of an impending liquidation. Later that night, as the family was preparing to go to work at the factory, Rachela suddenly balked. She was not in the mood to go to work. The other family members tried to persuade her that it was much too hazardous for her to remain in the apartment overnight. "What if the liquidation takes place tonight?" they asked. But Rachela remained adamant. She cried and pleaded, "I don't want to go to work. Leave me alone. There isn't going to be a liquidation tonight anymore than there was last night, or the night before, or the night before that." Since, in fact, there was no indication that this night would be any different from preceding nights, the family finally left for work— all except Rachela and Father, who would not leave Rachela in the apartment alone. Perhaps nothing eventful would happen this night. And they retired for the night. All was quiet and peaceful.

At approximately 4:45 the next morning, Wednesday, October 28, a loud, pounding knock was heard on the door, accompanied by a shouted order, "Jews, you must leave your homes immediately and appear in the town marketplace without delay!" The liquidation of Starachowice was underway. It was now impossible for our cousins K'silush and Moisheleh Greenbaum, Lalunya and Moisheniu Schreibman, or little Samush to be given over to the Polish families who had agreed to take them. It was too late. Quickly, Father grabbed two of the knapsacks he had prepared earlier, one for himself and one for Rachela. He packed each with several pieces of bread and a bottle of water. Then they set out for the marketplace.

Father, fully aware of the fact that Rachela looked dangerously like a child, exhorted her not to dare go with her aunts or young cousins. He was certain that they could not possibly end up in the group to be chosen as laborers and that if Rachela tagged along with them she would undoubtedly, God forbid, perish. Father deliberately tarried until our aunts and young cousins had gone some distance. He deliberately detached himself and Rachela from them, as the throngs of Jews were being chased and gathered into the marketplace. As they were marching along, Father carefully instructed Rachela, "As soon as you see that I have been chosen for work, you must then jump immediately into that same line as fast as you can, and as forcefully as necessary. If you have to, you must push, squeeze in, crawl in, do whatever you have to, but you must get into that line."

Soon the entire Jewish community of Starachowice was herded into the market square. Above the turmoil of the thousands milling about within such a tightly crowded area under the terrifying circumstances of a liquidation under way, orders were heard being shouted for those with laborers' identification cards to move into the lines of the group selected for work. What chaos ensued! What confusion! Sounds of shouting and

Grandfather Nus'n Szachter

A group photo taken in Kraków in 1938 upon the occasion of the wedding of Uncle Moishe Szachter to Chavtche Gitler of Kraków. (*Left to right:* Simcha Weintraub, Cousin Chantche Ehrlich, Mother, Aron Silberberg, Irka, Pola Gitler, Uncle Yank'l Szachter)

Uncle Leib'l Szachter

Mme Surowjecka in front of her house in Świętomarz

Mme Zofia Surowjecka

Sir Józef Surowjecki

Mother, 1938

Rachela and Golda at
Mother's gravesite,
1949

Irka, Cousin Rivtche, Golda, and Rachela

Golda Szachter, c. 1946

crying were heard coming from all directions, as people with and without workers' cards struggled, competed, shoved, and pushed with all their strength in a desperate effort to land in the group selected for work. Germans were shouting orders, cursing, and beating and shooting Jews who failed to jump quickly enough to their commands. Families cried for mercy as they were torn apart.

Amid the horror and the suffering, Rachela saw Father make his way into the workers' group. As he had instructed her, she now fought as forcefully as she could, but was pushed out of the workers' group. She tried again, and again she was shoved out. Determined to get in, Rachela struggled several times until she finally succeeded, with help from a few older and taller friends from Bodzentyn, including two Grossman sisters, relatives of the Y'chiel Grossman family, who deliberately surrounded her to make her less visible.

Within this group were the more fortunate five hundred or so survivors of the liquidation. On the other side of the market square were the less fortunate, the overwhelming majority. Here the old, ill, and feeble were tossed and shoved. Here young children were torn from their young parents to be condemned. Heartbreaking good-byes were heard and seen everywhere. In some families, quarrels erupted over which parent should go with the children. For the most part, mothers chose to go with their beloved offspring. Many men fought their way into the lines of the workers, abandoning wives and children, but there were others who chose to go along with their wives and children. These masses of our brethren were hustled onto trucks, one after another. Truckload after truckload, they were driven off to the railroad depot, where they were transferred onto cattle cars and transported to the Treblinka Concentration Camp.

As the truckloads of human cargo were being driven away, many in the workers' lines who had abandoned their families began to feel pangs of guilt. How could they in good conscience have spared their own lives while allowing their dear ones to go to their deaths? On the other hand, what would they have accomplished by not having saved their own lives? Could they have prevented the slaughter of their loved ones? Of course not. But who could say that a father is more deserving of survival than a mother? On the other hand, if the situation were reversed, why would it have been more proper for the mother to have survived at the sacrifice of the father? Then why torture oneself with self-inflicting blame? Yet despite all logic, such feelings of self-reproach and guilt haunted many and deepened their agony even more.

By around noon, the last truckloads had been driven away. The liquidation of Starachowice was completed. The entire host of survivors to be workers were marched in rows of five to the labor camp beyond the city limits. It was a hot autumn day, and the German patrols, their rifles pointed, ordered the workers to jog. With the handle of their rifles, the Germans struck any Jew hesitating to keep pace. Moniek Grossman related how, anticipating the confiscation of any excess clothing, he was wearing two shirts and two pairs of trousers. Forced to jog continuously, so overdressed on such a miserably hot day, he saw the ordeal as impossible. Bitterly challenging his miserable predicament, he mentally rebuked his creator, "O God! You seem to be on *their* side! How could you? Is there no limit to the suffering you will allow them to inflict upon us?"

When the group finally reached the labor camp, all were ordered to be seated on the ground. From there, they were ordered to rise and pass through controls, single file, along one of two lines simultaneously being processed. At the focal point of each of the two lines was a station with a table and a number of trunks. As each person reached the station, officials ordered that all valuables—money, gold, silver, and jewelry—be deposited into one of the trunks. Any extra clothing was ordered to be deposited in a second trunk. As a warning to potential resisters, one Jew was shot outright for hesitating to relinquish his few possessions.

With Rachela's turn at the station approaching, she realized she had a considerable amount of money in her knapsack and decided she was not willing to part with it. So she took a piece of wrapping paper out of her knapsack, covered the paper money with it, then twisted the wrapping paper until the money was securely stuffed inside of it. She then removed the bottle of water from her knapsack, tossed out the cork, and replaced it with the wad of wrapped money so that the wad appeared as a makeshift substitute for the cork. When her turn came at the station, Rachela passed the inspection with the bottle of water unsearched.

And the lines continued on and on. As one trunk was filled to capacity, it was sealed, hauled away, and replaced by another. At the conclusion of this long, tedious procedure, the people were directed into one of two groups that were assigned to specific places of work within the factory.

The total factory complex consisted of two main areas, in addition to one smaller area. The latter, which was named Tartak, included a lumberyard and sawmill. Only a few selected people worked here. The two main work areas were the Hermann Göring Werke, which was the munitions factory proper, and the Wielki Piec (Giant Furnace), which was a huge foundry. When the division of workers was completed, the people were marched to one of the two camp complexes: Camp Strzelnica or Camp Majówka. From there, they were led to the camp barracks, where the men were separated from the women. After being settled in the barracks, each person was then officially registered into his or her respective camp.

The total experience was traumatic for all, especially the recent wave of refugees into Starachowice. Within a short space of a few weeks, they had been uprooted from lifelong homes, thrust into temporary crowded conditions in a strange city, and driven from there, if graced by Divine Salvation, not to some remote, unknown destination to be done away with, but to crowded, unsanitary workers' barracks. Hence, their thoughts all revolved anxiously around one primary concern—survival—from moment to moment, and from day to day. Their minds were plagued with tormenting questions: What will be done with us here? Will we be able to survive? If so, how long will we be kept here? Where will they send us next, and what will they do with us then? A second concern was for the fate of family members: Which ones survived and which ones had not?

There were three work shifts in the factory: the morning shift, from 7 A.M. to 3 P.M.; the afternoon shift, from 3 P.M. to 11 P.M.; and the night shift, from 11 P.M. to 7 A.M. Not until several shifts had gone and returned from work was it possible to know with certainty which of our family had been sent to their deaths and which ones had survived in camp. Of the Greenbaums, Aunt Brucheleh chose to die with her dear children, K'silush and Moisheleh; only Uncle Pintche survived. Of the Bidermans, it is not known whether Aunt Gitteleh chose to go with her oldest son Moishe because he had failed to force himself into the group of workers or vice versa. The fact is that Cousin Moishe was so sensitive a soul that he could have fainted at the sight of blood even under normal circumstances. In any event, neither he nor his mother, our aunt Gitteleh, survived; only Uncle Froyim Biderman and his two younger sons, Itche and Shloime, remained alive.

Cousins Chantche and Rivtche Ehrlich survived and told the heartbreaking details of the fate of the families of Uncles Moishe Szachter and Yoss'l Schreibman: When ordered to vacate their places of residence and appear immediately in the marketplace, all of them—Uncle Moishe, Aunt Chavtche, and little Samush, Aunt Dineleh, Uncle Yoss'l Schreibman, Lalunya and Moisheniu, together with Cousins Chantche and Rivtche—walked together to the city square. When they heard the orders for peo-

ple with workers' cards to line up within the group of laborers, Aunts
Chavtche and Dineleh resolutely chose to remain and accept for themselves whatever fate awaited their children. Uncles Moishe and Yoss'l
chose at that moment to stay also. Protesting that it was utterly senseless
for both her and her husband to sacrifice their lives, Aunt Dineleh, pressing her children next to herself, pleaded in tears with Uncle Yoss'l to leave
and join the group of workers and save his life. He responded merely by
grabbing Lalunya from Aunt Dineleh and holding her securely, as he
insisted adamantly that he would not leave. Cousin Chantche, at the
insistence of the adults, grabbed her sister Rivtche by the hand and left for
the line of workers. They both succeeded in edging their way into the line.

The sad irony of the near superhuman courage, devotion, loyalty, and
self-sacrifice displayed by Uncles Moishe and Yoss'l was the cruel fate that
awaited both of them: the horrifying experience of having to witness their
loved ones—their wives and children—being torn away from them before
their very eyes, as they themselves were returned as workers to the labor
camp. The Nazi tormentors had decided that some two hundred male
workers in addition to the group selected at the time of the liquidation
were needed in the labor force. So, the same afternoon following the
liquidation, Uncles Moishe Szachter and Yoss'l Schreibman were brought
to the camp, along with the additional laborers. Of course, their wives,
Aunts Chavtche and Dineleh, together with their small children—baby
boy Samush, Lalunya and Moisheniu—all perished.

Both our grandfathers, Nus'n and Meier, survived, as did Uncles Leib'l
and Yank'l. Of all the family units descending from Grandfathers Nus'n
and Meier, the only one to survive in its entirety was our own: Father,
Mother, my brothers, and my sisters. Thus of the twenty-eight members of
our family who gathered together at Aunt Dineleh's, only eighteen survived the macabre liquidation of Starachowice. Ten of our dear family
were transported to the Treblinka Concentration Camp to their deaths—
four adults and six children.

The desperate pursuit of their own survival deprived the remaining
adults even of the peace of mind in which to mourn the slaughter of their
many dear ones. The younger survivors, on the other hand, were not even
fully aware of what had taken place. They naively harbored the belief that
perhaps those relatives had been sent elsewhere, to some other camp, and
their elders had more immediate concerns than to tell them the grim
realities. In spite of everything, who knows how many more beloved ones
of our family would have had to be sacrificed, had it not been for Father's

sagacious foresight and astute planning, as he anticipated almost to the minutest detail every diabolical move of our foe.

All the family survivors but one were now settled in Camp Strzelnica—all except Grandfather Meier, who was placed in Camp Majówka. To be sure, all were now interned prisoners, slave laborers for the enemy. But at least all were alive.

19

Ups and Downs at the Surowjecki Farm

SOON AFTER the family had settled in at the Starachowice Labor Camp, Mme Surowjecka was contacted by a Pole who worked in the munitions factory. He had been sent by Father to inform her that my immediate family was alive and well at the camp. Other relatives had survived also, he told her. They included my two grandfathers, Uncles Moishe, Leib'l, and Yank'l Szachter, Pintche Greenbaum, and Yoss'l Schreibman, Uncle Froyim Biderman and his two sons Itche and Shloime, and Cousins Chantche and Rivtche. All the rest had been sent away and were no more.

I breathed a sigh of relief to learn that most of the family had survived, especially the entire immediate family. However, I could not possibly grasp the depth of the tragedy of my ten dear departed. Knowing that my own life depended on my ability to adapt to my new surroundings without revealing my Jewish identity prevented me from dwelling on the tragic slaughter of Aunts Gitteleh, Brucheleh, Dineleh, and Chavtche, and Cousins Moishe Biderman, Moisheleh and K'silush Greenbaum, Lalunya and Moisheniu Schreibman, and Samush Szachter. I could allow myself neither the luxury of diverting my thoughts from the ever-present danger surrounding me nor the liberty of overburdening Mme Surowjecka with my own inner sorrows. The fact that verbal messages as well as an occasional letter could now once again pass more or less regularly between Father and the Surowjeckis indeed served as a great boost to my morale.

Adjustment to my new home at the Surowjecki farm, away from the family, was still slow and painful. Nonetheless, as time passed I adapted to my surroundings. I fully realized that my situation left me no alternative. Moreover, Mme Surowjecka gradually began devoting less attention to me, not so much because she felt less empathetic to my predicament, but rather because by pampering me less and by showing me less pity openly, she thought I would probably adjust more quickly and be forced to strengthen my own resolve sooner.

In addition, she started teaching me some of the chores of village farming and began expecting me to assist responsibly in the various work routines of rural farm life. Ironically, Sir Surowjecki, who was totally unaware of the fact that I was a Jewish child and was under the impression instead that I was his wife's niece from Kraków, openly disagreed with his wife in the demands she placed upon me. "Halinka is a big city girl," he would say. "She is neither trained nor accustomed to the hard work of village farm life, and I think you should leave her alone."

"Never mind," Mme Surowjecka would counter. "Halinka is a young, completely normal, and healthy girl. She will learn, and she'll get used to the work. Nothing will happen to her."

To be sure, in the beginning I was terribly awkward. One of the first chores assigned to me was that of taking the cow out to pasture for grazing. It was the only cow the Surowjeckis owned at this time, because the Germans had confiscated their other cows and two of the four horses they possessed before the war. The responsibilities of tending the remaining horses and feeding and milking the cow belonged to her farmhands, Marysia and Juzia. The two girls would tend the cow in the stable. My responsibility was merely to take the cow out and watch after it as it grazed in the pasture. As I led it out for the first time, the cow began to run from the meadow through the garden. I ran after it, but I had no idea how to control it. In its flight, it trampled and killed one of the little yellow chicks. When she learned of the accident, Mme Surowjecka was clearly disappointed in me and angry. I felt terrible and was frightened. I had failed to meet the expectations of the one person upon whom my security and very life depended. But what was there for me to do or say? All I could do was agonize inwardly.

The next day, as Mme Surowjecka was returning from one of her marketing trips to Starachowice, she stopped to tell me that she had just seen Father and had brought him some strawberries for the family. Later that evening, however, she related to me the tragic news that my cousin Itche, the middle son of the three Biderman boys, had been killed in an accident at the munitions factory. Somehow, a giant mallet had fallen on him and crushed him instantly. The news shocked me, and I was deeply jolted. The thought flashed through my mind that I should have known something catastrophic was impending when, the day before, the little yellow chick was trampled to death by the cow and Mme Surowjecka had become so visibly irritated with me. Was not all this a bad omen presaging the horrible tragedy that had now befallen my beloved cousin Itche? Once again, I had no choice but to bear these pains inside me and carry on as best I could, as if nothing had happened.

In time, I learned to rise early in the morning and to tend and control the cow. I also learned to work in the garden. When the weather was warm, I worked out there every day. Soon Mme Surowjecka asked me to carry pails of water out to the garden in order to water the vegetables. When he saw me exerting my utmost strength to carry them, Sir Surowjecki quarreled with his wife. "You should not be requiring Halinka to carry out those pails of water. They are much too heavy for her."

Mme Surowjecka indignantly countered, "What makes you think they are too heavy for her? She'll get used to the work. It's good for her." And as usual, she prevailed.

Another chore of mine was weeding. At other times, I would take the vegetables out of the soil, cut off certain parts, arrange them in bundles, and place them in baskets for marketing. Once I saw Marysia and Juzia taking about a dozen apples apiece from the pile they were preparing for marketing. They told me they were going to hide them in the attic for themselves. I knew that Mme Surowjecka would be angry if she knew, but I could not decide whether to tell her. On the one hand, they were friendly to me, and I sought to avoid harming that relationship. On the other hand, I realized that the danger to me would be very great indeed if they became angry with me and chose to be vengeful. I therefore withheld that information from Mme Surowjecka.

Soon, however, I was faced with a far more serious situation. When our family was all still at Aunt Dineleh's in Starachowice, as I related earlier, Mme Surowjecka had once sent her male farmhand, Juziek, to deliver a box of apples to us. He now unfortunately recognized me and whispered into the ears of Marysia and Juzia that I was a Jewish girl. Suddenly they began addressing me in jest, "*Żydówica*" (Jew girl), and in no time all the farmhands began snickering at me, "*Żydówica*." I fully realized that this new situation was extremely dangerous and that I could definitely not afford to withhold this information from Mme Surowjecka.

When I informed her of the situation, she instantly sensed the danger to herself as well as to me and wasted not a single moment. She called out to them immediately and forcefully, and with unwavering and unequivocal clarity said, "I understand you've been amusing yourselves in some name-calling. What's this I've been hearing about '*Żydówica*'? I'm warning you, I had better not hear that word out of any of you again. If I do, I shall have to teach you how to mind other people's business. Now on with your work. And you had better do what you are told, if you know what's good for you." Apparently they feared some possible punishment or perhaps being fired by her, or simply they respected her prominent image among the villagers. In any event, they ceased calling me "*Żydówica.*"

A subsequent incident, however, caused Mme Surowjecka to act differently. A friendly merchant was passing by one day on horseback. When he saw me, he stopped. "Good morning," he greeted Mme Surowjecka. Then he added, "I am simply curious. Tell me, who is that child who seems to look so different?"

She spontaneously responded, "Oh, she is my niece from Kraków."

"I see," responded the merchant, but he seemed to be examining me from head to toe with an intent gaze. Then, with a gentlemanly "Good day," he rode off.

Mme Surowjecka realized she must act quickly to minimize as much as possible the differences in appearance and demeanor between me and the native, village peasant girls. She proceeded to lengthen my dresses to make them closer in style to those worn by the Polish girls. For the same reason, she also combed out and stretched my curly blond hair until it was long and straight.

Gradually, Mme Surowjecka taught me the prayers and rituals of the village church services. She showed me how Christians brought their hands together in prayer, and the proper movements they made when they crossed themselves. Soon she began taking me to church with her. In time, either she or Sir Surowjecki were taking me almost every day. Before long, I became accustomed to the rituals and procedures and learned the hymns and melodies. Although nothing in the world could have veered my heart away from the faith of my family and from all that had been sacred to our parents and grandparents for generations and centuries, I nevertheless recognized the beauty of the spirituality of the church services as well as its sanctifying influence on the Polish peasant household in general. In time, I found attendance at the church services a pleasant and enjoyable aesthetic experience. Mme Surowjecka was pleased with my progress in every respect, and life in Świętomarz began to take on a degree of normalcy for all concerned.

Village life for Poles under the Nazis could be described as paradise when compared with the cruel edicts and persecutions to which the Jews were subjected in Bodzentyn, Starachowice, and throughout Poland. No curfew was imposed, and Poles were free to go about their work and business. They could shop, travel, or play freely. Still, they were made to feel the yoke of foreign occupation in several respects. For example, they were deprived of certain luxuries, as when they were forced to surrender some of their horses and cows to the Germans. In addition, the Nazi authorities occasionally searched Polish homes, which terrified the population. For when the Germans caught a Pole even suspected of being a Communist, an anti-Nazi activist, or a violator of any of their laws, they were no less brutal to that person than they were to the Jews. It is therefore not surprising that the Poles generally had no pro-German sympathy. Clearly they looked forward to the day when the Germans would be driven from their soil. Their sympathies were expressed in the optimistic view of the peasants: "They may be clothed in fur underwear, but they will not win the war."

Apart from their anti-German sentiments, however, the average Pole was not unsympathetic to the conquerors' treatment of Polish Jews. On one occasion, for instance, a villager commented to Mme Surowjecka, "The Germans are really taking care of the Jews, aren't they? We're almost rid of all of them."

Mme Surowjecka quickly countered, "Don't leap so fast for joy. In the meantime, you haven't survived yet yourself. The Jews are their breakfast; they have us in mind for supper."

Hearing such callous anti-Semitic utterances or being called "Żydówica" while being alone in a Polish village away from the family invariably sent a jolt through me. Inwardly, I would have preferred being in the labor camp with the family than to be exposed to anti-Semites everywhere around me. I found comfort from four sources. One was the loose page from the Hebrew prayer book that I had found in my bag of belongings I had brought from Starachowice, and which I kept carefully hidden among my clothes. That one page provided me with a link to my past, to my family, and to my people.

The second great source of comfort was the frequent exchanges of messages between Father and me that were passed along through Mme Surowjecka and her nephew. These exchanges were possible because of the particular physical layout of the munitions factory and the camp. The workers had a considerable distance to walk from their barracks to the factory. Both Jews and uninterned non-Jewish Poles worked at the factory, so the factory itself was not guarded with extreme strictness by the Germans, and it was therefore possible for Jews to meet and make contacts with Poles, even those not associated with the factory. In this way were Mme Surowjecka and Ben able to convey messages and greetings between the family and me during their trips into Starachowice to market their produce. On occasion, a letter could be smuggled in or out as well. These means of communication were of inestimable comfort to me. Between letters, I found comfort in the small picture of Father I had brought with me. Whenever I was alone, I would take it out and look at it.

A fourth source of comfort was the unrelenting efforts and kindnesses of the Surowjeckis and Ben toward me. Ben had his own room in the house, where he listened to the radio, studied the news, and perused maps. He was often away from home, probably working with the underground Communists, but when he was home he was as kind as he was liberal. Once during mid-November 1942, he attempted to show me on a map how far the Germans had advanced into Russia, deep into the Caucasus region, all the way to Stalingrad, near the Volga River. Often when it was cold, he would come into the kitchen to warm himself. While each member of the household would be occupied with his or her own activity, Ben would take the hand of one of the female farmhands and begin dancing a fast polka. In this way, he strove to demonstrate that he did not consider himself above them, but rather wished to treat them as equals.

Mme Surowjecka similarly used to relate how she was once a farmhand herself, and for a time had worked as a cook in a restaurant. Therefore, despite the fact that she now owned fields and acres of land and had farmhands of her own, she was always able to imagine herself in their situations and exercise compassion in dealing with them.

Sir Surowjecki was much older than Mme Surowjecka, and seemed very old to me. Nevertheless, whenever he spoke on any matter relating to me, or whenever he spoke directly to me, he was always kind, soft-spoken, and understanding.

I also made friends with village girls my age and enjoyed playing with them. At no time, however, could I allow myself to become lost in play. I was constantly on guard to avoid revealing my true identity and heritage to anyone, child or adult, for fear of that knowledge somehow leaking to the Germans. In spite of this unceasing vigilance, I managed to enjoy their company and the toys they shared with me.

Before long, it was Christmas time. At the Surowjecki household, Christmas Eve was a festive occasion. A particularly elaborate seven-course meal was prepared and served, along with wines and delicacies. Carols were sung, and festivity and merriment filled the air. The occasion was further enhanced by a short visit from the village priest, Father Eugeniusz Skrzypczyk, who came to offer his personal Christmas Eve greetings. This special honor was probably because the Surowjeckis were prominent members of the church and village communities.

Tall, lean, in his late thirties, and dressed in a traditional priestly black suit and starched collar, he made his dignified entrance, greeting the assembled household with "Pochwalony Jesus Chrystus" (Praised be Jesus Christ). Standing near him as he pronounced the greeting, I returned his greeting with the appropriate response, "Na wieki wieków, amen" (Forever and ever, amen), to which he smilingly nodded approval. He then proceeded to engage in social pleasantries, to the delight and honor of the entire household. Before leaving, he walked past each person and placed a wafer on his or her tongue. Being familiar with the ceremony, I once again responded properly, in careful emulation of the Christian custom and ritual. Father Skrzypczyk then went over to Mme Surowjecka for a final word. Before leaving, he bade one and all "Wesolego Bożego Narodzenia" (Merry Christmas). Then he left.

Later that evening, when I happened to be alone with Mme Surowjecka, she seated herself beside me and said, "Halinka, I never told you this before, but the priest is aware of the fact that you are a Jewish child. I informed him of that from the very beginning, at a Confession. I want you to know that he was very impressed with how much you've learned and the manner in which you conducted yourself tonight. He complimented me on the progress you've made in the short time you've been with us, and added that he is very proud of you."

It was a custom in the village for children to find Christmas gifts under their pillows when they awoke Christmas morning. Indeed, I had not expected to receive a Christmas gift at all, but as I peeked under my pillow out of curiosity that Christmas morning, I found—to my surprise—one loose, long, broad, and coarse strand from an old broom. I felt deeply hurt. I realized that either Marysia or Juzia had probably placed the ugly broom strand under my pillow as a crude joke. But I knew there was more to their joke than that. They were in fact intimidated by Mme Surowjecka from openly calling me "Żydówica," but nothing could prevent them from perceiving me as precisely that. To be sure, I recognized the beauty of the Christmas celebration, with its ceremonies and carols, but the more I was made to feel their resentment toward me merely for being what I was, the more I felt estranged from that which was sacred to them. It was all simply not mine. The entire scenario merely strengthened my resolve to cling even more tenaciously to that which was mine—to my heritage and to my Jewishness.

Thus I could never be free or at peace from being hounded as a "*Żydó-wica*," even within the Surowjecki household. I was continually reminded that I was a lonely Jew surrounded by Poles who were, with relatively few exceptions, at best conditionally sympathetic and at worst deeply anti-Semitic. From the very outset, my housing arrangement was plagued with inherent and unavoidable flaws. On the one hand, Father would never have entrusted my safety and very life to anyone he did not know well, nor to anyone living so far from Starachowice as to make regular contact impossible. On the other hand, these precise limitations would be the inevitable cause of my being recognized by one or another peasant sooner or later. In fact, the male farmhand Juziek had spotted me instantly at the farm.

In addition, the village of Świętomarz was located but five kilometers from Bodzentyn. It was therefore hardly surprising when, on a cold winter day, a beggar woman came to the Surowjeckis in search of food. She happened to be the same beggar woman who had periodically come to our house in Bodzentyn to beg for food. The instant she saw me she remarked, "I know that girl."

Mme Surowjecka quickly retorted, "You couldn't possibly know her because she is my niece from Kraków who came only recently to visit me."

Whereupon the beggar woman summarily countered, "Never mind all that. I assure you I do know her, but you need not worry. I will tell no one anything they should not know. Her mother was nice to me. She used to give me bread whenever I came to their house."

Soon after that, who appeared at the Surowjecki home if not Zwada, the Bodzentyn shoemaker our family had frequently patronized. He naturally recognized me immediately. Before Mme Surowjecka had a chance even to try to deny my true identity, Zwada interjected, "I know this girl. As a matter of fact, I not only know her, but the very shoes she is wearing at this moment are the work of my hands and were made in my shop in Bodzentyn. But do not fear. Her parents were good to me. You may be sure I will not inform on either her or you to the Germans."

We were fairly confident that these good people would not betray Mme Surowjecka or me to the Germans. But could they be expected never to mention to their peasant friends and acquaintances the fact that a Szachter girl from Bodzentyn was being sheltered incognito at the Surowjecki farm? And how long would it be before the Germans might overhear this fact in conversation or be directly informed by some Pole?

Despite these potential dangers, days and weeks passed uneventfully.

An incident did occur, however, some three to four months after I moved in with the Surowjeckis that, although not actually threatening, aroused some feelings of unpleasantness for all concerned. I had begun attending daily church services soon after arriving at the farm and was by now able to participate in the rituals and hymn singing quite routinely, almost to the point of habit. One day, however, when I was in church with Sir Surowjecki, I subconsciously crossed myself with my left hand instead of my right hand. Although Sir Surowjecki noticed the slip on my part, he did not make me aware of it until we returned home.

"Halinka," he began slowly, "I realize now that you are not Mme Surowjecka's niece from Kraków but, rather, a Jewish girl my wife agreed to shelter without my consent. Had I originally been asked, I must tell you candidly that I would not have agreed to allow you to live in our house, because both your life and ours are now endangered." Fortunately he hastened to add, "However, since you are already here, I shall treat you no differently than I have until now. Of that you may be assured." And, in fact, neither he nor Mme Surowjecka ever treated me any differently than before.

In some ways, Sir Surowjecki was even nicer to me and more considerate than Mme Surowjecka. It happened at around this same time that some of my clothes began needing mending. Mme Surowjecka asked me to repair them on her sewing machine. Inasmuch as we had no sewing machine at home in Bodzentyn, I had not the slightest idea how to use one. When I admitted my lack of ability to her, Mme Surowjecka revealed in her facial expression both disappointment and irritability. Sir Surowjecki, intervening on my behalf, said, "How can you expect such a young city child to know how to use a sewing machine?"

Mme Surowjecka quickly snapped back, "Halinka is old enough. She should know how."

I was unhappy to see and hear Mme Surowjecka so disappointed in me. I therefore waited for an opportunity when she was away from the house, then experimented with the machine until I succeeded in mending my clothes and restoring my pride in my own eyes as well as in hers.

After several weeks, the relative calm at the farm was suddenly broken. In the middle of a cold winter night the Surowjecki household was rudely awakened by a pounding on their door and men's voices from outdoors demanding, "Open the door. Open the door or we will break it open."

Both Mme Surowjecka and her husband cried out at the top of their voices, "Help, Police! Help!" But there were no police within earshot of the Surowjecki home. The intruders continued to demand entry into the house. One of them called out, "I am Policeman Gałązka. You must open the door for me."

To him Mme Surowjecka replied, "I know Policeman Gałązka very well, and you are not he, and I will not let you in."

Finally, the intruders succeeded in breaking into the house. They began searching everywhere and demanded that Mme Surowjecka hand over to them the materials from the Biderman yard goods store in Bodzentyn. When I heard those words, I became petrified from fear. Perhaps they would recognize me, I thought. Perhaps they knew I was here. I instantly sensed grave peril. My predicament was relieved slightly by the fact that Marysia and Juzia were also terrified. They apparently feared for their own safety, knowing full well the possibility of being kidnapped, raped, or shot. They both jumped into my bed and huddled close to me, pulling the covers over us. When the robbers came into my room and saw the three of us huddled closely in bed, trembling from fear while hiding under the covers, they spoke to us in an assuring tone, "Children, children, have no fear." Before they left, however, they helped themselves to a substantial volume of the Biderman yard goods.

Mme Surowjecka was not the type of person who would relinquish to robbers merchandise with which she had been entrusted without a battle. She decided to inform on the scoundrels to the Germans. Her resolve in bringing them to justice was so determined that it even blinded her to the dangers she was courting for herself, to say nothing for me. She had been robbed of merchandise she was holding for safekeeping for a Jew. She was illegally sheltering a Jewish child, a fact that was by now no secret to at least several of the local peasants. And she was coming to the Germans for assistance in retrieving that same Jewish-owned merchandise from robbers who knew of her own illegal activities. Still, she was determined to do exactly that, and her mind was irrevocably made up.

The next morning, Mme Surowjecka informed me she had made arrangements for me to spend the day at the home of Sir Bugajski, the church organist. She explained that she was going to the police to inform the German authorities of the preceding night's robbery and that it would obviously be dangerous for me to be at her house in the event the Germans came into the village. I was to remain at the home of the organist until she came for me.

I had enjoyed many a good time playing with the organist's daughters, Alicja and Bogusława, and this time was no different, except for two conspicuous moments. First, as we were playing a particular game, and I had just completed my turn to leap, one of the girls remarked, "Halinka, I have to tell you, you jump just like a Jewish girl." We all laughed, but inwardly my laugh was accompanied by a pang of fear and recharged insecurity. Later, when we were in the house, Sir Bugajski engaged me in conversation. Generally he was very courteous and hospitable to me. This time, while we were talking, he somehow mentioned in passing that he knew a very nice Jew in Bodzentyn by the name of Biderman. In all probability, he was curious to see how I would react upon hearing the name of my uncle, Biderman the Jew, being mentioned as an acquaintance. I pretended to be detached and unimpressed, as I exercised the most strenuous effort to show no visible reaction.

By evening, Mme Surowjecka came calling for me. When we arrived back at her home she informed me, with obvious satisfaction, that the Germans had searched for and caught some of the robbers and had brought them to her house. She described how, after she had identified them, the Germans beat them, tortured them, and broke some of their fingers until they finally confessed the robbery and told the Germans where the yard goods were being kept. Then the Germans left with the robbers. After a few hours, they returned with a substantial portion of the retrieved merchandise and gave it to Mme Surowjecka. She was quite pleased that the robbers had been justly punished and that much of the stolen Biderman yard goods had been recouped. I, however, was terrified at the prospects of vengeful consequences as a result of her actions, but there was nothing I could do or say. I had only to keep all such fears to myself, while hoping from moment to moment and from day to day.

Days and weeks passed once again in an atmosphere of relative calm. Then one day, Mme Surowjecka informed me that she had reason to believe the Germans might be coming into the village any day and that it was not safe for me to be visible until the danger of possible searches had passed. In the cow stable, there was an opening in the ceiling that led to an atticlike area where straw and hay were stored. Mme Surowjecka took me up into that little attic and instructed me to remain there for as long as necessary. On the floor of the attic was a loose straw door that they used to cover the opening. Mme Surowjecka handed me the loose door and instructed me that, in the event I heard someone entering the cow stable, I should cover myself with it so that only the straw and hay would be visible.

Three times a day, morning, noon, and evening, she brought food for me into the stable, moved a ladder to the attic's opening, ascended the ladder, and handed me the food. Being confined to the cold stable attic for hours on end gave me a general feeling of uneasiness and apprehension, especially during the night. But such apprehension by now already felt like a normal condition of life.

Once during the day, I suddenly heard someone entering the stable. Unprepared, I instinctively bent over to peek down and see who had come in. There stood a young man whom I had never seen before, apparently a new or part-time farmhand. The sound caused by the moving straw as I bent over attracted his attention, and as he looked up to the attic he saw me. I rolled back out of sight as he worked in the stable. He was there only a short period of time, but I became very frightened. "Who is this fellow?" I thought. "Will he tell Mme Surowjecka he saw someone hiding in the attic of her cow stable? Might he be a German?"

I was afraid to tell Mme Surowjecka of the incident because I feared she might think to herself, and rightly so, that I had disobeyed her explicit instructions to lie quietly and remain hidden and out of sight. I already knew my being in her house was causing her much difficulty; my carelessness now could possibly endanger the lives of us both. If I told her, I feared she could become angry and perhaps punish me, who knows how severely. So I decided to tell her nothing.

She continued to bring food to me three times daily for several days, until one day she finally came calling, "Halinka, all is clear now. You may come down." Needless to say, I was delighted. It felt so good to resume normal village life once again. For the time being at least, the danger seemed to have subsided. I continued to be mindful of the potential danger caused by my having been seen in the attic by the strange young farmhand, but I never found the courage to inform Mme Surowjecka of the incident. The more time passed, the more I feared she could become angry at me for having withheld such vital information for this long a period of time. I could only hope now that I would never see or hear of the young peasant or suffer any adverse effects from his having seen me in the attic.

As time passed, and as I was continually thrust into and escaping from the dangers of being recognized and reported to the Germans or of making a wrong move that would put me into exactly that situation, my thoughts turned often to my family in the labor camp at Starachowice: to Father and Mother, to Moishe and Shloime, to Irka and Rachela, to Grandfather Nus'n and Grandfather Meier, to all my surviving uncles and cousins. I hoped they were all well and safe. I hoped that their conditions were not too uncomfortable, and that they were not being overworked. If only I could be with them and share their conditions and their fate. If at least I could be with them long enough to be assured that they were okay.

20

The Family at the Starachowice Labor Camp

THE Starachowice labor camp consisted of two separate camp complex areas: Camp Strzelnica (Shooting Range) and Camp Majówka (May). Both were originally Polish army bases that had been converted by the Germans into internment quarters for their Jewish slave laborers. Each of the two camps was enclosed by a high fence, and in the center of each camp complex were two towers. At the top of each tower, German guards were stationed with machine guns, watching constantly, ready to shoot without warning anyone whose movements aroused as much as the slightest suspicion. Above their heads was a rotating light that made a full revolution approximately every second, making the prospects for escape extremely risky.

Only Grandfather Meier was interned at Camp Majówka. The rest of the family were detained in Camp Strzelnica. The entrance to Camp Strzelnica was at ground level. To the right of the entrance were the guard house, the administrative offices of the German guards, the kitchen, and the laundry. On the left were the camp infirmary and one barracks for the *Judenrat* and their families. The Judenrat was a committee of seven Jews selected by the Germans to administer the execution of their orders through approximately ten subordinates—Jewish policemen appointed by the committee.

Two flights of stairs led to a terraced area where about twenty one-time army barracks structures were located and numbered. About five were used to house women prisoners and about fifteen were used for men. Each barracks consisted of one huge room, somewhat like a barn. Each of the four huge walls of the room was lined with two-level tiers on which the inmates slept. The tiers were made of wood and were constructed in a manner suggesting narrow shelves. Because they were so close together, they were difficult to get into and left little room for inmates to turn about freely. In the lower tier, the average person could sit up only with head bent. While at first there was not any bedding except for a few afghans strewn about here and there, straw sacks were eventually placed over the bare wood, one for each inmate. People rotated positions within the tiers so that the few windows could be shared. Thus, most of the time people sat, lay, or slept crowded together, and without the benefit of a bit of fresh air.

Father, Moishe, and Shloime were together in one of the men's barracks, while Grandfather Nus'n, Uncles Moishe, Leib'l, and Yank'l Szachter, Uncle Pintche Greenbaum, and his brother Moishe were together in another. Uncle Froyim Biderman, his youngest son Shloime, and Uncle Yoss'l Schreibman were in yet a third barracks. Uncle Yoss'l, more than the others, had become terribly morose. He simply could not accept the bitter fate that had claimed the lives of his beloved wife and two precious children. On the women's side, Mother, Irka, and Rachela were together in one barracks, and Cousins Chantche and Rivtche Ehrlich were together in another.

Inmates worked, with little exception, on one of the three shifts at the factory. Although our immediate family had been assigned to the night shift at the time of the liquidation of Starachowice, this arrangement did not continue indefinitely, since assignments to the various work shifts continually rotated. When inmates left the camp area en route to the factories, Jewish policemen took a strict count of their number. The workers, patrolled by Germans, were then marched in rows, five abreast, to the factories. As one shift arrived for work, it relieved the workers on the preceding shift. Workers were counted again before reentering the camp from the factory. In this way, the Nazis were able to minimize through intimidation the chances of any Jew's escaping, for they realized the Jew, who would be aware that his escape would be known to the Germans, would be held back for fear of retaliation against his family members still in camp.

The trek from the labor camp to the factory was approximately four kilometers. It soon became apparent that Mother would not be able to make this daily trip back and forth for very long. Father was able to arrange through Shloime Ehnesman, now a member of the Judenrat, for Mother and Rachela to work in the camp laundry. Favors such as these were by no means had for the asking. While it is true that Father and Shloime Ehnesman were boyhood friends, and that Shloime may have been more inclined to extend a favor to Father than to other Jews even without payment, special treatment was gained for a price. *Lapowka* (bribery) was a byword, a way of life in camp. Father paid off Ehnesman handsomely for the countless acts of intervention on behalf of our family, though not necessarily for each one.

When Mother and Rachela were first transferred to the laundry room, they were also allowed to be placed in a barracks on the lower, ground level so they could walk directly to the laundry room for work. This was a highly exceptional privilege. However, because the guards between the lower level and the upper level were strict and ruthlessly cruel, Mother and Rachela were effectively cut off from the rest of the family. Father therefore arranged, again through Shloime Ehnesman, for Mother and Rachela to be reassigned back to one of the women's barracks upstairs, where they were once again with Irka.

Father similarly arranged for himself to work outside the factory, where he helped transport large iron pieces into the factory, to be worked on and assembled into munitions works. He had sought this position for himself, not in order to be spared from a heavy labor assignment, but rather because this particular situation better enabled him to remain in contact with Poles, especially Mme Surowjecka and Ben Kazimierz. From them, he not only bought food and other items but also was regularly brought up to date regarding my situation and general well-being at their farm. Messages were exchanged and occasional letters were smuggled through.

All the other men in the family worked in the munitions factory, as did Irka and Cousins Chantche and Rivtche. Irka and Chantche's job was to clean and polish new cannon shells, while Rivtche worked with the youngest laborers in the factory, oiling machines and motors. For a short interval, Irka worked at distributing soup in the factory mess hall. She was fired when the German officer in charge considered it unnecessary to retain two girls to distribute soup per shift, and she was reassigned to her old job. Father, in an effort to keep Irka on the job she preferred, took a ring off Irka's finger, sought out the officer, and offered it to him, asking that Irka be allowed to return to the mess hall. Although the German hated most Jews, he liked Father. He refused to accept the bribe or to allow Irka to reclaim her old job, but he agreed to reassign her to a less strenuous job than cleaning cannon shells; she now painted them. Our friends the Grossmans from Bodzentyn also worked in the munitions factory, while the Weintraubs were among the select few who worked at Tartak lumberyard and sawmill.

In most instances, workers were unaware of the function or purpose of their particular jobs, whether they were working on parts for tanks, guns, or any other kind of military machinery. Nonetheless, many of the jobs could be and were highly dangerous. Moniek Grossman related how one day, as he was on the way to the factory, he saw an acquaintance, a Jew from Bodzentyn—with a missing leg! A cannon shell had fallen on his foot and blown off his entire leg. Similarly, when Cousin Itche Biderman was killed in the foundry, he had been working in a huge smithy where large iron parts were being cast. He had been operating a gigantic mallet that fell upon him and instantly killed him. Itche had been working on the night shift; my sister Irka learned of the tragedy as she was going to work on the ensuing morning shift. Itche and Irka were both about sixteen years old at the time.

Upon returning to the barracks after work, people generally went directly to bed. For one thing, what else was there to do, or where could one go? In addition, milling about the camp grounds was not risk-free. Anyone needing water had to leave the barracks, secure permission, and only then walk down the two flights of stairs to the kitchen and back. Toilet facilities were at an outhouse in back.

At Camp Strzelnica, even these movements were potentially dangerous due to the prevalence of guards, especially the trigger-happy ones in the watchtower. Included in the German armed corps were Ukrainian pro-Nazi sympathizers who were born and bred in a centuries-old climate of anti-Semitism. The German guards as well as their Ukrainian puppets were unreasonably strict and barbarously cruel in the execution of their orders. Although it was not explicitly forbidden for inmates to mill about or for men and women to visit each others' barracks, it was nonetheless dangerous because of the carefree, whimsical inclinations of the guards to shoot at the slightest movement that might be alleged to be a provocation. Still, family members did see each other almost daily, either in brief visits to each others' barracks or on the way to or from work.

"Meals" were served twice a day. First, on the way back from work, the laborers were led to the mess hall in the factory, where they were served a bowl of soup by a Jewish policeman, as he punched a ration card. If he so chose, or was given "adequate reason" to so choose, the Jewish policeman could serve an additional slice of bread or a potato to selected individuals. However, if a worker was caught attempting to steal a potato, he might be shot on the spot. In addition to receiving the soup after work, the inmates lined up at the kitchen once a day to be served a slab of bread with jam. The workers in the kitchen were also allowed a slab of bread, as well as a potato or a bowl of soup from the kitchen. Obviously these servings hardly constituted a nutritious or even the most minimal, subsistence diet.

There were alternatives, to be sure, for people of means. Food and other necessities could be bought at high prices from Poles in the factory, who served as clandestine middlemen between the interned Jews and the outside world. It was a problem, however, to smuggle the purchased items past the Jewish policemen as they carefully counted the workers reentering the camp from work. But the Jewish policemen could be bribed to look the other way.

Because Father had stored money in our boot heels and in the women's girdle stays, our family suffered no lack of food, clothing, or any other necessities throughout our entire period of detention. Mother would prepare the bought food, using the laundry heating facilities as needed. The men of the immediate family would visit Mother and the girls at the laundry room and join them for meals. Uncle Leib'l also managed to purchase foodstuffs that he shared with the other men of the family as well as Cousins Chantche and Rivtche.

People with less means sold any dispensable clothes or valuables that they had managed to bring from Starachowice for a bit of supplementary food. A girlfriend of Irka on one occasion stole an extra dress Irka happened to have in order to sell it for food for herself. Other people, with no money and nothing to sell, were left no other recourse than to starve. Not surprisingly, resentment was felt toward families such as ours by some less fortunate, especially natives of Starachowice, who could be heard grumbling, "Look at the newcomers. They buy up all the food; they buy favors; and we sit here and languish and starve." Mother, out of sensitivity and compassion, shared with some of the less fortunate, and they were genuinely grateful.

The Judenrat were a privileged group in the camp. They were awarded to the top-ranking overseers directly under German command. Like the Germans, they were allowed adequate amounts of the highest quality of food, cooked for them by Jewish women assigned to the kitchen. They also were given a special barracks on the lower, ground level alongside that of the German military staff. Their barracks was equipped with a stove, and their families were allowed to live with them there. As long as they carried out the orders of their German masters to the letter, they were allowed considerable freedom of action in the administration of the camps. When the opportunity arose, they freely exercised nepotism in their appointments of policemen and *Blockenältesten* (barracks officers), which was understandable given the circumstances. They could be bribed to a certain extent for special favors, such as changing one's job assignment or granting permission to move to a different barracks. Their acceptance of bribes was justifiable because of the inherent risk of incurring Nazi ire, as well as the possible need to bribe a German superior. The Judenrat members were generally considerate to our family, especially Shloime Ehnesman, due to his lifelong friendship with and respect for Father. Their reputation in camp, however, was not enviable because of the high expectations their inmates had of them, expectations that went beyond their capabilities to perform. For granting requests considered too excessive by the German authorities, or for giving special treatment to too many people, their positions, their lives, and the fate of their families could have been jeopardized at any moment.

The Jewish policemen were given no special barracks. They and their families were assigned to barracks with all other inmates. They were, however, issued uniforms and were charged with the execution of German orders, handed down from the Judenrat, such as patrolling the camp-grounds, counting the inmates going to and from work, ordering inmates in and out of the barracks, distributing food in the mess hall, and the like. They too could be bribed, and at least some were not unkind, especially to our family. They acted sternly, however, particularly in the presence of Germans. Such behavior was understandable, in light of the fact that through their positions as Jewish policemen, they, like the Judenrat members, were saving their own lives and the lives of their wives and children. In fact, a few of them were shot for exercising "excessive" leniency toward fellow Jews.

Nevertheless, in many an instance they abused their power unnecessarily and beyond even their "call of duty." Their behavior toward onetime friends and fellow townspeople often degenerated to the level of a strictly official overseer-inmate relationship.

Moniek Grossman relates how he once purchased a couple of shirts from a Jewish policeman in charge of overseeing the storage building where the trunks of clothes confiscated at the time of the liquidation of Starachowice were being kept. A second Jewish policeman caught Moniek with the illegally purchased shirts in hand and began beating him mercilessly. As one other Jewish policeman and a onetime friend of the Grossman family happened to be passing by, Moniek cried out to him, "Please help me. I'm being beaten for no reason." The onetime friend looked on for a moment, unmoved, as the beating continued, and walked away. The general feeling in the camp was that a genuinely fine person did not become a policeman for the Germans for any reason.

Each barracks had a barracks officer, who was charged with overseeing the barracks, making sure it was kept neat and clean and that no stealing occurred. Some of these officers were not abusive. Others, fearing to appear lax to the Germans, shouted orders or slapped inmates, thereby creating resentment for appearing to flaunt their nominal authority.

A special group was housed in the *Konsum* (cooperative) barracks near the administrative offices in Camp Majówka. It included tailors, shoe-makers, and bootmakers who produced all clothing ordered by the German command. Unlike all other inmates, these craftsmen worked at their trades and, like the Judenrat, lived with their wives and children. With kitchen facilities and ample food, theirs was a privileged group in their communal barracks.

After three months of massive malnutrition within insufferably crowded and unsanitary conditions, it is little wonder that a fierce typhus epidemic broke out in the labor camp in January 1943. A highly contagious disease, the typhus fever spread quickly among the inmates, disabling a large segment of the work force in both camps. As many as 75 percent of the interned people contracted the disease. In our family, everyone fell ill, with the single exception of Mother, who had had the disease as a young girl during World War I and who was therefore immune to it now. With only one physician available for the entire camp, Mother was forced to care for all the stricken members of the family. Irka not only fell victim to typhus, but she suffered complications as well that caused a kidney ailment that, in turn, resulted in high fever and even hallucinations. Father immediately contacted the one physician in camp, a Jew from Starachowice named Dr. Kramasz, who prescribed and sent appropriate medication. Even before Irka had become ill, but particularly now, she dreamed of being located near a window. Since she was so ill, her co-inmates cooperated and allowed her to be at the single window in a corner of their barracks for the week her illness lingered.

The Nazis and their Jewish subordinates succeeded in forcing many of the sick, through threats and beatings, to go to work. However, many were so ill and infested with lice that they simply refused. They seemed to have broken down and to have given up the struggle for survival. They merely remained in their tiers, allowing events to fall as they might. These unfortunate people, in turn, were the first to be taken out of their barracks and shot to death.

Meanwhile, the Germans, determined to sift out the afflicted inmates in order to stem the epidemic, ordered all the surviving diseased to the infirmary, which was designated as Barracks Five. In no time, that barracks became unbearably overcrowded. The German officialdom of the camp was headed by one Kommandant Althof, whose very nature and personality set the tone of camp life. The mere sight of suffering, beatings, and shootings brought him visible delight. The sound of his shrieking voice and the cracking sound of the big horsewhip he habitually snapped became commonplace under his command. Typically shouting at the top of his lungs to the accompaniment of the whip, he terrified not only the inmates who heard him from one end of the camp to the other, but also the Jewish policemen and other privileged Jews. Even the Ukrainian guards and Althof's subordinates were petrified by his hysterical outbursts of fury. Only regular beatings and shootings seemed to assuage the hunger of his sadistic nature.

One day, Kommandant Althof paid a personal visit to Barracks Five and, without provocation, took out his revolver and shot to death every single person in the barracks, perhaps as many as two hundred. After they all had been shot, the grounds outside Barracks Five was drenched with blood. When news of this savage massacre spread throughout the camp, those who were already stricken feared and desisted from going to the infirmary, opting to wait out their afflictions in their barracks. But when absenteeism in the factories reached intolerable limits, the Germans and their Jewish underlings began coming to the barracks and ordering all inmates outdoors for a procedure soon to become infamously known as a "selection."

The object of the selections at the Starachowice labor camps was to single out the most severely ill—for extermination. The procedure began by ordering those people who looked the sickest to walk quickly down the two flights of stairs, with the obvious intention of identifying those faltering from weakness or high fevers and ejecting them from the rest for the preplanned executions.

Moniek Grossman, himself extremely ill at the time, recalls how he realized what was taking place and, knowing he was too ill and unsteady to hurry down the stairs, chose to defy the risk and escape back to his barracks. There, while hiding himself under the straw sack that covered his tier, he looked out from a window to observe the goings-on, and saw a Jewish policeman walking into various barracks buildings to hustle out the inmates. With interest, Moniek noted how the policeman missed—or, more accurately, passed over—a barracks building in which his own ill son-in-law was interned. Moniek also saw Kommandant Althof standing and deciding which of the inmates who stumbled or fell he would direct to Barracks Five.

From Barracks Five, the ill selectees were loaded onto a truck, together with a group of healthy inmates, and were driven to a forest area outside the city, never to be heard from again. It was later learned that the healthy were first ordered to dig graves for the ill. The ill were then shot into the graves, together with the healthy people, after which the Germans and their Jewish subordinates covered the graves with soil.

Not long after that incident, Moniek informed his brothers that his mind was irrevocably made up. "As soon as I am fully recovered, I will not remain in this place," he asserted. "I am not going to stay here until those bastards decide to kill me. At the first opportunity, I'm getting out of here." Soon Moniek was trying his strength out, attempting to walk, to judge if he was well enough to go back to work in the factory. Mimicking his still unsteady efforts, a Ukrainian guard standing nearby ordered, tongue in cheek, "Jews, sing! This young man needs some music so he can dance!"

Grandfather Nus'n, who was on the same tier as Moniek, wryly quipped, "Well, Moniek, go ahead, sing. Why don't you sing?"

"You will see," Moniek replied in quiet but deadly serious determination, "One day soon, I will no longer be here."

Attempting to desert the camp was surely a life-threatening risk; many inmates were shot on the spot with far less provocation. But one night during the month of January 1943, Moniek, together with his two brothers, Alter and Nuter, dared to evade the rotating lights above the two camp towers, jumped the fence surrounding the camp, and escaped into the dark of the forest. And they were gone. The administrative policy of the camp apparently called for no punitive measures in retaliation for successful escapes. Nevertheless, the twin perils of being shot if caught and not surviving in the forest anyway continued to leave serious doubts in the minds of any who dared contemplate the attempt, and few braved the risk.

As the typhus epidemic raged in the camps, many were too feverish and weak to go to work. They were constantly harassed, however, with the threat, "If you're too sick to go to work, we'll have to send you to Barracks Five." A number of them heeded the threat and forced themselves to go to work. Still, when absenteeism was too high in the factories, periodic selections continued, to the terror of all inmates, the healthy as well as the ill. During a particular selection, Grandfather Nus'n took ill. Because of his age, he would surely have been selected for Barracks Five. He was saved only by the efforts of one of the younger Jewish policemen who, for a generous bribe, hid him in the barracks attic until the selection had been completed.

During the same selection, a German officer went in to double-check a barracks nearby and discovered an ill inmate who had remained "unnoticed" by the Jewish policeman. An immediate investigation revealed the identity of the policeman responsible for the barracks in question. He was summoned to the front of the assembly and, as an example to all, was summarily shot dead.

The most frightening selection, as far as our family was concerned, occurred one day when orders were issued for all inmates to leave their barracks and walk briskly down the stairs. As usual, the Nazis and their Jewish appointees were seeking those who would falter from high fevers caused by typhus. Rachela at that time was in the midst of a bout with the disease and looked very ill. On her way down the stairs, she faltered and stumbled and was ordered to go onto the truck of the condemned. Mother followed her. Murmurings quickly spread through the crowd, "Mrs. Szachter is not sick, but she went onto the truck."

At the square near the foot of the stairs stood Kommandant Althof, together with his entourage of senior-level Jewish overseers. Shloime Ehnesman, looking in the direction of the murmurs, saw Mother on the truck. He instantly remarked to Kommandant Althof, "A woman who is not sick just went on the truck." The kommandant countered, "Well, get her off." Quickly Shloime Ehnesman walked up to a Jewish policeman standing near the truck and whispered an order into his ear. The latter immediately climbed onto the truck and ordered Mother to get off. He whispered to her, "Don't worry; I'll take care of your daughter. You hurry and get off the truck." The policeman, Yank'l Szczęsliwy, a good friend of our family, milled about in the crowd for a few moments until he saw the kommandant's attention diverted. He quickly climbed back onto the truck, picked Rachela up in his arms, and, carrying her, descended from the truck, took two big steps, and placed her among the inmates, who immediately moved to shield her from view. That night, approximately 120 people were driven out to a field outside the camp where they were ordered to dig their own graves. Then they were murdered.

We were fortunate that Irka was at work at the factory when this selection took place. It is difficult to imagine how she could have survived seeing Rachela and Mother getting onto the truck of the condemned. On her way back from the afternoon shift that day, she met a friend named Reiz'l Rabinowicz, who was on her way to work. Reiz'l informed Irka, with a broken heart and choking in tears, "My mother and sister were taken today during the selection. Your mother and sister were also taken, but they were ordered off the truck. How lucky you are." Irka attempted to offer Reiz'l her most empathetic expression of condolences. As the girls went their separate ways, Irka was beside herself until she got back to the barracks and actually saw Mother and Rachela with her own eyes, alive and safe.

One typhus victim of the family, however, was Grandfather Meier. Isolated from the rest of the family in Camp Majówka, he had no source of supplemental nourishment. Quite aged, fifteen years Grandfather Nus'n's senior, a longtime diabetic, and starving, of course, his chances of surviving the typhus disaster were practically nil. He expired in the spring of 1943.

Shortly after the death of Grandfather Meier, a decision was made by the Germans to close down Camp Strzelnica. Apparently the death toll had shrunk the ranks of the laborers to the point where maintaining two camps was no longer efficient. Hence the two camps were consolidated into one, and all surviving inmates of Camp Strzelnica were moved into Camp Majówka. Conditions in Camp Majówka were decidedly better than they had been in Camp Strzelnica. Although the camp experience in Majówka continued to be traumatic for all, life was nonetheless not as restricted. Movement was less monitored and less risk-laden. The inmates were able to breathe somewhat more easily.

Around this time, Father decided he now needed to obtain some of our valuables that he had buried in the treasure boxes in Grandfather Meier's garden in Bodzentyn. But how could this be done, with the entire family interned in camp? Fortunately, Father had the foresight before leaving Bodzentyn to decide on precise spots within the courtyard garden to bury our family fortune and to draw a map designating clearly those precise locations. While he was in the camp, he solicitously guarded that map in an inner pocket of his clothing at all times. He now had only one feasible option: the Surowjeckis. Father decided to present the problem to either Mme Surowjecka or Ben the next time one of them stopped over to see him outside the factory.

Before long, Ben was in Starachowice on one of his marketing trips. As usual, he stopped by the factory area to see Father. Father automatically asked how I was faring, and Ben replied that, except for an occasional scare, as well as for normal ups and downs, all was well at Świętomarz. Father then proceeded to explain his predicament to Ben and told him of the detailed map. Father requested only the gold and silver coins contained in one specific location, and offered Ben all the other valuables interred with it, if only he or Mme Surowjecka would locate it, dig it out, and bring the money clandestinely to Father outside the factory area. Father apparently felt that the gems would have little, if any, value in the labor camp situation.

Without responding to the offer of reward, yet in the same spirit of generosity and charitableness with which his aunt had originally agreed to take me into her home, Ben now replied to Father that he fully understood our predicament and would make every effort to locate and bring him the money. Father placed the folded map in Ben's hand, as Ben once again assured Father he would study it and dig up the treasure. They decided that they would meet one more time to arrange a specific day, time, and place to deliver the treasure. Father then expressed his heartfelt thanks. Ben bade Father farewell and returned to Świętomarz.

21

Perils and Tragedy at the Surowjecki Farm: Świętomarz Becomes Too Unsafe to Remain My Haven

IT WAS NOW the spring of 1943. The days were much longer, and I was working full days out in the garden and pasture. No new threatening situations had occurred in Świętomarz for several weeks now, and village life under German occupation proceeded as usual. Events, however, were soon to unfold that would radically worsen my situation at the Surowjecki farm and ultimately necessitate my being sent away from Świętomarz.

I learned of Father's need for the family valuables only after Mme Surowjecka and Ben had successfully located them in Grandfather Meier's garden and brought them back to Świętomarz. One evening, Mme Surowjecka called me over to the table where she was sitting and showed me a very impressive collection of valuables that were spread out before her. "Halinka, these are all your Father's," she said, and she told me of Father's recent meeting with Ben. "They were exactly where the map showed them to be," she added. "They are really beautiful, aren't they?"

I saw the many gold and silver coins Father had requested from Ben. In addition, I saw Mother's plush, pliable silver mesh purse that Rachela and I used to play with, as well as numerous pins, necklaces, watches, and rings, all of which were familiar to me. Mme Surowjecka informed me that Ben would be going in to Starachowice the next morning and would be meeting with Father in order to deliver the coins to him. She added that Father had offered her and Ben the gems as a reward, but that she would merely retain them for safekeeping.

The next day I was working, as usual, in the garden. By midafternoon I became increasingly anxious to be called in for supper, eager to hear that all had gone smoothly according to plan. The day seemed unending, and I began to feel more and more uneasy about not being called in. The sun began to descend, and still I was not called in. This delay was totally unusual. Dinner had never been this late. I began to worry and feel ill at ease, but I didn't dare to go in without being called. What could I ask, and how could I ask it? I was frightened.

At long last, I heard the call from Mme Surowjecka: "Halinka! Supper-time!" I hurried in and joined the Surowjeckis and the farmhands at the supper table. Not a word was offered concerning Ben or the day's events in Starachowice. I asked nothing. I was too terrified. The evening passed in unbearable suspense, as the subject remained unmentioned, as if nothing eventful was to have taken place that day. The entire household retired for the night.

The next morning began no differently. I was still too frightened to ask how events had transpired the preceding day, and no one uttered a word on the subject. Finally, after breakfast, Mme Surowjecka motioned to me to follow her into Ben's room. There, Ben lay on his bed in obvious, intense pain. When he saw me, he sat up in the bed, lifted his pajama jacket, and showed me the terrible wounds on his back. In a subdued voice, he related to me that he had met with Father the day before outside the factory at Starachowice as prearranged and that he had handed Father the bag containing gold and silver coins. Apparently, a Ukrainian guard had caught sight of the delivery and alerted several guards. As soon as Ben began to leave, they charged after him. Father somehow disappeared as Ben attempted in vain to run out of the range of danger. Ben was caught, however, and was forced back to the factory area, where he was clubbed and beaten mercilessly before he was let go.

I felt terrible about what had happened, but I was too afraid to say anything. I was not only being housed by the Surowjeckis and therefore automatically imperiling their lives, but now Ben was suffering from a torturous beating resulting from yet another personal sacrifice he had made for Father. In spite of all this, neither the Surowjeckis nor Ben ever expressed or revealed in any way the slightest resentment toward me. It seemed that Father had escaped the incident unharmed, but I could not muster the courage to ask.

After the next market day in Starachowice, Mme Surowjecka brought me Father's regards and informed me that he had indeed been unhurt and that all was well with the family. She informed me also, however, that at the time Ben was caught and beaten he had been questioned as to the contents of the bag he had been carrying. More than that, he had been brutally tortured until he revealed the name of Szachter as the man to whom he had handed the bag. Further, he had been forced to yield a physical description of Father. How fortunate I had learned of this now, I thought, since Mme Surowjecka had just seen Father and he was well and unharmed. It was obviously prudent for me to not reveal my thoughts to Mme Surowjecka, but I assumed that Father had escaped being caught because the guards were undoubtedly searching for a man of his description named Szachter, while Father's false identification card, prepared while he was in hiding in Bodzentyn, was made in the name of Y'chiel Silberberg. What a relief that was.

For a short period of time, conditions seemed to normalize at the Surowjecki farm, until a crushing tragedy befell their household. Mme Surowjecka, although outwardly strong, sadly yet unemotionally related to me a few days after the fact that Ben had been caught again. This time he had been caught engaging in Communist underground anti-Nazi activities—and had been executed. He had been shot dead. She did not show it, but the tragedy must have been a dreadful shock and crushing blow to her. For not only had Ben been very highly regarded and respected in the community, but he had also been a pillar of courage, strength, and moral support for Mme Surowjecka in all her endeavors, ranging from the conduct of the farm to providing shelter for the child of a Jewish family. Now he was gone.

Of course, she still had her husband, Sir Surowjecki. Being many years older than Mme Surowjecka, however, his support consisted primarily in his involvement in matters related to the conduct of their farm business. He would oversee the farm help and make sure the work got done; at times he would work in the garden himself. He frequently transported produce to the marketplace. But it was Mme Surowjecka who was clearly in charge of the household and the management of the farm. Sir Surowjecki was decidedly unhappy with the German occupation, and he approved of the political activity of Ben. But only her beloved nephew, Ben, with his innate wisdom and exemplary compassion, could give Mme Surowjecka the moral support she needed during these difficult times. No one now, including even Sir Surowjecki, possessed the education, astuteness, and moral fiber to fill the void in Mme Surowjecka's life caused by Ben's death.

After some time, while in one of her more pensive moods, Mme Surowjecka broached with me the subject of my future in Świętomarz. "Halinka," she began, "I do not know whether you have given this matter much thought, but one can never know. With a war going on, and the situation with Jews being what it is, who knows? There are hardly any Jews anywhere anymore. It is just possible that your parents will not survive the war. And if they don't, as I told you some time ago, you are welcome to stay and grow up here, and live here for the rest of your life. As you know, I have no children or close family, and in time you could inherit all I own."

After a moment, I replied, "You are very kind, Mme Surowjecka," and then I remained silent. Inwardly, however, I was not moved. On the one hand, though she never directly said so, I sensed that she would have been quite pleased if I were to remain at the farm, become baptized, and live my life as a Christian in Świętomarz. Perhaps she would have considered such a possibility a significant missionary achievement on her part. On the other hand, I could not imagine life without Mother and Father and the family. I certainly could not imagine myself living there indefinitely, surrounded by the anti-Semitism that seemed to pervade the village of Świętomarz. Deep down, I had faith that all would turn out well eventually and that the family would somehow survive. My hope at this time was that I would be able to remain safely in Świętomarz until the present danger came to an end.

But Ben Kazimierz was no more. And once he was no longer on the scene, circumstances in Świętomarz could never again be the same. My identity was no longer a taboo subject among the villagers, a piece of gossip to be hushed. Although never totally silenced, the peasants now felt less intimidated and began to treat the subject more normally, that is to say, without restriction. Word soon began to spread more loosely that Mme Surowjecka was sheltering a Jewish child in her home.

One night, villagers learned that the Germans were coming into Świętomarz. Mme Surowjecka became frightened and felt she had to act quickly. She came into my room and woke me up from sleep to warn me. Hurriedly, she explained, "Halinka, I am afraid. I must hide you. Come quickly with me out to the garden." In an instant I had changed clothes and followed her. In the garden were a number of beehives. She led me to an empty one and instructed me to squat down and squeeze myself into it. It was built low, like a small doghouse, with a sloping roof, and so I had to sit bent over and squashed in it. I was more terrified than ever before. Despite the fact that it was springtime and the air was mild and balmy, I felt extremely cold.

When Mme Surowjecka saw my teeth chattering and my body trembling from cold and fear, she ran back to the house and brought out a blanket for me to cover myself with and an aspirin to calm my intense anxiety. Still I shivered and my teeth would not stop chattering, so she went back to the house again and brought out a second blanket. Unfortunately, the space in the beehive was too tight for another blanket to be squeezed in.

I sat bent over and squatted in the beehive for what seemed like an eternity. My legs were crammed into the hive. If only I could stretch them out for a moment, I thought. But I knew that would be too unsafe. Mme Surowjecka came out every fifteen to thirty minutes throughout the night to assure me all was well. Every time she implored me, "Don't be afraid, Halinka, everything is all right. Try to relax." At times, she would simply call out, "Halinka, Halinka." When I did not respond, she knew that I had fallen asleep and went back into the house. A mother could not have been more kind, understanding, or sensitive than she proved to be.

Not until the break of dawn did she finally come out and open something like a little door, so I was at least able to stretch my legs. She told me that the Germans had left the village and that the immediate danger had now passed. She added, however, that the situation in Świętomarz had deteriorated to the point that my returning to her house was no longer advisable. It had simply become too dangerous for both of us. She informed me that I would be taken directly to another village, named Jadowniki. She instructed me to remain in the beehive until she came back for me.

22

A Short Interval in Jadowniki

LATER THAT DAY Mme Surowjecka drove me in a horse-led wagon to Jadowniki, seven kilometers northeast of Świętomarz. I brought with me only a bag of belongings she had prepared for me.

Mme Surowjecka owned several acres of farmland in Jadowniki that were leased and worked on by a friend of hers whose name was Maria Sawiczka. On the way, she explained to me that I would be staying in Jadowniki only temporarily, until she could work out a more permanent arrangement. She continued to explain that she had informed her friend of the fact that I was Jewish, and that Mme Sawiczka had agreed to allow me to stay with them temporarily, but only reluctantly so, and even then only on certain stringent conditions: Under no circumstances would she allow me to reside in her house; she wanted no part of any arrangement that could possibly incriminate her for sheltering a Jewish child. She would, however, allow me to stay in the barn, but only because it belonged to the Surowjeckis. She faithfully promised to bring food into the barn for me three times daily.

In the event I was caught by the Germans, however, I must not in any way suggest that her friend was sheltering me, but I must instead lay the blame and responsibility on Mme Surowjecka alone: She explicitly emphasized that if I were ever discovered and interrogated by any Germans, I was to refer them directly and unequivocally to her, and only to her. Mme Surowjecka's assurances were certainly noble and brave. Still, I was apprehensive of my new, limited and conditional living situation.

When we arrived at the Jadowniki farm, Mme Surowjecka stepped down from the wagon, helped me off, and introduced me to her friend, who was walking toward our wagon as we arrived. Mme Sawiczka proceeded to show us the barn where I was to stay. As soon as I was settled in it, Mme Surowjecka bade us farewell and returned to Świętomarz.

My initial feelings of apprehension were somewhat assuaged now by my new hostess's amiability. Rather plump in build, her manner of speaking seemed to reflect that of a basically good-natured person. She was a widow and a mother of three daughters, Zosia, Hania, and Stasia, whose ages were approximately nineteen, sixteen, and twelve.

Although I was confined to the barn at all times, day and night, the experience was not as traumatic as I had initially imagined. First of all, the barn was huge and spacious, which minimized the reality of my confinement. Inside the barn were huge, comfortable piles of straw on which I could sit or lie at any time. More important, however, was the realization that my life was being sheltered from the dangers currently rampant in Świętomarz. Moreover, I was brought food, as promised, three times a day, and I was greeted kindly and spoken to each time, so that I was able to feel my long solitude being broken on these three mealtime occasions at least. In addition, I was brought a number of storybooks, which I enjoyed reading very much. The thought of their providing me with these books revealed a consideration and sensitivity on the part of my hosts that I considered very kind.

I recall perhaps two occasions when Sir Surowjecki came to the Jadowniki farm to collect several dozen cabbages from his garden to take to market. Each time he came into the barn to see me and spent a few moments speaking to me. These short visits also helped break the many hours of quiet solitude I had to spend in the barn.

It was by now near the beginning of May, and the weather was beautiful. I was therefore able during the day to peer out through the cracks in the barn walls and see the bright, radiant sunshine over the abundant wheat fields and cabbage patches and over large expanses of rural beauty that I had always loved and now longed for so much. I was fully capable of accepting my situation, and even perceived it as a welcome protection, but I do recall thinking to myself, "If only I were free. If only I could go out and be a child once again. If only I could."

During the nights I slept on a pile of straw. The first two nights, I was frightened at being in such a huge, pitch-black barn all alone. From time to time, a bird or two would fly into the barn. The sudden flapping of wings, which seemed so close at times, rudely disturbed the stillness of the dark night. The sound was jolting and unpleasantly loud, particularly since I was able to see nothing. Once a cat ran in, stopped, and ran again through the barn. Being unable to see it, and not realizing at first what caused the noise I heard, I feared perhaps a strange, unfriendly human being might have come into the barn who could possibly harm me. After two nights, however, I overcame my fear of those noises and grew accustomed to the strange surroundings. I reminded myself of the time back home in Bodzentyn when the dark shadows in our parlor frightened me at night. That time, Father had lit a lamp and proved to me that the shadows were harmless, and from then on I was no longer scared by them. Similarly, here in the barn I was able to convince myself of the harmlessness of the various animal sounds and even began anticipating them calmly.

Excretions of body waste posed another problem, especially at night, because of my fear of the dark. I had to singlehandedly open the two huge barn doors, go out alone into the strange, dark village farm, and then return and close myself back into the barn again by pulling back together those two gigantic doors. As with the sounds, after the second such occasion I realized that no source of harm roamed about the farm during the night, and so I began to enjoy coming out of the barn precisely then. The quiet stillness of the outdoors and the balmy air of the May night breezes were exhilarating and refreshing. I delighted in staying out, walking about, taking in the wonderful farmland air before returning to the barn.

On one single, exceptional occasion, I was allowed to come into my hostess's house, where I slept the night, sharing the bed with her oldest daughter, Zosia. We got into a pleasant conversation about dreams. She asked me if I recalled any of my own, and when I did relate a few, she attempted to interpret them in a manner that revealed her religious training and background. It also revealed an impressive level of intelligence and perceptivity, and I even suspected she might have known I was Jewish.

After I had spent about two weeks in Jadowniki, Mme Surowjecka concluded that Mme Sawiczka's initial reluctance to shelter me might have even intensified. Moreover, Mme Surowjecka was a highly principled woman, who genuinely feared for my safety and well-being; with my staying in Jadowniki, she did not have a firm enough grip on the unfolding of events to her satisfaction. Finally, she rationalized that perhaps my absence from Świętomarz for the two-week period had allowed tensions to simmer down there as well. So she decided to bring me back to her farm and home, and hope for the best. I felt good seeing Sir Surowjecki once again at the Jadowniki farm. But this time he had come to take me back home with him. Before leaving, he loaded his wagon with several dozen cabbages and bade Mme Sawiczka farewell. Then he brought me back to the Surowjecki farm.

I was happy to be back where I could once again spend entire days out in the open air working in the garden and pastures, and where I could sleep nights in my own warm bed. For the next several days, life resumed its familiar routine, and I was able to feel relatively contented and at ease.

During that time, I learned how fortunate I had been to have been away when I was. One night, Mme Surowjecka related to me that a gang of peasants had come to their home, pounded on the door, and demanded, "We know you're hiding a Jewish brat in your house. Hand her over to us so we can take care of her, once and for all. And make it fast."

Mme Surowjecka had replied to them, "Which Jewish kid? You probably mean my niece from Kraków. But she is no longer here. She went back to her parents." And indeed, I was no longer there, and the confrontation was laid to rest.

In passing conversation, Mme Surowjecka mentioned that a Jewish woman she knew from Bodzentyn was living with her child incognito in a large city in Poland. The woman had managed to obtain official papers as a Polish citizen and somehow was surviving, thus far at least. Mme Surowjecka added that she was exchanging mail with the woman because it was extremely important that the woman receive mail from the outside. Only that way could she appear to be maintaining normal, long-standing relations with friends and acquaintances, and thus minimize suspicions of being a new resident who no one anywhere seemed to know.

As a passing thought, I asked, "Would it perhaps not be a good idea for me to be sent to stay with that woman? If she is living in a large city as a Pole and has a child of her own, could I not possibly fit into her situation without arousing excessive suspicion to herself or to me?"

"Perish the thought, child," Mme Surowjecka instinctively replied. "The poor woman is in more hot water than she can cope with as is. Neither she nor you need anymore troubles than you both already have."

A few days later, as I was grazing the cow in the pasture, I was startled by the voice of a Polish peasant girl about my age. She happened to be passing by and, as she saw me tending the cow, she snickered at me maliciously, "Żydówica." When I saw her I was alarmed, because I had never seen her before, and instinctively I began to fear that practically everyone in the village must now be aware that I was Jewish. This possibility was more dangerous now than ever before. As soon as I had returned the cow to the stable, I ran in to inform Mme Surowjecka of this incident.

Dejected, she remarked pensively, "If only my nephew Ben were alive. If he were around, they wouldn't dare be so loose-tongued and behave so boldly. Nor would they have ever had the audacity to come and demand that I surrender you to them so they could kill you." She added, however, that under the present circumstances she had no choice but to pursue the alternate plan she had prearranged in the event of this type of emergency. I would have to be sent away once again, this time to Świślina.

23

A Longer Interval in Świślina

ŚWIŚLINA is a tiny village that was located midway between Świętomarz and Jadowniki. In the village, there lived a young peasant couple named Stefan and Julianna Galek. Julianna at one time had worked for a year as a farmhand for Mme Surowjecka. The couple and Mme Surowjecka were now close friends. In fact, only a few months before, a baby girl had been born to the couple and Mme Surowjecka was among the guests at her baptism. She felt close enough with them to request their assistance in this weighty matter of shielding me. However, even to them she realized she could not disclose my true identity, because anti-Semitism in Świślina was even more ingrained in the local cultural environment than in Świętomarz.

Instead, Mme Surowjecka explained to me, she had "informed" her one-time farmhand that I was her niece from Kraków, named Halinka Bertusówna, and that my parents were Communists who were being sought by the Germans in Kraków. Inasmuch as it was obviously dangerous for me to be living with my parents under those circumstances, she, Mme Surowjecka, had agreed to take me in to live with her. However, it was also unsafe for me to remain in Świętomarz for an extended, uninterrupted period of time because suspicions of the villagers could then be aroused in Świętomarz, as well as those of the Germans, over what would seem like my unusually long stay away from home. It was therefore necessary for me to be away from Świętomarz for occasional periods of time, to enable Mme Surowjecka to claim that I had gone home to my parents in the meantime.

Parenthetically, I should add that, despite what seemed to be common knowledge in Świętomarz that I was a Jewish child, Mme Surowjecka nonetheless harbored the hope that my extended absence from the village would enable her to convince the native peasants that I was indeed her niece from Kraków and that I had gone home to my parents.

In any event, Mme Surowjecka exhorted me, it was of life-and-death importance that I most solicitously play the role of Halinka Bertusówna, the niece of Mme Surowjecka from Kraków, and never reveal with any word or gesture or act my Jewish identity.

Arrangements were made for Stefan to come early one morning to Świętomarz to escort me back to his home in Świślina, which was but three-and-a-half kilometers away. At the designated time, he arrived by foot and was introduced to me by Mme Surowjecka, who had prepared a bag of belongings for me to take along. Before we left, Mme Surowjecka handed Stefan a huge chunk of a side of pork as supplementary compensation for the charitable act he and Julianna had agreed to undertake on her behalf. Only later did I learn that this compensatory reward constituted a highly valued item for the young peasant couple, who were so impoverished that such a substantial portion of meat was truly a luxury to them.

Soon we were on our way, along the several-kilometer walk from Świętomarz to Świślina. The balmy springtime air was divine on this morning in late May. We walked through lovely fields and spacious meadows, one after another, and I took in the magnificent fragrance of the cool, open air. Once again, I dreamed of freedom. As I breathed in the smell of the flowers and plants and as I observed how they seemed to be perspiring from the droplets of morning dew on their leaves, I thought to myself, how exhilarating, how inspiring all this used to be, and could be now. How ironic that I am out here enjoying the free and open space of the wondrous world, while I am indeed anything but free—with my life being perpetually placed in danger. At any moment, I could be discovered and sent away to some sinister location where I would probably be put to death. These thoughts were interrupted only by sporadic conversation between my escort and me that, together with the sublime springtime morning air and rural environs, caused the journey to be surprisingly short.

We reached Świślina before noon. My new host invited me into his small house, where he informed me that his wife was working out in the fields and that he too would now have to be leaving for work. He showed me where I could find some lunch for myself, and then he asked that I make myself at home until they returned toward evening.

That afternoon, I took a brief stroll outdoors and read a book I had brought from the Surowjeckis. Otherwise, the day passed uneventfully. Toward evening, the young couple returned home with their baby, Zosia, who had been looked after during the day by Julianna's mother, who lived in the house next door. Stefan then formally introduced me to Julianna, and she asked me to assist her in getting supper. The sight and smell of the rendering pork fat and the roasting pork were unappetizing to me. But the overpowering awareness of my situation gave me the strength to feign an appetite. I could hardly afford showing any displeasure with the non-Kosher meat for fear of betraying my Jewish identity, nor could I afford to be a nuisance to my hosts through appearing difficult to please. I sat down with them and partook of the supper meal without ado.

We passed the evening pleasantly in light conversation, until the time came for the Galeks to go to bed. I was then shown where I would be sleeping, on a bench on the opposite side of the same room in which they slept. Over the bench they had placed a flat, canvas-covered, straw mattress. Small insects leaping out from the filthy mattress made the bench very uninviting for a bed, but I had no alternative. My life depended on my ability to adapt to the prevalent circumstances, regardless how difficult they might be. Soon all were in bed, and my first day in Świślina had passed peacefully, if not in optimal comfort.

In the morning, Stefan left for his work in the munitions factory in Starachowice. He frequently walked to and from work through a forest, to the very same place where our family and several hundred other Jews were working as slave laborers. Julianna left the house soon after, for the fields where she spent her workday. Before leaving, she instructed me to perform a few household chores and also to care for Zosia, who was not yet able to crawl. If the baby cried, I was told, I should put some sugar into a rubber nipple for her to suck on. Looking after Zosia became my daily responsibility for as long as both Stefan and Julianna were away from home.

On his way back from the factory, Stefan would from time to time stop in at the Surowjeckis, where Mme Surowjecka would give him a slab of meat to bring home. He would also convey regards to me from the Surowjeckis. In this manner, of course, Mme Surowjecka remained continually apprised of my welfare. In turn, she constantly shared news of my welfare with Father.

One evening Stefan was telling Julianna and me that on his way home through the forest he had encountered some Jews. "There's nothing I would have liked better," he indignantly claimed, "than to have killed off a few of those damn Christ-killers myself!" His words sent a chill through my body. "What a backward bigoted peasant," I thought. But I struggled to maintain a dispassionate composure, to reveal no external reaction. Still, the thought ran through my mind that I dare not emit a Yiddish word in my sleep. How dangerous that could be. I dare not. I dare not.

Julianna's mother and two unmarried sisters lived in the house next door. We would, on occasion, go over there after supper to spend the evening. Other young adult peasants also used to come there to socialize. The ladies would knit socks and gloves and other items as they passed the evening in light conversation. Much of their small talk revolved around Jews, as they amused themselves with frequent anti-Semitic slurs. All Jews were one stereotype in their imaginations. Most had probably never seen a Jew, nor would they have recognized one anyhow. Amid their remarks and brave assertions, they would chant a little ditty:

Żydóweczka Chajusia	A Jewess named Chayusha
Miała żydka Lejbusia;	Had a Jew named Leibusha;
Rzuciła go w pokrzywy	Into ivy she tossed him
A Żydek już nie żywy.	And her Jew there got poisoned.

All of this ripped through my entire being. How bitter to have to sit through such malicious abuse, acting unmoved and totally unaffected. Yet my life depended on my doing exactly that. Again, I prayed that I would not mumble a Yiddish word in my sleep.

I had been introduced to the villagers as Mme Surowjecka's niece from Kraków. To these natives of Świślina, Kraków and Bodzentyn and even Świętomarz seemed like metropolises. They had never seen a big city and so were curious to know about Kraków. At times they would ask me to describe what big city life was like. Of course, I too had never seen Kraków. I had, however, visited my Aunt Brucheleh in Kielce, which was a big city compared to Bodzentyn. I proceeded to tell them that in Kraków people had ready water in unlimited supply in their houses.

"You mean to say that you don't have to fetch it from a river or well?" they asked in amazement.

"No," I replied.

"Well, how does it get into the house?" one peasant asked. I replied, "Steel pipes are built and installed underground which connect the water from the river or well directly to the house. The water flows through the pipes and into the house."

They seemed awestruck and asked, "But how do you stop it from flowing in through the pipes and flooding the house?"

I could hardly believe their ignorance and backwardness. I realized, though, how important it was for me to be impressing them as the big city girl they believed me to be. Taking full advantage of the situation, I related with exaggerated enthusiasm the wonders of big-city plumbing. I explained that the water-filled pipes led through a small hole in a wall.

Attached to the end of the pipes was a small piece, called a faucet, that directed the water flow into a tublike enclosure called a sink.

"But how do they stop the water flow from overfilling the tub?" they demanded.

Speaking in the increasingly confident tone of an enlightened pedant, I explained that a handle at the top of a long screw was attached to the faucet. "When the screw is tightened, the flow of water is completely blocked. But as the turn of the handle slowly releases the attached screw, the water gradually begins to flow, and, as a turn of the handle back in the opposite direction tightens the screw, the water flow decreases until it is finally stopped entirely." They seemed overawed at each and every wondrous detail of big-city plumbing. They marveled with openmouthed amazement.

On another occasion, when I informed them of the miracle of electric light, they reacted with even more surprise and astonishment. Although it was important that they believed me and were impressed with the exaggerated manner in which I spun my detailed yarns of modern city life, nonetheless their extreme provincialism, ignorance, and naïveté were astounding. To think that I, a small-town girl of eleven, was able time and again to completely bedazzle them—adults ranging from their upper teens to midtwenties. And they never even suspected that I was capitalizing on their backwardness or that I was Jewish.

And so the summer days and weeks passed in Świślina in relative calm. I experienced no great immediate dangers as long as I carefully played the role of Halinka Bertusówna from Kraków. One day, however, it was learned in the village that the Germans were coming into Świślina. Julianna's primary concern was that the Germans might discover and confiscate the slab of pork Stefan had just brought home from the Surowjeckis. She instructed me to take the slab with me and go out beyond the meadow to a sloping valley and remain there with the meat until she called me to return to the house.

I, of course, had more serious concerns. What if Germans were to find me holding onto a huge chunk of meat? And upon questioning, what if they were to terrorize me until I unwittingly revealed that I was Jewish? Obviously, I could express no such thoughts to Julianna, so I took the meat from her and ran through the meadow, but as I was running down to the valley I tossed the meat off to a side. In the event the Germans were to discover either the slab of pork or me, I thought, they would not be able to connect me with it.

After several hours, I heard Julianna calling me back into the house. But on my way back, I was unable to locate the hunk of meat. I could not recall where I had thrown it, and I became paralyzed with fear as I searched everywhere for it. Surely I could not tell Julianna the truth. Luckily, after what seemed like an eternity, I at last caught sight of the meat slab, embedded in a spot amid tall grass that was pressed down by the weight of the meat. I quickly grabbed hold of it and hurried back to the house.

When I arrived back, I gave the meat to Julianna, who remarked that the Germans had left the village, much to everyone's relief. It was already near suppertime, and so she asked me to help her by peeling some potatoes. As I sat down and began to peel, a sudden harsh pounding was heard at the door. "Oh, no," I thought. "It could not be."

A few German soldiers came stalking into the house. Julianna had been mistaken. The Germans had not left the village. I became so terrified that I could feel my heart leap up to my throat. I tilted my head downward, fearing that if they saw my face they might recognize my Jewish identity. With my head crouched downward and with my eyes fixed on the potatoes, I kept peeling and peeling. As I sat there busily at work, the Germans milled about the little house, apparently searching futilely for something. They walked close by me, but they neither addressed me nor asked me anything. After some fifteen terror-filled minutes, they left the house and the village.

The summer months were soon coming to a close. Toward the end of August now, it was almost three months that I had been in Świślina. By this time, Mme Surowjecka had decided that I should return to Świętomarz. She was hoping that, after my long absence, she would be believed when she claimed that I had been with my parents in Kraków for the summer. So, one Sunday morning in early September, Stefan drove me by horse and buggy back to the Surowjecki farm in Świętomarz.

Once again, I was happy to be back with the Surowjeckis. I felt much more comfortable being with them and welcomed a return to my old outdoor chores in the cow pastures and the garden. Unfortunately, my three-month absence from the village did not alter the situation I had left in May. It was simply common knowledge throughout Świętomarz that I was a Jewish child. Whether I was directly referred to or addressed as "*Żydówica*" or merely victimized by unfriendly glances, my Jewish identity was known to one and all. And the presence of an unwelcome Jewish child in the village made for good gossip among the peasants. The situation was as unpleasant as it was dangerous, both for the Surowjeckis and for me.

Being with the Surowjeckis once again enabled me to resume communication with my family in the labor camp via letters Mme Surowjecka delivered to Father through a bribed Jewish policeman. I wrote to Father telling him how badly I missed being with the family. I also wrote of my experiences in Świślina and Świętomarz. I wrote that I could no longer bear to hear time and again the malicious anti-Semitic remarks of peasants and their boasts about how happy they were that all Jews were being deported and killed, and that there were hardly anymore Jews left anywhere. I would much prefer to perish together with the family, I added, than to survive with such miserable anti-Semites.

In the meantime, Mme Surowjecka informed Father of the deteriorating situation in Świętomarz and of the fact that my life was no longer safe there. Clearly something decisive would have to be done soon. Świętomarz could obviously no longer remain my haven. At one point, I questioned Mme Surowjecka about the Jewish woman from Bodzentyn who was living with her daughter in a large city as a Pole, only to learn that she and her child had been discovered and executed. Mme Surowjecka informed me she had suggested to Father that she could arrange for me to be taken into a Christian orphanage, where I could be baptized and live safely as a Pole indefinitely. However, Father found that proposal unacceptable, she said, because he feared the family would lose contact with me.

I wrote Father again, this time pleading that I wanted to be brought into the labor camp if at all possible. I longed to be with the family once again, I said. Regardless of what fate awaited them, I wanted to share it. Father finally concluded that, with conditions being what they were, indeed I would be no less safe at the labor camp than at the Surowjecki farm in Świętomarz or in any of the surrounding villages. Further, I was now only three months away from my twelfth birthday. Father reasoned that I could probably pass as a worker, if only he could devise a scheme to smuggle me safely into the camp.

24

Back with the Family at the Labor Camp in Starachowice

THE FAMILY was still interned in Camp Majówka, where all inmates of Camp Strzelnica had been transferred following the administrative decision to close it down. In general, conditions here were a considerable improvement over those of Camp Strzelnica. Mother and Rachela once again worked in the laundry; the rest of the family worked at various assignments in the munitions factory; and day-to-day activities essentially proceeded uneventfully until a new eruption of the typhus epidemic.

The most recent epidemic occurred in early September. By this time, the German Kommandant Althof had been replaced by a Kommandant Kolditz. Like Kommandant Althof, Kommandant Kolditz was efficient in carrying out the orders of his superiors. Unlike Kommandant Althof, he did not terrorize by shouting and beating, or by whimsical shooting to kill. Nor did he reveal sadistic satisfaction at causing human suffering, as had his predecessor.

In dealing with the typhus epidemic, however, he more than proved his mettle in meeting the highest standards of savage Nazi brutality. Aside from random shootings of suspected typhus victims, he once threw the camp into an uproar and total chaos by ordering all the inmates out of their barracks for an unspecified period of time, until the premises could be thoroughly fumigated. In this manner, he was determined to root out the disease once and for all, ruthlessly disregarding the extreme human distress and suffering he caused in the process.

This procedure lasted for several days, as the inmates remained outdoors without any shelter. Conditions were as miserable as they were chaotic, with the several hundred inmates milling or sprawled about in undefined spaces along the campgrounds. Their only possessions were whatever they had managed to grab when the barracks were emptied out. Everything else that remained in the barracks was burned to ashes, and people were afraid of even thinking what horrors the morrow might bring. It was during this period that arrangements were made for me to be smuggled into the camp.

In devising a scheme to bring me in, Father had several serious obstacles to overcome. To begin with, I could not possibly be brought in either to the camp or to the factory unnoticed; I would have to be mixed in with a group working outdoors and smuggled into the camp as that group returned from work. Second, as had been the case in Camp Strzelnica, a strict count was taken by a Jewish policeman as the workers left the camp area on their way to work and as they returned to camp after work, for each of the three workshifts; and the number of workers leaving had to correspond to the number of workers returning. Therefore, an increase in the number of returnees, which would be caused by my entry into the camp, would be noticed immediately. Moreover, I would have to know precisely where to come in, what to do in order to appear credibly as a worker, where to go after work, how to get into the camp, and, once in the camp, where to find the other members of the family among the several hundred internees.

As in so many other situations, Father devised an ingenious plan. It was a complex scheme, however, and involved several stages of careful planning. Of all the places where inmates worked, there was only one in which people worked outdoors. That was in a quarry just outside the camp where a considerable number of people were engaged in excavating stones. The area itself was only lightly guarded by a handful of Jewish foremen and a couple of German soldiers, apparently because the authorities believed few Jews would risk escaping into the decidedly unfriendly Polish environs. Because the area was accessible to general noncamp traffic, however, Father believed that I could casually become intermixed with the group.

Fortunately, Cousin Rivtche happened to be working out in the quarry at that time. Nevertheless, Father felt that someone from our immediate family should also be there at the time of my arrival. After studying the situation, he learned that a girlfriend of Rachela, named Nachtcha Baum, was also working in the quarry. Furthermore, she was approximately the same age and size as Rachela. With that information, the other pieces of the puzzle began to fall into place.

First he arranged for Rachela to take Nachtcha's place in the quarry on the day I was to be brought into the camp. Father also bribed the Jewish policeman in charge of counting the workers leaving and returning to the camp on that day in order to overcome the problem of numbers. In addition, he "hired" one of the Jewish foremen guarding the quarry to "keep an eye" on the situation on my behalf on the day I would be entering the camp.

When Father met with Mme Surowjecka on her next market day trip into Starachowice, he instructed her to bring me with her the following Tuesday morning and to drop me off near the quarry. I was to be on the lookout for Rachela, who would be wearing a sweater from home in Bodzentyn that I would positively recognize. Rachela and Rivtche would also be on the lookout for me. I was to walk nonchalantly into the quarry and move unobtrusively toward them. Then I was to proceed to do whatever I saw the other people doing and simply stay with them and follow them from that point on. With plans thus consummated, Mme Surowjecka left Father and returned to Świętomarz.

That evening, she informed me that plans had been completed by Father for me to be brought into the labor camp, and she proceeded to convey carefully Father's instructions. Feelings of anticipation soon began to overcome me. I could hardly wait to be going, to be once again together with the family.

In Camp Majówka, Father double-checked all details of the complicated operation as the day of my planned arrival approached. He reminded Rachela to be on the lookout for me and to behave inconspicuously as she saw me coming into the quarry so as to attract no attention. He reminded her that I would be instructed to work with the rest of the group for the remainder of the shift and to follow them carefully until all had returned safely into the camp. Father similarly explained all details to Cousin Rivtche.

On the designated second Tuesday in September 1943, Cousin Rivtche went to the quarry as usual, anxiously anticipating my arrival. Rachela went also, in place of her girlfriend, Nachtcha, but first she dressed herself in a navy-blue skirt and a navy blue-and-white striped sweater from Bodzentyn that she was certain I would recognize. She also borrowed the blue babushka and white trench coat that Nachtcha frequently wore on her way to the quarry so that she could pass as her replacement. As the inmates left the campgrounds that morning, the Jewish policeman in charge of counting them, having been bribed by Father in advance, recorded one more worker than was actually in line.

Rachela, meanwhile, slipped past him unnoticed. Once she arrived at the quarry, Rachela removed Nachtcha's babushka and trench coat, so that her old blue-and-white striped sweater would be easily visible to me when I entered the quarry area. Then Rachela, who had never been in the quarry, proceeded to do whatever work she saw Cousin Rivtche and the rest of the group doing, as she too anxiously awaited my arrival.

In the meantime in Świętomarz, Mme Surowjecka was preparing to take me into Starachowice. As a precautionary measure, she placed a white patch over my left eye for the journey. She explained that, in the event we were stopped and questioned, she would be able to claim that I had an eye infection and that we were on our way to see a doctor in Starachowice. She then prepared her horse and buggy, and soon we were on the fourteen-kilometer journey to the labor camp.

As we were riding, my thoughts focused only on being together again with the family. I could hardly wait to be there with Mother and Father, with Irka and Rachela, and with Moishe and Shloime. I kept hoping we would not be stopped and that all would work out according to plan.

At one point along the way, we passed by the body of a man lying on the ground off to the side of the road. We realized he must be a Jew who had either starved to death or been shot. Who else, if not a Jew, would be left dead, unattended like that, to rot away so ignominiously on the street? Mme Surowjecka remarked, "It is terrible to see what the Germans are doing to the Jews. It is really awful and disgraceful. But who knows, perhaps the Jews are being punished for what they did to our Lord, Jesus Christ."

I made no comment, but her remark did reinforce my feeling that she would have considered it a praiseworthy personal achievement had she succeeded in converting me into a Christian. Nonetheless, she did risk her life for me on countless occasions and strove beyond any reasonable expectations on my behalf, in order to spare me from what otherwise would undoubtedly have resulted in death. No words of praise could adequately extol this rare, courageous, and highly principled woman.

At approximately 11:30 A.M., we approached the area of the labor camp. As we neared the quarry, Mme Surowjecka slowed down her horse and buggy until it came to a halt. We stepped down from the wagon, walked several feet to a lawn facing the quarry, and sat down on the lawn. Then I cautiously removed the eyepatch from my eye and began looking about for Rachela in her navy blue-and-white sweater that I remembered so well. Soon I caught sight of her and realized that she had seen me, too. I also saw Cousin Rivtche, who was near to us already and coming closer. The area was only guarded by two uniformed soldiers and a few men overseeing the girls at work.

Rivtche walked over to us and immediately began asking about our trip into Starachowice. Mme Surowjecka, meanwhile, was eager to know about my family's welfare and how safe I would be in the camp. She exhibited genuine concern and love for me. We were interrupted by a foreman who apparently knew Rivtche and who admonished her to remove herself from "auntie" and "the little girl." As soon as he moved away from us, Rivtche instructed me to follow her unobtrusively into the quarry area. Mme Surowjecka remained sitting on the lawn for perhaps an hour before she left.

We slowly made our way toward Rachela, and I soon mingled in with the group. Whatever I saw the other people doing—gathering stones, carrying them to a heap to be carted away—I did likewise, as we veered gradually and continually toward Rachela. Once we were together, we hugged and kissed, Rachela and I, then Rivtche and I, but only for a moment. Rachela and Rivtche were anxious to know how I was, but prudence and experience prevented them from talking too much. I, on the other hand, was unable to contain myself. "Where do people live out here?" I asked. "Do you sleep here—outdoors?" They pleaded with me to remain quiet and keep working, and so I did, gathering and carrying first stones, then pieces of wood, and later tree branches.

As the day wore on, I continued to ask questions: "What do you eat here? What do you drink? What do you wear? What does the camp look like?" And they continued to exhort me, "Don't talk so much. Just keep on working." Still, I had more questions. Thus, we worked at our chores amid sporadic conversations, hour by hour, until it was time for the morning shift to be relieved. The group then marched to the mess hall for their daily soup allowance, and so I followed them and was also served a portion. The paucity of the meal was easily compensated for by being back with the family.

From the mess hall, we proceeded in rows five abreast back to the camp. Rachela once again put on the blue babushka and white trench coat belonging to Nachtcha, and I was smuggled into the middle of the row in which Rachela and Rivtche were marching, as I had been instructed. At the camp gate, the Jewish policeman now counted the actual number of people entering the camp. He thus arrived at the same figure he had counted in the morning, when he counted one extra person to earn Father's bribe. I had now safely arrived inside the labor camp. All had gone smoothly according to plan.

I continued to follow Rachela and Rivtche, past the administration buildings, the kitchen and laundry structures, toward the barracks, all of which were on ground level here in Camp Majówka. Along the way, we passed by groups of people standing, sitting, or lying on the ground, as well as a number of uniformed guards. Finally, I saw Mother and Irka from a distance, obviously looking for us, while standing among many other women milling about. As soon as Mother saw me, she broke into tears, weeping and trembling continuously. Cousin Rivtche continued on to her barracks group, as Rachela and I walked toward Mother and Irka. I felt wonderful to have finally arrived and to be standing together with Mother and Irka once again. It had been almost a full year since we last saw each other, before I was sent away to stay with the Surowjeckis. We had so much to talk about.

My first questions concerned the chaotic outdoors situation. "How is it that everyone is out here in the open?" I asked. "Do you always stay out here, eat, and sleep in the open air?" "Does Mother light candles on Friday night?"

Amused by my naive questions, my sisters informed me of the current uproar created by the recent typhus epidemic and Kommandant Kolditz's order to fumigate all the barracks. They assured me that the conditions were only temporary and that, as horrible as they were, they constituted paradise compared to those in Camp Strzelnica. "You don't know what you missed by not being there," I was told.

As we talked, we were continuously interrupted by friends and well-wishers who were aware of my recent arrival. The whole barracks, camping outdoors for the time being, seemed to know I had just arrived. My arrival, in fact, was somewhat of a novelty in the camp; I was greeted by the women inmates as a celebrity of sorts.

Noting that I had seen no male inmates, I asked where Father, Moishe, Shloime, and the rest of the family were. I was informed that the men were normally in different barracks anyhow, and therefore were separated now. Likewise, Cousins Rivtche and Chantche were not in the same barracks as Mother and my sisters either, so they too were in a different area at present. When conditions stabilized, I was assured, men and women would be able to visit each other's barracks, as had been the case before the current turmoil.

Conversation then veered to my experiences at the Surowjeckis. At one point, Irka remarked how impressed she was at how good my Polish was in the letters I had written the family from Świętomarz. She was, of course, alluding to the fact that formal schooling had ended for me after only the first few days of the second grade, when Jewish children were officially forbidden from continuing their public school education in Poland. Beyond that, I had had but limited and irregular private tutoring in Bodzentyn.

Subjects that first day focused on the current epidemic; how many and which friends and acquaintances had been stricken ill; who had most recently died; and how many and who were the most recent victims of whimsical shooting by the guards. Irka pointed out Kommandant Kolditz, who was standing not far away, overseeing the camp. He was apparently seeking out the most ill-looking inmates for his next group to be slaughtered. Who knew what horrors awaited whom the next day?

Meanwhile, the hours passed. Soon it was time to go to sleep. Like everyone else, I lay down on the bare ground under the open skies, with a pillow under my head and a light blanket as my cover. I was too uncomfortable and perhaps too excited to be able to sleep. I was thrilled to be reunited with the family. Whatever was tolerable for them would have to be tolerable for me.

The next day, as the morning shift left for work, I went along with Mother and Rachela to the camp laundry. Although I had no specific assignment, I assisted them in folding clothes. This became my regular job at the camp, and I found it pleasant, as long as I was together with Mother and Rachela.

Later in the day, Father stopped in at the laundry to see us. It was wonderful to see him, especially after the long year I had been away. Aware, though, that we were not in our barracks, and not necessarily among friends only, I stifled my urge to embrace him for fear the Germans might discover I was an illegal inmate. Our eyes, however, communicated the joy we felt at seeing each other again. His face seemed pale and aged compared to the time I had last seen him, reflecting the enormous burdens he endured to ensure our survival as a family. Moreover, his facial expressions betrayed his doubts about his decision to smuggle me into camp. Could my chance of survival possibly be better in this atmosphere, where Jews were dying every day?

About two days later, all the inmates were ordered back into their barracks, and camp conditions returned to their "normal" state once again. Like Camp Strzelnica, there were several barracks for the women and considerably more, a short distance away, for the men. In addition, the internal structure of the barracks at both camps was similar in that they contained two tiers along all four walls of the barracks, and the tiers were subdivided into sections, each of which accommodated approx-imately ten people. Unlike the barracks of Camp Strzelnica, however, the barracks at Camp Majówka were large and spacious, and the tiers ex-tended out further from the wall. Our family had a corner with a window we could open. Each person lay on a straw-filled coarse-cloth sack and was given a pillow and a blanket. Thus the sleeping conditions here were tolerable.

At Camp Majówka, movement in general was decidedly more relaxed than in Camp Strzelnica. That is not to say it was totally risk-free, but at least inmates could visit briefly at other women's or men's barracks to check on a relative's welfare, chat slightly, and learn of recent develop-ments. In this manner, not only the immediate family but also our total family managed to see one another on a near-daily basis, if not in one of the barracks then by passing one another on the way to or from work, at work, or in the mess hall after work.

The daily food situation was much the same as it had been in Camp Strzelnica, with soup being served in the mess hall after work, and a slab of bread and jam being served one other time. As in Camp Strzelnica, people with money, including Father and Uncle Leib'l, purchased neces-sities from Poles in the factory and brought them covertly into camp. Father would frequently come to our barracks to bring us food, and Uncle Leib'l brought food to Cousins Chantche and Rivtche, as well as to the men of the family.

Whereas in Camp Strzelnica Mother had access only to the stove in the laundry room, in Camp Majówka there was a heating stove in the center of each barracks that she and other women used for cooking. The use of the stoves was always uncertain, however, due to the fierce competition for the extremely limited facilities. Mother frequently found herself either unable to get to the stove altogether or in the process of cooking only to be pushed away by other inmates before the broth, potatoes, or fowl were sufficiently cooked. Frustrated, she would break down in bitter tears, not knowing whether she would fare any better the next day, or the day after that.

Realizing that our health depended on her being able to prepare the supplemental food, she alternately used the stove in her barracks and the stove in the laundry room. Unfortunately, competition in the laundry room was equally intense. As a rule, she found the use of the stove in the men's barracks to be less problematic, particularly during the day when most of the men were away at work. Whereas in Camp Strzelnica, it was far too dangerous to carry cooked food into the men's barracks, at Camp

Majówka, Mother, Irka, Rachela, and I would often go there with the food Mother had prepared and eat together with Father, Moishe and Shloime.

Because Mother was generally able to prepare supplementary food for us, we were often able to dispense with our daily servings of bread and jam. This was unfortunately not the case with some of the men of the family. Thus, on a number of occasions Mother would send me over to the men's barracks to give our portions of the bread and jam to Uncle Pintche Greenbaum and his brother Moishe. Similarly, Cousins Chantche and Rivtche frequently cooked a soup from the raw foodstuffs Uncle Leib'l brought them and then brought it into the men's barracks to share with Grandfather Nus'n and Uncles Moishe, Leib'l, and Yank'l.

The combined circumstances of overcrowded, unsanitary barracks and sub-subsistence food allotments ensured future typhus epidemics. As soon as a new wave of the disease reached the point of preventing large numbers of workers from performing their assignments at the factory, Kommandant Kolditz resumed his dreaded selections and exterminations of the afflicted, which spread terror anew throughout the camp.

A few weeks after I was brought into the camp, I contracted typhus. Despite the high fever and intense sensations of weakness and general physical discomforts which accompany the illness, I nevertheless found strength merely in being with the family in the camp. Fortunately, all the rest of the family was by now immune to the malady, having contracted it while still in Camp Strzelnica. Thus Mother, with help from Irka and Rachela, cared for me until my illness abated.

But, while I was still ill, a selection was announced. All inmates were ordered to assemble outside the laundry room. Mother was beside herself, petrified for me; she was worn pale, thin, and weary from the conditions of camp life. Irka and Rachela, however, acted quickly. They put lipstick and rouge on my face and put shoes with high heels on me to make me appear older. They also put makeup on Mother in order to mask her paleness and make her look younger and healthier than she appeared despite her mere forty-one years. We went out for the selection in front of the laundry room and took our places among the assembled inmates. As Kommandant Kolditz and his cohorts sought out the diseased and the weak, they looked past Mother and me, apparently noticing nothing unusual. We had survived the selection. We returned to our barracks relieved that, in the aftermath of our most recent encounter with death, all the family were still together.

One day, not long after this selection, Mother, Rachela, and I were working as usual in the laundry room and Irka happened to be visiting us. Suddenly none other than the Nazi camp kommandant himself, Herr Kolditz, stalked into the laundry room unannounced. Instantly, we became terror stricken. What if he were to notice me and realize that I was hardly twelve years old and that I was as yet not even totally cured of typhus? This could be very dangerous. I happened to be standing near the huge kettle used for heating water so, at the moment when the kommandant was facing away from the kettle, I swiftly and quietly moved behind it. Irka, noticing that I was still partially visible, began to move toward the kettle in order to cover any view of me.

The kommandant, suspicious of her sudden movement, struck Irka with the handle of his rifle. Instantly seeing the grave danger I was in and taking full advantage of the kommandant's momentary diverted attention, Rejnia Laks, a friend of Irka who was standing near me, boldly stepped in front of the kettle, covering me entirely from the kommandant's view. In a moment he turned around and looked suspiciously in the direction of the kettle. He began walking toward it, looking about here and there but noticing nothing unusual. He then turned away, looked about the room as if searching for something he could not locate, and left.

In between selections and incidents such as these, life in Camp Majówka was comparatively quiet and relatively normal. On an evening when the guards were out, a girl sitting up in the barracks might hum a tune or sing a song. Boys and girls would take an occasional stroll on the campgrounds outside the barracks. They would be seen promenading, necking, and making love. At night, young men would come into the women's barracks, ascend one of the tiers, and lie down beside a girlfriend. Sometimes they would make love, openly engaging in intercourse.

Mother would attempt to block our view of such goings-on, exhorting us, "Go to sleep, children, go to sleep." Her efforts, however, were in vain. On the one hand, it was impossible for her to totally prevent our awareness of the actions themselves. Moreover, all the women were fully aware of what was taking place and commented freely and critically. In general, they held in contempt any girls willing to let themselves be so used—or, who were "visited by a cousin," as the procedure was described in cover-up jargon—and considered such girls tramps and prostitutes.

Before long, winter came, and we were already into 1944. On a cold winter morning, Father appeared early in our barracks to inform Mother that he had heard from his sources that the kommandant would be visiting the camp later in the day. To minimize the risk of my being discovered, he added, he thought it would be wise for me to go with him that day to the factory, instead of remaining in camp. He asked me if I would like to go with him, and I instantly welcomed the opportunity to be with Father for a day, as well as the diversion from my daily routine.

I went along with him, past the gate where the departing workers were counted and all the way to the factory, which was approximately four kilometers from the camp. Once we were in the factory, with whom did I cross paths but my three-month host from Świślina, Stefan Galek! When he saw me with Father, he instantly realized that I was not Halinka Bertusówna, the niece of Mme Surowjecka from Kraków. Gaping in astonishment, he remarked to Father, "I can't believe this. She was in my house for three months, and I never dreamed she was Jewish." How fortunate for me that he did not know it then, I thought to myself. If he had, I probably would not be here today.

The day passed pleasantly, and at the conclusion of the work shift I went with Father and his group to the mess hall for our daily soup. We then proceeded to make the long walk back to the camp, where the entire group was counted as each five-person column passed the gate.

In February, a special group of Jews was transferred to the Starachowice labor camp from the Majdanek Concentration Camp. These people attracted more attention than was usual for new inmates because of their particular behavior as well as their outward appearance, which betrayed their activities in the camp from which they had come. They were known in Camp Majdanek as the *K-L (Konzentrationslager) Sonderkommando* (Concentration Camp Special Squad). Their function there, it was said, had been to remove masses of asphyxiated victims from the gas cells and transport their corpses to the crematorium where they were to be burned. As the armies of Soviet Russia were pushing to within approximately one hundred kilometers of Majdanek, the camp was dismantled and the bulk of the inmates were transferred to the Auschwitz Concentration Camp. The K-L Sonderkommando, however, was transferred to Starachowice. The individuals of this group were conspicuous by the unusually large letters *KL* followed by a series of numbers that were tattooed on the top of their right forearms.

Hardened by the fiendish, inhuman activities that had become commonplace to them in Majdanek, they were exceptionally aggressive in their demands to be given positions of Jewish leadership within the camp. They were ruthlessly determined to obtain the special privileges granted individuals such as Shloime Ehnesman and his Judenrat associates or at least be appointed to positions of authority, such as Jewish policemen or *Blockenältesten*. The Judenrat, however, operated as a clique that zealously guarded the status quo of the group. When openings did occur, members of the in-group would offer positions to relatives or long-standing friends. In no way would they succumb to the bullying, belligerent advances of an outside group that they dared not trust. Nevertheless, the pressures exercised by the K-L Sonderkommando posed a serious threat to the Jewish leadership, because the Nazi command would surely tolerate no infighting within the ranks. Nor would they tolerate any indication of weakness or lack of control on the part of their Jewish lieutenants. Nothing less than the very lives of the Jewish administrators, as well as those of their wives, children, and relatives, were at stake. Hence the Jewish camp leadership stood its ground, exercising the full authority assigned to them, in order to resist and keep in line the persistent demands by the K-L Sonderkommando for comparable special privileges.

Periodic resurgences of the typhus epidemic continued to be a pattern of life, together with the terror-filled selections that accompanied them. We were primarily concerned about Mother, whose health was visibly deteriorating. In Bodzentyn, she had been an active, good-looking, and hard-working wife and mother. Under pressure when Father had been in hiding, however, her sciatica and arthritic pains kept her almost totally bedridden for the better part of that eight-month period. Now, in Starachowice, she was obviously quite ill; she had lost so much weight that she was hardly more than skin and bones, and her flesh was yellowing.

Nonetheless, she did not complain. She was determined to carry on to her last ounce of energy in order to keep the family fed and cared for, to the extent the miserable camp conditions allowed. We feared for her health, but we dreaded even more the possibility that her sickly appearance would cause a German to single her out in a selection. We worked at encouraging her to eat more, in order to stem her dangerous loss of weight and to recoup some of her waning strength. Friends from Bodzentyn and Starachowice also gave us makeup to put on her, as well as on me, for each selection that took place, and we all heaved a sigh of relief after each one that we survived.

Father, however, also began to feel the burden of camp conditions. He told Mother he had seen the doctor and had learned he was showing signs of what could be the beginning of a heart ailment. There was little, however, that could be done under the conditions of camp life. His feet ached and got swollen from the daily four-kilometer walk to and from the factory, regardless of weather conditions. He had to soak his feet every evening after work. On one occasion, as I was going to visit the men in our family, I noticed stacks of straw on the ground near their barracks. Inside the barracks, I saw Father in discomfort, soaking his feet, sitting on a thinned-out straw-filled coarse-cloth sack, and I had a thought. I asked Father to stand up for a moment. Then I took the sack and carried it out of the barracks to the stacks of straw. I pulled out the old, flattened straw and discarded it, refilled the sack with ample fresh straw, brought it back to Father's barracks, and placed it on the tier where he was assigned. I then repeated the procedure for Moishe and Shloime.

With Father's feet causing him so much pain, he asked Shloime Ehnesman whether there was a possibility of his being reassigned to some work within the camp so he could avoid the increasing strain from the walk. Later, during one of his visits to our barracks, Father told Mother that he had been offered a position of Blockenältester, but that he had refused the offer. "I do not want to be a barracks officer; I do not want to be a policeman," he said, "because I want no one to harbor any resentment toward me. If indeed we survive the war, I wish no one to have any cause to bear a grudge against me. What is more, I wish to remain anonymous and inconspicuous to the Germans—completely unknown to them." And he chose to continue suffering, rather than accept the dubious distinction of being a barracks officer.

By mid-July 1944, the Soviet army was already approximately one hundred kilometers from Starachowice, and the Germans apparently decided to abandon the labor camp in its entirety. The number of inmates at the labor camp had been greatly reduced because of the many outbreaks of typhus and the repeated selections and exterminations of the afflicted. So, during the waning days of July, a road made of small stones was constructed, leading from Camp Majówka to the nearby railroad tracks. On the final Wednesday of the month, the two remaining camps of the complex were consolidated into one in Majówka.

It was by now common knowledge in the camp that in various concentration camps Jews were being placed into showerlike stalls, where they were gassed to death, and that their corpses were then placed into huge crematoria and reduced en masse to ashes. We now feared that the entire labor camp work force was about to be transported to one of those camps—Auschwitz.

As the inmates of the Camp Tartak lumberyard were herded onto trucks to be transported to the new camp, an ominous incident served as a sign of the momentous event about to befall us all. Before the trucks left, a top-ranking German officer climbed onto each of them to make a count of the inmates being transported. On one of the trucks, a young lady calmly stepped up to the officer and boldly slapped his face once, and then a second time. To the shock of all, the German officer stood calmly and merely walked away. The lack of a response from a high-ranking Nazi officer in view of such an overt act of defiance signaled to us, with relative certainty, that plans had been finalized for the entire camp population to be sent to its death.

With the word spreading in camp that our being sent to Auschwitz was imminent, inmates began contemplating possible avenues of escape. Following one day's work at the factory, Uncles Leib'l and Yank'l, instead of returning to the camp, hid out near the factory area. From there they succeeded in escaping into a nearby forest, and for the time being at least were freed from death at the hands of the implacable foe. Their escapes caused no outward reaction or retaliatory efforts by the Nazi authorities in the camp.

As expected, the next day, Thursday, July 27, all inmates were taken from their barracks and led to one large area. The Germans, realizing that people with boots might be tempted to risk escape, ordered that all boots be placed into a single huge pile. With Nazis standing with pointed rifles along each side of the new stone road, all inmates were herded four abreast to the railroad tracks and onto freight cars bound for the Auschwitz concentration camp. But, for reasons unknown to the inmates, the trains did not roll on to Auschwitz that day; some surmised that the Germans had underestimated the number of freight cars needed to transport so large a mass of human cargo. We were all unloaded from the trains and returned to the barracks.

It was now absolutely certain, however, that the trains had been bound for Auschwitz and that we were all definitely marked for our deaths. A frantic rush toward the wooden camp fence ensued, with Shloime Ehnesman and his son leading the way. As the Ehnesmans were seen making a desperate effort to jump over the fence and flee to the forest and into safety, scores of others followed. The Nazi guards in the towers immediately opened machine-gun fire, shooting down on the determined, prospective escapees. Other Nazi guards and their Ukrainian cohorts rushed to the fence and to the gates and opened fire in all directions.

As I looked out from the window of our barracks close by, I saw Shloime Ehnesman and his son shot dead. The sound of the machine guns was relentless, as some 150 people were shot near the fence, on the fence, or past the fence. Many who were contemplating escape lost their nerve, while others felt they had nothing to lose and braved the odds. Some of the people did indeed succeed in escaping into the woods, including Uncle Yoss'l Schreibman.

While sitting together in a barracks with Mother, Irka, Rachela, and me, Father told us that he had been devising a plan of escape. But we were now no longer in possession of our boots, where most of our money had been hidden. Father related how vigorously he had endeavored to retrieve them, but to no avail. Now, he said, we would have no way of securing the most basic necessities of sustenance, nor could we buy favors from the generally unfriendly Polish peasantry. Escape, then, would be tantamount to suicide. My brother Shloime, however, vowed that under no circumstances would he go to Auschwitz. He insisted he would jump off the train at an opportune moment.

Late the next afternoon, Friday, July 28, as the setting sun ushered in the Sabbath, all surviving inmates were herded for the second time onto the trains bound for Auschwitz. We were pushed and packed into the train cars so tightly that there was standing room only. The men were separated from the women. Mother, Irka, Rachela, and I were in the same car. Cousins Chantche and Rivtche Ehrlich were together in another car. In the men's cars were eight men of the family: Father, Moishe and Shloime, Grandfather Nus'n, Uncle Moishe Szachter, Uncle Froyim Biderman and his youngest son Shloime, and Uncle Pintche Greenbaum.

When we had been packed into the train cars, all windows and doors were shut. This time there were no false alarms. This time the trains rolled on, and on, and on, toward their notorious, infamous destination.

IV

TO THE DEATH CAMPS

25

The Journey to Auschwitz

THE TRAIN JOURNEY from Starachowice to Auschwitz during the closing days of July 1944 was another unique experience in suffering. As might be expected during those peak summer days, the air was extremely hot. Some of the more fortunate passengers rode in open cars, but most rode in closed cars. Standing squashed together for endless hours in the closed cars in the stifling heat of summer brought people close to suffocation.

In addition, we had neither food nor water nor toilet facilities for the duration of the journey. There were no provisions for changing clothes, for washing, or for any other sanitation. At one point, I moaned to Mother when my hunger pangs reached limits I had never before experienced. Although no one on the train had any food, Mother had with her a lump of sugar she gave me to munch on. That lump of sugar had to suffice for the entire journey. And at that, how much more fortunate I was than all the other wretched passengers.

Each car was monitored by German guards. At the suggestion of some older women, a few young, attractive Jewish girls approached the young German soldiers in the hope of appealing to their masculine instincts and pleaded with them to provide water and some air. On occasion, the guards actually did open a window for a brief interval.

Nonetheless, the ordeal remained traumatic and dismal. Much shooting took place, especially at night, as many Jews attempted to escape by jumping off the train. Some succeeded; most were shot. In addition, the guards fired many shots into the air in an effort to frighten would-be escapees from attempting the jump.

Fear gripped all passengers, regardless of what options they chose. Attempting to escape was dangerous and yet not attempting to escape was equally dangerous. We were tortured by untold, horrible thoughts: If we did not escape, would we survive the journey? And if we did survive the journey, how long would it be before we would be gassed in Auschwitz anyhow and our corpses burned in the crematoria? How horrible is the experience of being gassed? How great is the torture before one expires? Some were wailing; others were screaming; others were quietly resigned to the idea that we were riding our last journey in life; still others were able to maintain a slight hope that we might yet come through the current period in Gehenna.

Within our family, no one dared discuss one's thoughts for fear of exacerbating the already horrible apprehensions we were all experiencing. Instead, we deliberately kept our thoughts to ourselves. Many were the fears in my mind, and I became quietly resigned to my unknown fate.

The distance from Starachowice to Auschwitz was no more than 120 kilometers and should have taken no more than three hours by train, but the journey dragged on through Friday and Saturday, and not until Sunday morning did the train arrive at its dreaded destination.

It was dawn on that fateful Sunday morning of July 30, when the train pulled in at the Auschwitz concentration camp. Jewish tradition ordains that the ninth day of the Hebrew month of Av be observed as a fast day and as a day of Jewish national mourning to commemorate the destruction of the Holy Temple in Jerusalem by first the Babylonians in the year 586 B.C.E. and then the Romans in the year 70 C.E. Tradition also ordains, however, that when the ninth day of Av occurs on the Sabbath, the fast must be postponed to the following day to prevent the Sabbath day from being marred by fasting and mourning. The ninth of Av this year was, ironically, the Sabbath just past. Thus, as our train rolled into Auschwitz early Sunday morning, it had arrived on the day when indeed Jews the world over were fasting to commemorate the two most tragic events in Jewish history. As a number of passengers caustically noted, world Jewry was observing the fast and the day of mourning by choice; we, however, were experiencing a fast and cause for mourning—but through no choice of our own and in the extreme.

26

Arrival and Initiation at Auschwitz

WE WERE DETAINED on the train for a long period of time, perhaps several hours. Looking out from the window of the train, I saw a large, two-door, arched metal gate, above which was the slogan *Arbeit macht frei,* which means "Work brings freedom." As I peered about, I saw groups of inmates with shaved heads, walking or running about, some wearing what looked like striped union suits as outer garments, others wrapped in blankets— on July 30. I imagined we had been brought to a gigantic insane asylum. Everything seemed so bewildering, and I wondered just how horrible this strange place would prove to be. I was afraid and felt like crying and screaming, but all such impulses were numbed by the dreadful reality of this macabre setting. All weeping and screaming had ceased. People were terrified and sobered into quiet resignation.

Finally, the trains were unloaded, in a relatively quiet and orderly manner. Most striking were the grisly, unbearable stench of burning flesh and the sight of the burning furnace nearby. The grotesque, simultaneous recognition of these ghastly realities, with the musical performance of a band in the background, with sniffing dogs here and armed SS troops there, with the demented-looking shaved-headed inmates running about, with the cynical slogan *Arbeit macht frei* appearing above the arched gate—all combined to dramatize the insanity of our new surroundings at the infamous institution known as Auschwitz.

As the inmates from Starachowice walked out from the trains, some women were able to see their husbands, brothers, and other relatives. We, unfortunately, could not. We soon learned, however, that many people had perished on the trains during the journey to Auschwitz. Rachela happened to cross paths with a friend from the Starachowice labor camp. She said to Rachela, "I don't know how to tell you, but—I just learned from my brother that your father and younger brother are no longer alive. I am terribly sorry."

When Rachela questioned the veracity of her friend's utterances, Rachela's friend explained sadly that when the Judenrat stepped into the train at Starachowice, the K-L Sonderkommando who had arrived in Starachowice from the Majdanek Concentration Camp aggressively forced its way into the same car. Father, Shloime, and the brother of Rachela's friend were there also. The heat and lack of circulation in the closely packed car brought people close to suffocation. As some of the former Judenrat members were attempting to maneuver themselves into a less awkward standing position, individuals of the K-L Sonderkommando began taunting: "Who do you think you're pushing around? What do you think, that you are the same big shots you were in camp? What makes you think you're better than anyone else?" Tempers began to flare on both sides until the K-L Sonderkommando thundered, "All you pigs refused to share your privileges with anyone except those who were willing and able to make you rich. We'll show you what big shots you are now." And a fight broke out. Father desperately attempted to calm the violence, only to incur the wrath of the K-L Sonderkommando, who now turned on him. As Shloime moved to defend Father, the ruffians began assaulting Shloime. The fight resulted in a number of fatalities, including Father and Shloime. Father was only forty-four years old; Shloime was sixteen.

Before Rachela had a chance to absorb the impact of this devastating news, she realized instantly how knowledge of these tragedies would totally crush Mother's spirit, particularly at a time when she had so little strength to endure anything, so she quickly sought out Irka and me, and also Chantche and Rivtche, in order to share the news with us before Mother had a chance to learn of it. Rachela whispered to the four of us in a manner that would not arouse Mother's attention. Irka urgently suggested, and we all agreed, that under no circumstances should Mother be told of the tragic deaths of her husband and her son Shloime.

Within moments the mobs of new internees were marched through the large gate into the camp. All the while, the band stationed at the gate played the popular sentimental song "Rosamunde" and several German marches.

As a rule, each new transport arriving at Auschwitz first underwent an initial "selection," where the oldest and the youngest of the new internees were weeded out to be sent directly to the gas chambers. Sometimes, a new transport might be sent in its entirety to the crematoria. On the morning we arrived, however, no selection took place and no new internees were sent to the gas chambers. This was a highly unusual and exceptional occurrence. Word had it that the Nazi authorities had received orders from their superiors to forgo the routine selection from our transport.

By the summer of 1944, the tide of battle had clearly turned against the German forces, and as the advancing armies of Soviet Russia pressed westward, the Nazi campaign to rid Europe of its Jews was stepped up. Conceivably, the crematoria at Auschwitz on the Sunday morning of July 30, 1944, were loaded to capacity and were simply unable to absorb any additional victims that day. That circumstance probably spared my life, for if a selection had taken place that day, as a girl of twelve I would almost certainly have been pegged for extermination.

Instead of lining up for selection, we were marched on and on for perhaps three kilometers, until we arrived at Birkenau, an adjunct camp of Auschwitz that inmates generally referred to as part of Auschwitz, presumably because it was originally conceived as an extension of Auschwitz. There, we were led directly into a barracks and hustled into a huge room.

In the room, we were then ordered to undress completely and to leave all clothes, valuables, and shoes behind. Standing in the nude, and terrified from embarrassment and fear of the unknown, we covered ourselves with our arms and huddled near one another, as Nazis ran all about amid much commotion. All clothes and shoes were gathered and heaped up in two huge piles, as Nazis searched for gold and other possessions. Our boots had been taken from us before we boarded the train from Starachowice, but our family had come to Auschwitz with money still hidden in our shoes and girdles. These too were now all taken away. We attempted to steal them back from the pile, but all was in vain. Our money was now gone.

We were then moved to an adjoining room where we were required to take a shower and be disinfected. We had learned while yet in Starachowice that people were being gassed in showerlike booths, so we were certain that these disinfecting machines were the gas chambers and that we were now going to be asphyxiated.

To our surprise, we were not gassed but, indeed, merely disinfected. We were then inspected for cleanliness by the Nazis. To be sure, after the near three-day train journey, many women did have lice in their hair. Those women's heads were shaved almost totally. In our immediate family, only Rachela was not shaved. All were then given ill-fitting prison clothes and wooden shoes. Some inmates were given the striped suits we had seen others wearing as we arrived in Auschwitz. Apparently, there were not enough suits to accommodate the thousands of inmates who were at

Auschwitz at that time. Word had it that the clothes and shoes we were now being given were those worn by others who had already been gassed. It was said that Jews who worked in the crematoria sometimes found clothes belonging to their loved ones who had already been put to death, and that the workers themselves were subsequently put to death as new workers were selected to replace them.

We looked at each other with our new "clothing" and shaved heads, and we could hardly recognize one another. Were our circumstances not so macabre, so grotesque, we might have laughed at each other's appearance. But our circumstances were indeed dreadful and tragic. Before we had a chance to dwell on our plight, we were slapped about and ordered to line up again to go to yet another room for registration. Before leaving, our registration numbers were given out to us.

In the adjoining room, the registration numbers were being tattooed on the left arm of each inmate. As my turn to be tattooed approached, I saw a pointed tool with the short needle with which the operation was executed, and I began to cry hysterically. Cousin Rivtche, seeing how afraid I was, walked over to assure me that the operation didn't hurt very much. Seeing that she had already been tattooed and hearing her calming tone of voice as she held my hand partially assuaged my fear. And so I was tattooed in medium blue on the bottom side of my left forearm with the number A14313. The terror of anticipation proved to be much greater than the essentially slight physical pain.

The disinfection, head shaving, allotting of clothes, registration, and tattooing took the entire day. Not until the sun began to descend were we finally led to our barracks.

27

Auschwitz: Structure and Order

AUSCHWITZ-BIRKENAU was a gigantic complex and structure consisting of three huge camps: A, B, and C. Each of the three camps was surrounded by two electrically charged barbed wire fences that separated it from the other two camps. The overall area was surrounded by an inner chain of sentries posted around the camp. At a distance of two kilometers beyond the ring of the inner chain of guards was a second, outer chain of sentries that was posted around the entire complex.

Within the two-kilometer area separating the inner and outer rings of guards, there were watchtowers five meters tall every 150 meters. These watch towers were equipped with machine guns and search lights, and were manned at night. Hence it was practically impossible for an internee to escape from the camp. Inmates were forbidden to cross from one camp to the other, but individuals could at times pass through the official gate and enter into another camp by informing the attendant of their desired destination.

Of the three camps, Camp A consisted exclusively of workers, while Camp B had a more transitional nature, housing some inmates who did not work. Camp C was considered to be the worst of the camps, because inmates there were the next most likely selectees for the gas chambers. Each camp consisted of as many as fifty or sixty wooden huts, called *Blocken* or barracks, where the inmates slept. Other barracks served other purposes. For example, a group of eight such huts constituted the *Krankenbau,* the infirmary and clinic. Another was the *Krätzeblock,* the barracks where inmates with infectious diseases were quarantined. Still another was the *Schonungsblock,* the barracks for convalescents. One hut with showers and latrines served every six to eight barracks.

The barracks consisted of a large room or hall, approximately thirty meters long and nine meters wide. They contained no inner ceilings and were open to the gabled roofs. Three tiers of boards were attached to the walls to form bunk beds. The tiers were covered with thin straw sacks and two blankets, as well as downward-slanting boards attached to the walls that served as "pillows." The bunk areas were too narrow for all inmates to be able to stretch out fully and insufficiently high for all to be able to sit up straight. In addition, the corridors were extremely narrow, so with perhaps 250 inmates in each barracks, the residence-sleeping quarters were terribly crowded.

Each barracks was supervised by a hierarchy of appointed officials. The senior barracks officer was the *Blockenälteste* or, as the Jewish inmates from Poland referred to her in Polish, the *Blokowa*. A subordinate official was the secretary or *Schreiberin*. Each barracks was in turn supervised by a minor official, known as the *Stubenälteste*.

Although Auschwitz was primarily a death camp for Jews, it was also a detention camp for political prisoners, criminals, prostitutes, homosexuals, and others. These prisoners were allegedly given subsistence levels of food and less severe working conditions than Jewish inmates. There were, in addition, groups who were treated with civility and who were granted privileges denied to other groups. A group from Belgium and Holland, for instance, was reputed to have been treated with genuine consideration and given truly comfortable barracks and beds so that the Nazis could exhibit them to the International Red Cross as typical examples of German humanitarian treatment of political prisoners. This was done in an apparent attempt to dispel reports and rumors that were leaking out regarding the true savagery that the Nazis were perpetrating against political prisoners, especially the Jews.

The workers at the I. G. Farben paint and chemical industries at Auschwitz were likewise said to be given clean, comfortable barracks, with genuine beds, pillows, and blankets. Similarly, the members of the musical band stationed at the entrance gate were reputedly well fed and were clothed in handsome uniforms. The musicians were said to be drawn from all the inmates, including Jews. The band's primary functions were to provide background music to accompany the entry of each new transport of victims arriving at Auschwitz and to accompany the daily marches of the inmate laborers to and from work. In addition to these routine functions, it occasionally performed fine music as well, for the entertainment of the Nazi hierarchy.

The primary function of the camp, of course, was to exterminate Jews en masse and in the most expeditious manner. Toward this gruesome objective, four crematoria were located in the camp, two larger ones and two smaller ones. All four operated at full speed, at times for days and nights on end, and were surrounded by Nazis armed with machine guns and dogs. The two larger crematoria each contained a huge chimney that rose from the furnace room and from which tall columns of fire continually surged and raged. The two smaller ones worked at half the capacity of the larger two. The sight of the flames, as well as the powerful and penetrating stench, perpetually served as a grim reminder of the foremost objective of the camp.

In cynical contrast to these heinous, lawless activities, the strictest scheduling and cleanliness procedures were maintained at Auschwitz. Meticulous neatness was demanded in the barracks. For example, every morning inmates were woken at dawn and were immediately required to fold their blankets perfectly flat and smooth above and below their box-like pillows. Inmates were also required to polish their shoes with a particular machine grease and to scrape mudstains off their clothes. Any inmate who failed to measure up to these highest standards of Teutonic discipline and order would typically receive a severe beating from the Stubenälteste, who was commonly referred to in the women's barracks as "the whore." Once a week, all inmates were required to take showers regardless of the weather, summer or winter, and periodic *Entlausungen* or delousing procedures were an integral part of regimen at Auschwitz.

All inconsistencies and contradictions notwithstanding, the morbid existence at Auschwitz was determined by the fact that selections were conducted at the camp on a regular basis. The head camp doctor would order all inmates of one or more barracks to be marched into some large barracks room and to stand at attention. Then he would peer about and examine the inmates, acquiring impressions of their general state of health. He might order them one by one to trot before him at a rigorous clip. He would then signal either *Rechts* (right) for those permitted to remain in the group or *Links* (left) for those designated to be hauled away. He typically sought out those who looked young, sick, and old. Once the ill-fated selectees were hauled away, they never returned. It was common knowledge that they were placed in the showerlike facilities where they were asphyxiated, and common sense determined that the continuing, persistent flames of the crematoria were reducing human corpses to ashes.

The population of the Auschwitz Concentration Camp thus decreased rapidly, but not only as a result of the selections. The routine, regimented existence itself was designed to decimate and incapacitate the population at an ever-accelerating tempo.

28

Settling into the "Life" of Auschwitz

FOLLOWING the day-long initiation procedures of being disinfected, shaved, given clothing, registered, and tattooed, we were led to our barracks in Birkenau, Camp B-2-b. Although they were in the same barracks as ours, Cousins Chantche and Rivtche were not placed adjacent to Mother, Irka, Rachela, and me. At the registration, they, with the family name of Ehrlich, were listed under the E's; whereas we, with the family name of Szachter, were listed under the S's. Other people had deliberately given false family names in order to be able to remain together with other family members or close friends, but the thought did not occur to any of us until it was too late. Nonetheless, we were able to see each other at all times.

The senior officer of our barracks, the Blockenälteste, was a small, fat young Czech woman with a pretty face, who was as mean as she was pretty. Her function was to oversee and supervise inmates and the routine and decor of the barracks, the details of which were carried out by the barracks Schreiberin, and the Stubenälteste of the barracks or *Stube*.

Our pretty Blockenälteste was at all times dressed impeccably in fine clothes and sweaters. She worked as hard as her small fat body allowed in order to please her Nazi superiors. Typically, she would sit with a small whip in hand. She supervised efficiently and ruled with an iron hand, ordering her subordinates to hit inmates who failed to follow orders to the minutest detail. She acted mean and screamed out her authority, particularly when her superiors were within earshot.

The barracks Schreiberin was, by contrast, a basically fine human being; whereas the Stubenälteste of our Stube proved to be a base, unprincipled brute. Older and decidedly meaner than her superior, our Stubenälteste was also far more insensitive and coarse. She dressed ostentatiously in ostrich-feather jackets, in fancy pink, yellow, or white sweaters, and in elegant clothes taken from inmates and given to her by Nazi officials. In general, she impressed us as being a whore. More than that, her extremely elegant outfits contrasted so dramatically with the miserable, ragged clothing provided for the thousands of inmates, that we wondered how callous a human being could get. Displaying a total absence of compassion, she would flaunt her authority by demanding swift and precise conformity to routine orders to irrational extents and was not in the least averse to using her whip or directly hitting inmates for the slightest infraction.

The day began at dawn. At the sound of the morning reveille, lights went on, and immediately all inmates began bustling about frantically: shaking out blankets, making up beds, polishing shoes, dressing quickly, running half-dressed to the latrines and washrooms. The Stubenälteste would mill about in haste, screaming and hitting people, rushing them to be out and back far sooner than necessary. By no means atypically, the Blockenälteste would suddenly hit an inmate or kick another, and scream at her for not having made up a bed absolutely perfectly. The entire barracks was made to rush feverishly in order to be back in time to receive a slab of gray bread and some horrendous blackish coffee substitute.

Immediately following these preliminary rituals, the *Zählappel* or morning roll call took place. Columns and columns of inmates rushed out in front of our barracks buildings to the enormous roll call square located in the middle of the camp. There we quickly lined up in groups of five for the dreaded roll call, which took place outdoors twice daily, morning and evening, regardless of extremes in the weather conditions—heat, rain, snow, frost, or storm. As the whistle blew, the Stubenälteste immediately began bustling: counting, talking, and running around, beating one for moving too slowly, yelling and screaming at another to impress the Nazi officers, forcing yet another to stand erect, and the next to straighten out the line.

If the count agreed with the known number of inmates, the assemblage was released. If, however, even one single person was not accounted for anywhere within the camp complex, the entire assemblage was ordered to stand and wait—indefinitely. The inmates were at times held for hours, until all figures agreed. People were terrified if any discrepancy surfaced, because the Nazi authorities contemptuously ignored any degree of human inconvenience and suffering. One morning the roll call lasted until noon before all numbers were finally brought into agreement. On that occasion, no one was singled out for punishment. On another occasion, however, a woman who had escaped from the camp and been discovered and caught was brought back and publicly tortured in front of the entire camp, as we stood mute and at attention to take note.

Roll call procedures were trying under the best of weather conditions. In the winter, however, the mornings were dark, dreary, and dreadfully cold, especially when it was raining or snowing outdoors. The Stubenäl-testen, while busying themselves counting and recounting the inmates of the Stuben, were adequately dressed in warm sweaters, some made from fine materials. The wretched inmates, by stark contrast, had no warm clothing, only summer rags. At times, some even had no shoes or merely one shoe. Irka once had to stand in a freezing puddle with one slipper, which naturally became thoroughly drenched with the ice-cold water. Inmates who were clad in the odd-looking striped prisoner uniforms were more fortunate than others because the suits actually provided a degree of warmth. But for most, the only source of warmth was their body heat. Inmates therefore huddled up close to one another, as their teeth chattered uncontrollably in the freezing temperatures.

Upon conclusion of the morning roll call, the inmates were released. The workers then were marched in groups to work and the many non-workers were rushed, slapped about, and hustled back to their barracks. Mother and I never went out to work. We merely remained in our bar-racks. Irka and Rachela, and Chantche and Rivtche, however, were as-signed to work outside the camp area in the *Ausserkommando* or outside detachment.

One time, a Mrs. Polska, who was a Stubenälteste in a barracks not far from ours, and her assistant, a young woman named Lydia, came to our barracks seeking a couple of girls to help in their barracks. Mrs. Polska selected Irka and Rachela, then requested and received permission from our Stubenälteste to take them for the day. Mrs. Polska was exceptional in her genuine desire to be helpful to the inmates of her Stube. She saw to it that the barracks were made clean and that the bunk beds were made up neatly while the inmates in her charge were away at work. In this manner, they were spared the need to rush feverishly as other inmates were re-quired to do. Blankets as well as possessions belonging to the inmates were placed under their pillow boards and guarded. Mrs. Polska used Irka and Rachela on several occasions, and each time she gave them extra food and clothing for their efforts. She truly proved herself to be a fine human being.

Unfortunately, Stubenältesten with the civility and decency of Mrs. Polska were rare at Auschwitz. Average working conditions were some-thing of a radically different order. Typically, inmates were lined up in columns of five and marched from the Zählappel off to work, in time to the music from the band stationed outside the camp gate. As the inmates marched, Nazis with their German shepherds and Doberman pinschers marched alongside the formations to keep watch over them. If a worker accidentally moved out of step or was too tired to maintain the pace of the marching, she could be struck with a handle of a rifle or shot. If a Nazi were more gentle, she might snicker, "*Schmuckstück!*" (Jewel piece) and shove a worker back into step.

The labor assignments, as often as not, merely amounted to busywork. For two days, workers might be required to carry bricks and stones from one place to another. In the ensuing few days, they could be ordered to move them back to their original location. At other times, workers might be handed shovels and ordered to dig ditches as part of a project to "regulate a river." We were seldom sure if these were actual projects since so many Nazi schemes were totally incomprehensible. At other times, genuine construction took place—of buildings designed to facilitate and expedite the gigantic death industry, barracks, or roads leading from the barracks area to the gas chambers and crematoria.

Inmates were forced to work from dawn to dusk, with only one break for midday "lunch," which consisted of a serving of a watery soup. One would at times find a large hunk of pig fat in a serving; at other times, one might find pieces of white sugar beets or potato. Inmates were constantly watched during work by Nazis, their puppet Jewish *Kapos,* and their huge ferocious hounds. If anyone slackened her pace of work, a Kapo would beat her back into the proper tempo. The only relief came when the Nazis and Kapos went indoors for a break themselves, especially in winter, when they would go in to warm up from the bitter cold. On those occasions, and only then, could the workers relax and rest slightly.

In the evening, as the sun began to set and the long day's work came to an end, the workers at last would rush to line up at the latrines. On the way back to camp, the workers again marched five abreast under the fearsome eyes of the Nazis, their Kapos, and the dogs. The inmates would then hurry into line for the evening ration, which was usually one more serving of soup. These two daily servings of soup were supplemented only by the one slab of gray bread that was served in the morning. The whistle was soon heard for the evening Zählappel. When the numbers agreed and the assemblage was released, the working inmates returned to their barracks, hardly able to endure until they could at last simply collapse into bed.

In order to urinate at night, we had to leave the barracks to get to the latrine. From there, the sight of the huge columns of fire billowing from the enormous chimneys of the crematoria was awesome. Somehow the black background of the sky caused the bright flames to flicker more dramatically at night, as the fires, fueled by burning human flesh, ascended to the heavens.

It is little wonder that, when working up to twelve hours a day with such scant food rations to sustain them, people had to urinate often and were constantly hungry and losing weight. Little wonder also that most were unable to survive the ordeal for more than ten weeks. People's health naturally deteriorated and illnesses erupted. The ill, the dying, and the dead were in the barracks and along the roads, continually. To be sure, the so-called Krankenbau, or infirmary and clinic, at all times held at least 10 percent of the total camp population, and sometimes even cured some of them. For most, however, the Krankenbau was but a waiting station en route to the gas chambers. That was the first place the head camp doctor would come to seek out his selectees.

In addition to the rapid attrition caused by living conditions and the selections drawn from their ranks, many others lay dead on the grounds, shot and dripping blood, for having attempted to steal an extra morsel of food or for having failed to follow an order with utmost precision in accordance with the Teutonic standards of discipline. The corpses of the dead were continually ordered picked up by inmates, piled into pushcarts, and wheeled away directly to the crematoria.

Between the regular selections, on the one hand, and the attrition resulting from illness and random shootings on the other, the presence in camp of young and old persons became a rarity. One would also hear a surprised reaction when a half-crazed inmate would question an as-yet-unorphaned fellow internee, "You have a father?" or "You have a mother?" Auschwitz was one gigantic genocidal death enterprise, the likes of which have never been known or imagined throughout the annals of human experience. It combined technology, efficiency, neatness, and order to effect what could normally take place only in a nightmare, only in the subconscious recesses of a disturbed mind gone wild.

29

The Last Gold Coin

ONE DAY a few weeks after we had been brought to Auschwitz, we were standing at a morning Zählappel when a group of young men were seen in the distance, marching in prisoners' uniforms. Rachela happened to be watching and was certain she saw our older brother Moishe among them. In the row behind us, a friend tapped Irka and whispered, "Did you see the group of men marching a moment ago? They are from Starachowice, and I am certain I saw your older brother among them." Immediately after the Zählappel was concluded, Irka and Rachela excitedly corroborated each other's information and decided to follow in the general direction the men were being marched.

The girls' determination to locate the group of men was, to be sure, a decidedly hazardous undertaking. They had to pass through a gate leading from our Camp B into Camp A. The gate was guarded by young women attendants who were dressed in uniforms and special hats. Fortunately, the gates were open and the girls allowed Irka and Rachela to pass. Apparently it was permissible, at least at times, to go from one camp to the other within the Birkenau complex.

To be sure, however, Irka and Rachela were not free from the danger of being beaten, or sent to the prostitutes' camp, or even being shot. They continued walking in Camp A, closer and closer to the men's working area. As they approached it, a Nazi woman noticed them and snickered, "Look at those two whores, running to flirt with the boys." Fortunately again, the Nazi woman was preoccupied with some concern of her own. When she turned her back, the girls ran on, until finally they arrived at a site where they saw men at work digging. They caught sight of Moishe among them and attempted unsuccessfully several times to gain his attention through vigorous hand gestures and by calling out to him in muted shouts, "Moishe! Moishe!"

When at last he spotted them, Rachela motioned to him that she and

Irka were going into a nearby latrine. Then, as they entered the women's side of the latrine, he proceeded to enter the men's section on the other side. They were able to communicate through a crack in the wall. During their short conversation, Moishe, not knowing that the girls already knew of the death of Father and Shloime, confirmed, in a voice breaking from emotion, that they had indeed perished on the train journey from Starachowice to Auschwitz. Irka and Rachela told Moishe that they had already learned of the horrible news earlier.

Moishe then slipped a gold coin through the crack in the latrine wall, as he explained that it was the last and only coin he had managed to salvage and that he wanted the girls to have it. They argued, "No, Moishe, you keep it. It will be of greater use to you than to us. Perhaps you will be able to use it for food." He remained adamant, however, and tearfully insisted that the girls take it, so Rachela took it and concealed it in her bosom.

Inasmuch as it was extremely dangerous to remain conversing for any period of time, Rachela went out to check whether any Nazis or Kapos were nearby. None was, but the girls decided it would be wisest not to tarry. Rachela ran on, but Irka, who hated to leave so soon, remained a few more moments. When finally she did leave she happened to cross paths with a Nazi woman, who instantly berated Irka for having come to flirt with the boys. She then ordered Irka to kneel on pointed pebbles, which proved to be an extremely painful punishment.

When the Nazi woman became distracted momentarily with another matter a short distance away, Irka quickly jumped up and ran. She fled for her life and succeeded in escaping. Soon she caught up with Rachela, near our barracks. Before entering the barracks, they once again firmly agreed that under no circumstances should Mother or anyone else be told of Father's and Shloime's tragic fates. In our barracks, they approached Mother and me and informed us of their meeting with Moishe and of his insistence that they take the last gold coin. Rachela then cautiously removed the coin from her bosom and handed it to Mother.

30

Family Illness at Auschwitz

A FEW WEEKS after we arrived at Auschwitz, two friends told us they had learned from some men from Starachowice that our Uncle Moishe had become ill and that he and our beloved Grandfather Nus'n had been singled out in a selection and sent to the crematoria. This horrible news was told to Irka and Rachela, who once again agreed not to inform Mother. They kept the news from me also, for fear that something I might do would alert Mother of the tragedy.

In September, Cousin Rivtche developed an abscess on her knee and became unable to walk. The infection had seemed slight when it first began, some time earlier. Rivtche, however, had attempted to conceal it as long as possible, hoping to avoid being sent to the Krankenbau, for the Krankenbau was more often than not the most dangerous place to be in Auschwitz. It was common knowledge that the head camp doctor, Josef Mengele, came there regularly to make his own selections. Referred to by the inmates as the "Angel of Death," he made his rounds with a truck in which his selectees were carried off directly to the gas chambers. Rivtche's abscess, however, reached the point where she was totally immobile and, despite the fearful possibilities, she had to be hospitalized.

Our Blockenälteste was uncharacteristically pleasant in this instance and escorted Rivtche to the Krankenbau, where she caringly handed Rivtche over to the doctor there. The physician was one Dr. Luboff, a Russian woman who was a prisoner also and who determined that Rivtche's abscessed knee would require an operation. Following the surgery by Dr. Luboff, Rivtche was given a nightgown, instead of the hospital gown Jewish patients were normally given, and was covered with a blanket. Inasmuch as the Jewish ward was filled to capacity, she was placed in the last bed in the Polish ward, right next to the German ward. There, Rivtche's nurse was a Polish nun, who took special interest in Rivtche, probably because Rivtche was small and young. The nun, who obviously was overcome with compassion for Rivtche, seemed to be almost always in tears and conversed with Rivtche in Polish.

The day after Rivtche's surgery, a selection took place in the Krankenbau. During selections, patients were required to stand, undressed and unassisted, in the middle of the room so Dr. Mengele could observe them and judge who appeared most unfit physically and were therefore most deserving of being singled out for the gas chambers. It was, of course, impossible for Rivtche to stand unassisted on that day, and she defiantly refused to be helped or carried into the room for the selection, for fear she would most assuredly be selected.

As Dr. Mengele stalked through the hospital corridors, looking about in all directions, he noticed that Rivtche was lying down covered by a blanket. He stopped and began to shout in a growing rage, "Who is this girl? Why is she not standing up for the selection? Who is responsible for her failure to obey the orders of the selection process?" In the middle of his tirade, he grabbed the record card at the foot of Rivtche's bed in order to determine how ill Rivtche was, for whenever he saw a thick pack of cards, signifying a lengthy illness, or concluded from a record card that a patient was seriously ill, the person would automatically be doomed for the gas chambers.

As he was reading, Dr. Luboff and Rivtche's Polish nun-nurse ran up to Dr. Mengele and urgently insisted that it was the first day following surgery on the girl's knee, but that Rivtche was young and in perfect health otherwise. Certainly, they added, she would soon be up and about. The "Angel of Death" allowed himself to be convinced. He put the record back on the foot of the bed and moved on—and Rivtche survived. Unable to walk for weeks, she was detained in the Krankenbau for two full months, during which two more selections took place. On these occasions, Rivtche appeared sufficiently healthy to evade selection.

In the meantime, I too became ill. I had caught an infection and developed a high fever. For the same reasons as all inmates, I too dreaded going to the Krankenbau. I became so ill, however, that I had no alternative. I was first taken to the registry at the Krankenbau, where a preliminary examination was always required to determine if admittance to the hospital area would be allowed. My high fever, of course, revealed that I was truly ill, and I was placed in the hospital right away. In the hospital, various injections were tested on me, and a nurse came periodically to check my temperature. Not only did my high fever persist, but I felt so ill I was able neither to eat nor to drink. White bread and coffee were brought to me, but I was unable to consume either. I did hide the bread under my pillow in hopes of having it the moment I felt better.

For several days, I remained ill and showed no improvement. Consequently, the authorities decided that I should be transferred to a different unit. I was aware of the fact that I was now in one of those units where the "Angel of Death" routinely began his selection procedure. I also knew clearly that, if I continued to maintain a high temperature when he came for his next selection, I would certainly be sent directly to the gas chambers. I had become so ill, however, that all such concerns faded in my mind. The medication and my weakened condition put me into a deep sleep, from which I did not wake until the next morning.

That morning—miraculously—I awoke feeling better, much better. I had apparently passed the crisis and I became extremely thirsty. I stood up in my bed and was terribly anxious to be given some coffee. I also felt very hungry and let it be known to the attending nurse. Soon I learned I was to be sent back to the unit from which I had been brought only the day before. I was delighted. I remembered that I had hidden some bread under my pillow there. I could hardly wait to get back. As soon as I was back in my old bed, however, I stuck my hand under my pillow and to my deep dismay, there was no bread. It had probably been stolen. But soon I was again brought white bread and coffee, which I thoroughly relished and ate immediately.

Within a few days, I was totally recovered. Although it was now late October and the temperature was below freezing, I was taken outside for a shower. After the shower, I was given clothing to wear, but I still felt cold. I was brought to the Krätzeblock, the quarantine barracks, where I remained separated from Mother and my sisters and cousins. To be sure, it was a very nice barracks, even luxurious for Auschwitz, with real pillows and bedding. Still, I felt lonely. All the people there were strangers to me. I asked to be reunited with my family. I hoped and prayed to be with Mother especially. Two days later, I was sent back to our original barracks, where I was again together with her, Irka, and Rachela.

Mother now told me that she had had an unusual dream. She dreamed that she had a black shawl and that it had fallen into a stream of water. She strove to chase after it and catch it, but it seemed to flow away beyond her reach, constantly eluding her grasp, and at no point was she able to gain a grip on it. It flowed farther and farther away, until it was totally irretrievable. She was now certain, she said, that her father, our Grandfather Nus'n, had been selected and sent to the crematoria. Irka and Rachela attempted to convince Mother that her dream proved absolutely nothing, but they of course knew that Grandfather Nus'n had been sent to the gas chambers weeks before. Mother learned from friends soon after this that her father was no longer alive.

The news did not seem to come as a surprise to her. She avoided talking about it, apparently attempting to shield us, her children, from her deepest fears. Moreover, the fact that she never spoke to us or expressed concern about Father or our brothers tends to indicate that she surmised the worst, but desisted from frightening or depressing us, opting to keep her most morbid suspicions contained within her, to suffer alone.

31

Through the Valley
of the Shadow of Death

ONE LATE fall day in November, word spread in camp that the notorious Dr. Mengele was coming to various barracks, and possibly to ours also, in order to make a selection from among the nonworking inmates. Irka, Rachela, and Cousin Chantche were already at work, but Mother and I were in our barracks among the many nonworkers. Mother feared that the chances of our being selected were decidedly great and that probably the only way we might escape selection would be for us to manage somehow to be away from the barracks at the time of the selection.

It occurred to Mother that perhaps Mrs. Polska, the Stubenälteste of the nearby barracks for whom Irka and Rachela had worked on several occasions, might be sympathetic toward us and shelter us until the selection in our barracks was concluded. Mrs. Polska had indeed proved to be a truly fine, humane person in her dealings with Irka and Rachela. With nothing to lose, Mother and I proceeded toward her barracks. To get there, we had to walk past the gate leading from Camp B to Camp A. Fortunately, the gate was guarded by young attendants only, who allowed us to pass when Mother told them we were on our way to assist Mrs. Polska, a Stubenälteste.

As we arrived at Mrs. Polska's barracks, Mother approached her and explained that Mengele was believed to be due momentarily in the area of our barracks for a selection, and that because I was so young and Mother's health was badly deteriorating, our chances of avoiding selection seemed practically nil. Mother appealed to Mrs. Polska to allow us to stay with her until the selection was over. Proving true once again to her fine character, Mrs. Polska consented to allow Mother and me to remain in her barracks for the time being at least.

Minutes passed, then hours, with no indication that a selection was taking place or was about to take place anywhere in the camp. It was already beginning to get dark, and almost time for the evening Zählappel in our camp. We knew we could no longer remain at Mrs. Polska's barracks, for if we failed to appear for the Zählappel, the entire camp would be held up indefinitely until all were accounted for. Yet we somehow could not bring ourselves to simply get up and abandon the relative security we felt there. Ultimately, however, we had no choice, and Mother and I returned to our barracks for the Zählappel. By the time we arrived, the inmates were standing in columns, five abreast. We were already a bit late, and when our young Blockenälteste saw us, she struck Mother on the shoulder with a stick. As I moved to protect Mother, the Blockenälteste brutishly slapped me in the face. What a hateful bitch, I thought. How heroic she can look to her Nazi superiors against helpless prisoners. The Zählappel soon ended. The day had come and gone, with no selection having taken place.

A few days later, after the morning Zählappel had been concluded, and after Irka, Rachela, and Chantche had gone to work, Mother and I were, as usual, in our barracks. Suddenly, we were ordered by our barracks officers to line up outside the barracks hut. Several hundred nonworking inmates from a number of barracks were gathered together and then marched toward an unknown destination. The selection process had begun.

On our way, Mother urged me to run away and try to save my life. There was, however, no way I would leave Mother, even if I were certain I could save my own life. And there was surely no such certainty at Auschwitz anyhow. Running, then, was out of the question. So we continued marching. We marched on and on for some time until, at one point, Mother noticed our barracks Schreiberin walking near us. Mother inched her way toward her and, in a last-ditch effort to avoid our seemingly inevitable fate, handed her our last gold coin, imploring her to do whatever she could to save us.

"I appeal to you," Mother said. "Please do everything you possibly can to save my youngest daughter and me from being sent to our deaths. But if it will be impossible for both of us to be saved, please, I beg you, please see to it that at least my child is spared."

The large group continued marching until we finally reached our destination. There we were herded into a huge barracks room, and Dr. Mengele soon appeared. In his usual manner, he looked over each of the inmates under consideration before rendering his verdicts of Rechts or Links to signify his judgments of life or death for every internee present. Within moments it was my turn—and he pronounced the dreaded word

Links, signifying "to the crematoria." It was then Mother's turn—and he once again pronounced the fatal word, Links. Both Mother and I had been selected to be gassed and cremated.

The stark realization descended upon me. "This is it, the end," I thought. "I will never again see the family. How close and dear we have always been to one another. And now there is no way out. We are helpless. There is nothing anyone can do." With this death sentence, all the horrible thoughts and fears that had tortured our minds throughout our experiences in the different camps were now being realized. All hope was now in vain, crushed. I could not even imagine a possible way out. No one had ever come back from the gas chambers.

When the selection was concluded, Mother and I were among the approximately one hundred who had been selected. This group, among whom I was the youngest, was then herded onto buses and driven directly to a formidable looking concrete structure. There we were led into a gray painted room and locked in. Knowing we had been selected to be gassed, people were anticipating death momentarily. Many assumed we were actually in the gas chamber itself. Some people were sitting on the floor, others were lying. Some were weeping, others were praying. Some were reciting the *Shema Yisrael* (Hear O Israel, the Lord our God, the Lord is one), the Jewish credo, which is traditionally recited at the moment a Jew anticipates death.

There were no windows in the enclosed room, only a small opening perhaps the size of a vent located quite high up from the floor. Mother urged me to try and see if I could possibly escape through it and save my life. With the help of Mother and a few other women, I was lifted up high enough to be able to look through the opening. Unfortunately, it was much too small for a person to crawl through. Moreover, it seemed to be totally surrounded by water as well as barbed wire. I was then let down, with all thoughts of escape thus dashed.

Intermittently, Nazi officers would enter the room, speak to one another, leave, and relock the door. At one point, one of them spoke to some of the people in our group, asking cynically, "Do you wish to be gassed here, or would you prefer to be taken to the gas chambers?" Some of the women replied, "Gas us here, now. You may as well do it now and get it over with." Moments later, a few Nazis reentered the room, tossed some flourlike powder about, and once again exited. All were now certain that the powder thrown into the room was some form of poison, and death could be but moments away. All lay down, as the wailing and praying intensified. I thought to myself, "How young I am to be dying. I am not even thirteen years old. Why, oh why are they doing this to us?"

The wait seemed endless. People wondered, are we dying? Or are we perhaps already dead? Are we by chance already experiencing an after-death state? Moments passed, and hours passed. Germans continued entering and exiting, asking various questions. A woman whose mind had become affected spoke irrationally to some Germans as they were reentering the room. In response, they beat her repeatedly, pounding her savagely, and her face became swollen, black and blue.

This ordeal in the locked room continued for the remainder of the day and the ensuing night. In the morning, a group of Nazis suddenly entered the room and herded the entire assemblage out onto a truck. All were certain we were now being taken to the ovens. To our surprise, we were transported instead back to a barracks—not to our original barracks, but to the Schonungsblock, the convalescence barracks.

What could have happened? How was it possible that we had been delivered from the very maw of the beast? This had never occurred before at any other time in Auschwitz. What must have happened was that orders from Nazi superiors to dispense with the gassing had apparently reached Auschwitz after we had been selected but before we could be gassed. We had been detained, in all probability, during the period in which the Nazis were uncertain as to what they should do with our group. Should they carry out the extermination procedure already begun, or should they return us to the barracks? After they determined that we were not to be gassed, however, it defies comprehension how these savages could have played such macabre, cynical games with us, deliberately inflicting mental torture, allowing us to believe we were most certainly in the process of being put to death, and causing us to wonder whether we were indeed yet alive or dead—for fifteen hours or more. Although they had been ordered not to exterminate us, they nonetheless amused themselves in the joys of limitless cruelties inspired by their Teutonic command.

All their games and cynicism notwithstanding, the fact that we had been selected to be gassed and yet were not put to death constituted a miracle so unimaginable as to overshadow all the previous miracles of survival in my holocaust experience: It had been a miracle I was not identified by the robbers who had broken into the Surowjecki residence, demanding the Biderman yard goods. It had been a miracle when I happened to be in the barn in Jadowniki at the time a band of Poles came to the Surowjecki residence, demanding I be turned over to them so they could do away with me. It had been a miracle when the routine selection had been dispensed with on the day we arrived at Auschwitz. As a child of twelve, I most certainly would have been sent directly to the gas chambers. It had been a miracle when, in the hospital at Auschwitz, my fever broke the very day after I had been transferred to the unit of the critically ill, from which selections for the gas chambers were made routinely. But the miracle of having been locked into Death's antechamber waiting to be gassed and having come out alive surpassed all the other miracles.

In the meantime, Irka and Rachela had returned from work on the evening of the day Mother and I were selected for the gas chambers. When they returned to our barracks that evening after Zählappel, fellow inmates informed them that Mother and I had been selected and sent to the crematoria. Irka and Rachela were overcome by uncontrollable grief. The shock, the horror, the disbelief, and the loss seemed more than they could endure.

At the barracks, the Schreiberin called Irka into her office. There, she took out the last gold coin that Moishe had given Rachela and handed it to Irka. "Your Mother had asked me to do whatever I could in order to save her life and that of your younger sister," she explained. "In fact, she pleaded that I save at least your sister's life if at all possible. Unfortunately, I was powerless to do anything to save either of their lives, so I am returning the coin to you and your middle sister."

For days, Irka and Rachela grieved deeply, but they managed to carry on as best they could. As always, they appeared regularly for the Zählappel and were marched to and from work. One day at a Zählappel, some women remarked to Irka and Rachela that they had seen a group of people walking, "And we saw your mother and younger sister among them!" Irka and Rachela could not believe their ears. No one had ever returned from the crematoria alive. The dead do not return. Yet Irka and Rachela questioned the women. "Where did you see them? Where were they headed? Where did they go?"

According to the women, the group seemed to be heading in the direction of the Krätzeblock or the Schonungsblock. Immediately after the Zählappel was concluded, Irka and Rachela, too skeptical to allow themselves to rejoice and unable to believe Mother and I could be alive, wept as they hurried in the direction suggested by the women. They had to pass through several gates, but fortunately, the gates were being guarded by attendants only, who allowed them to proceed. At the Schonungsblock, Irka and Rachela entered and saw Mother and me there! They were totally dumbfounded. How could it have occurred that Mother and I were selected, taken into a crematorium—and brought back alive to the barracks!

Word now had it that the Russian army was quickly approaching Auschwitz and that the Germans had already begun to dismantle the camp. Moreover, it was said that all the crematoria except one had already been taken apart and that gassings were no longer being carried out at Auschwitz. Irka then told Mother how the Schreiberin had returned the gold coin because she had been helpless to save either Mother or me. As Irka returned the gold coin to Mother, Mother proudly asserted, "I knew I had picked the right person to talk to. I had a feeling all along that she was an honest and decent person and could be trusted."

32

The Last Weeks at Auschwitz

HAPPY as we all were to be together again among the living, we were nevertheless uneasy at being in separate barracks. Irka and Rachela made inquiries, in the hope of having Mother and me transferred out of the Schonungsblock and back to our old barracks. Their efforts, however, were to no avail. Moreover, Mother and I were soon transferred out of the Schonungsblock anyhow—not, however, to a barracks in Camp B but to Camp C, the "death camp" of Auschwitz, where the youngest and oldest people were sent along with those unable to work, to become immediate candidates for the crematoria.

Contact between us was obviously more difficult now. Still, Irka and Rachela managed to maintain contact with us. Each morning, they would get up at the crack of dawn in order to stop by and visit for a short while and be back in time for the Zählappel. In fact, through good fortune, they were even able to bring us some extra bread, which was so welcome in light of our near-starvation food allotments.

Shortly before Mother and I had been sent to the crematoria, Irka and Rachela had come in contact with a Henoch Schein, who had been an acquaintance of Father. The group in which he worked, they learned, was being brought to a location not far from our old barracks. Mr. Schein was thus in a position to render assistance, and he continually had extra bread sent to us. On one occasion, he even had shoes sent for Irka and Rachela.

The girls had to pass through a gate to make contact with the person who delivered the food or supplies for Mr. Schein. They then had to return through the same gate on their way back to our old barracks. In this manner, Irka and Rachela were receiving the desperately needed extra bread and managed to smuggle some of it to us. But such an arrangement, to be sure, was not risk-free.

One day he sent two loaves. Rachela had gone alone that day to receive them. At the gate, she placed them in her bosom and covered them with a coat she was wearing. As she passed through the gate on her way back to the barracks, an attendant noted something bulging in her bosom and stopped her, demanding to know what she was concealing. When the bread was discovered, the page struck Rachela repeatedly and forced her to kneel on an area that was covered with rocks. This excruciatingly painful punishment seemed to endure for an eternity before Rachela was finally released. Despite this mishap, Irka and Rachela continued to receive the bread sent by Mr. Schein. In turn, they would throw some of it over the electrically charged barbed-wire fence to Camp C for Mother and me.

By this time, Cousin Rivtche had been hospitalized for approximately two months. Finally, she was discharged and sent to the Schonungsblock for a short period. Then she was sent to Camp C, where she soon learned that Mother and I were there also. She lost no time in locating us. After having been separated from each other for such a long period of time, we were all thrilled to be in direct contact once again.

Events in Auschwitz were being determined now ever more rapidly by the steadily advancing Russian army forces, which daily were drawing closer. Irka and Rachela were working within a task force charged with taking the camp apart. In a move to concentrate the dwindling numbers of inmates while at the same time to dismantle the camp gradually, Camp B was closed down entirely. Irka, Rachela, and Chantche were then all moved to Camp A. From there, Irka and Rachela could still see us through the electrically charged wires, but they could no longer come to visit with us.

It was now late December, and Irka and Rachela were working outdoors in the dead cold of winter. Frigid temperatures made continual work a feat practically beyond human endurance. At one point, Irka boldly stepped into a bunker to warm her hands for a minute. Instantly, a Kapo walked up to her, slapped her, and fired her summarily. In a vitriolic diatribe, she informed Irka that as a punishment for such irresponsible behavior she would be sent permanently to Camp C. Little did the Kapo realize that Irka not only was not devastated by her verdict, but was elated to be transferred to the same camp where Mother and I were interned.

Rachela immediately pleaded with the Kapo to send her there also. All the young, healthy people in her group considered Rachela's request foolhardy and insane. Why would anyone wish to be sent to the "death camp," they wondered. Nonetheless, if Rachela herself asked to be sent there, thought the Kapo, why should I not allow her the "privilege"? So,

Rachela and Irka were sent to Camp C. Now, once again, Mother, Irka, Rachela, Rivtche, and I were in the same camp.

For work, we were taken to a long table, where we were assigned the task of *Weberei,* spinning and braiding ropelike strings to be attached to leather strips for parachutes. Gassings were by now totally discontinued, and people no longer feared being sent to the crematoria. The sub-subsistence food allotments and general camp conditions remained unchanged, but this period proved to be our most tranquil time at Auschwitz.

Because of the lack of food, however, I in turn lacked the strength to be able to pull the rope strings tightly enough for braiding. On one occasion, I slipped away from the table and out of the building unnoticed. Looking carefully about me and seeing no Germans or Kapos nearby, I ran toward the kitchen where food was being prepared for the Nazis as well as for the entire camp. There I saw a very large pile of potato peelings in a garbage heap. Quickly, I tossed them about in search of leftover potato pieces. I grabbed a pail set nearby on the ground and hurriedly filled the bucket with the discarded potato scraps. Just as I had filled the bucket, I realized I was being seen by a German. Holding fast to the pail, I fled for my life. I was lean and very light on my feet. I succeeded in running out of danger and reached our barracks unharmed. When Mother examined the contents of my stolen pail, she was not surprised to find that most of the potato scraps were rotten. Nonetheless, she managed to cook them, and we were all treated to some cooked, if partially spoiled, potatoes.

Our desperate food situation was also abated slightly by Rachela's friend from Starachowice, Nachtcha Baum, who bravely and generously slipped extra soup several times through the charged wire fences separating Camp A, where she was, and Camp C.

Soon the time drew near when the Germans were forced to evacuate Auschwitz in face of the imminent arrival of the Russian army. By then it was January 1945. The Germans were now looking for people able to perform the most difficult labor assignments. These people were to be sent to Bergen-Belsen in West Germany to begin building a new camp there. Among those chosen was Rivtche. Although she was certain she would be unable to work due to the pus that remained in her knee, she was selected anyhow and ordered to go.

On the day before her departure, the entire group from Camp C that had been chosen to be sent to Bergen-Belsen were sent temporarily to Camp A. There, Rivtche saw her sister Chantche. Chantche deeply feared

Rivtche would get hurt and be unable to survive, and so she appealed to Rivtche to run away and remain with her. At work that day, Chantche was working on the construction of a railroad track. Her mind, however, revolved about her sister and how dangerous it would be for Rivtche to be sent alone, with no family whatsoever, to a strange new camp. As Chantche's mind was absorbed with her concerns over Rivtche, she lost control of an extremely heavy rail. The track crashed down on her foot, incapacitating her instantly. She could not walk and was sent to the hospital.

In the meantime, Rivtche was sent to Bergen-Belsen along with the rest of the group from Camp C, which happened to consist of other girls from Starachowice. In Bergen-Belsen, Rivtche maintained an optimistic attitude by refusing to accept the extreme gravity of the situation. Instead, at all times she somehow harbored the hope that better days would yet come. Her knee continually oozed fluid, but she was still capable of going out to work. The Nazis always singled out the youngest and healthiest looking to go out to the factory, and Rivtche was among those chosen every day. However, inasmuch as transports with new inmates were arriving daily, Rivtche chose to escape going to work in order to search for the family in each transport and in the barracks. This incentive provided her with the urge to carry on from day to day.

By January 18, the Russian army had reached Kraków, no more than sixty kilometers from Auschwitz. The Germans apparently decided that the time had come for Auschwitz to be evacuated. Many of the inmates were transported to other concentration camps. Of the remaining inmates, it was ordered that all those able to walk would march toward Bergen-Belsen. Those too ill to walk were abandoned and left at Auschwitz for the Russians to deal with. Cousin Chantche desperately hoped to be sent with us—with Mother, Irka, Rachela, and me—but she was unable to walk because of the accident that had incapacitated her foot, and so she was not chosen to be in the group headed toward Bergen-Belsen.

On the night of January 18, approximately twenty thousand weary inmates, emaciated from months of hunger and starvation, were herded together. Mother, Irka, Rachela, and I were included in the group. The next morning, we began the infamous Death March to Bergen-Belsen.

33

The Death March to Bergen-Belsen

THE ASSEMBLAGE of the approximately twenty thousand "healthy" prisoners began the march toward Bergen-Belsen in the early morning. The air was bitter cold, and the ground was completely covered with snow for as far as we could see.

In this march, there were no regular formations. The group merely kept walking in lines of twos, threes, or fours. Mother, Irka, Rachela, and I tried to stay in the middle of the huge group, attempting to avoid being conspicuous to our German overseers. There were hundreds and hundreds of people as far as we could see in front of us as well as in back of us. We marched and marched, on and on, in what seemed like an endless trek.

The Germans, dressed warmly, were riding in jeeps and wagons, watching for those of us who appeared unable to continue walking or unable to maintain the pace of the group as a whole. Those prisoners the Germans shot dead. These prisoners, who were thoroughly undernourished and emaciated as a result of their near-starvation diet at Auschwitz, were being forced to walk for endless hours in subfreezing January temperatures, without food, water, or warm clothing. Many who were not murdered, collapsed or dropped dead anyhow. The road became littered with corpses, and the white snow path became increasingly lined with streams of fresh red blood.

Toward evening, we were placed in barns for the night, where we were at least able to rest together. During the night, however, some people were taken from the barn and sent to unknown destinations. Hardly rested from the insufferable marathon walk of the day before, at the crack of dawn we resumed yet another day of walking. Once again we were marched without respite in frigid temperatures, hungry, freezing, and becoming increasingly weaker.

Once, I found myself disconnected from the rest of the family. I apparently had walked faster gradually until I was ahead of the rest. I became frightened and realized that I simply must find Mother, Irka, and Rachela. It was terribly dangerous for us to have become separated. As inconspicuously as possible, I attempted to run back and forth past rows and rows of people marching in twos, threes, and fours—up and down, several times. At one point, I passed the two Grossman sisters from Bodzentyn. When they saw me, they informed me that my family was worried sick about me and admonished me to hurry and find them, and to then stay with them. I continued looking for them, running up and down the rows, past the Germans, who seemed primarily concerned with shooting the weary and the sick, until I finally found them. I was fortunate to have found them before dark. Had I been separated from them for the night, we might have been taken to different places altogether.

The march began exacting an intolerable toll on all of us, but especially on Mother. She was hardly able to continue walking. We were haunted by the fear she would become totally incapable of walking, no less than by the terrifying prospect of a Nazi taking note of her condition and, God forbid, shooting her. So, Rachela took hold of her, supporting her on one arm, as I took hold and supported her on the other. We practically had to drag her.

As we were now totally absorbed in holding up Mother to keep her from collapsing, an elderly woman from Starachowice, also nearing the point of collapse, lunged toward me in a desperate effort to gain a grip on my hand as a support for herself. All my strength was being sapped trying to support Mother, and without thinking I shook the elderly woman's grip from my hand. No sooner did she lose her hold on my hand than she was noticed by a Nazi, who summarily shot and killed her. My conscience began to plague me. Perhaps if I had allowed the woman to hold onto me, she might have survived. But if I had to choose between trying to save Mother or another, unrelated woman, what else could I have done under the circumstances?

Unexpectedly, Irka now became thoroughly exhausted and seemed to resign herself to whatever fate might await her. As we passed by a large stone, she suddenly and defiantly sat herself down upon it and declared, "I can't continue. I'm not walking anymore. I don't care what happens. Let them shoot me." Realizing instantly that the Germans would hardly be impressed by such protests and that Irka was placing herself in a position of mortal danger, Rachela and I cried out frantically for her to get up and start walking immediately. This she did, but not without lapsing back into that position and frame of mind another time or two.

Toward evening, this horrendous day also came to an end, and once again we were placed in barns for the night. Everyone dreaded the coming of the next morning, in anticipation of yet another endless day's march, not knowing if our starved, frozen, and thoroughly exhausted bodies could withstand yet a third day of such relentless torture.

The next day began promptly with the resumption of the Death March. Again we were marched on and on, and we were convinced we would have to suffer through the Gehenna of the past two days once again. We continued marching on this third day—but only until we reached a town along the pre–World War II German-Polish border, called Loslau. There we were ordered to halt. The hideous Death March had at last come to an end. After having exacted a terrifying toll of victims, who had either collapsed from maltreatment and starvation or who had been summarily shot because they were unable to keep pace with the bulk of the group, the Nazis now herded the remaining survivors into boxcars destined for the new Bergen-Belsen Concentration Camp.

Whereas the train journey from Starachowice to Auschwitz in late July was carried out in mostly closed train cars, causing some prisoners to suffocate from the stifling heat, the train journey to Bergen-Belsen in the latter part of January took place in open boxcars, causing the victims to freeze from the bitter frost. We were crowded into the boxcars, standing room only. My sisters and I attempted to place Mother in between us to prevent her from being stepped on or crushed.

After the trains had been rolling for several hours, a few women found just enough space to sit in a half-squatting position. Irka also found a tiny area, but when she began moving toward it she was struck on the head with a shoe heel by a Hungarian woman, who aggressively beat Irka to the tiny space.

After having traveled a considerable distance, Irka was standing against a door of our boxcar when suddenly, as the train was slowing to a halt, the door came open. Irka lost her balance and began to fall in the direction of a steaming hot kettle of soup. A Jew from Buchenwald who was part of the group in charge of distributing the soup saw Irka falling and grabbed hold of her, preventing a most serious, scalding accident. The prisoners were each then given one serving of the soup. The boxcars were closed once again, and the trains rolled on, until they reached Bergen-Belsen, in northwest Germany.

We arrived in Bergen-Belsen in the middle of the second night of our train journey. We were herded into barracks, where we collapsed from exhaustion. Our single consolation was that we were together: Mother, Irka, Rachela, and me.

When we awoke the next morning, one of Irka's shoes was missing. We searched all about but could not find it. It had apparently been stolen. The temperature was freezing, and finding new shoes for Irka became an urgent necessity. But where? We soon learned there were no extra shoes in Bergen-Belsen. All that could be found was a wooden shoe, which Irka tried on but could not wear. She wrapped her foot with rags until she finally found a soft shoe. The snow, however, penetrated the shoe and Irka felt miserable.

Cousin Rivtche Ehrlich had by now been in Bergen-Belsen for several weeks, assisting in the construction of the new camp. Somehow, though, Rivtche had managed to avoid going to work daily so she could await each new transport as it arrived in Bergen-Belsen in the hope of finding the family, especially her sister Chantche. When morning came, Rivtche as usual walked through the barracks checking to see if any family members had arrived the night before. This morning, finally, she found the four of us. She greeted us warmly and enthusiastically, and we were elated to see her. When we told her of Irka's problem, Rivtche could only tell us what we already knew: there were no shoes to be had in Bergen-Belsen.

Her first concern, naturally, was for Chantche's welfare. We explained to her that on the day the march to Bergen-Belsen began, Chantche had wanted very much to go with us but that, because she was unable to walk, she was not allowed to be in the march. Rivtche was understandably saddened and disappointed. Her youth and general optimistic nature, however, enabled her to quickly rekindle her hope that all would work out for the best and that her sister Chantche would somehow manage to survive on her own, wherever she might be.

34

Bergen-Belsen: Structure and Order

BERGEN-BELSEN proved to have but one characteristic in common with Auschwitz: both were death camps. Even in this respect, however, they differed in that Bergen-Belsen's genocidal effectiveness surpassed that of Auschwitz, if indeed that is possible. In every other respect, the two camps offered contrasts in styles of horror.

Whereas Auschwitz had been known for its strictness of regimen and routine, Bergen-Belsen had no regimen or routine whatsoever. Its only order was nonorder.

Whereas in Auschwitz, the barracks had tiers upon which the inmates slept, in Bergen-Belsen there were no tiers at all. Instead, inmates slept on the bare floors. Being all on a single floor level, we were far more crowded than at Auschwitz. We had absolutely no place to lie down or stretch our legs. Moreover, the inmates were frequently moved from one barracks to another.

Whereas in Auschwitz there were the two daily Zählappel, at Bergen-Belsen there were none. And while in Auschwitz the inmates were marched to and from work, where they were forced to slave from dawn to dusk, in Bergen-Belsen there was practically no work at all. Inmates lay in their barracks fading, starving, and dying.

Whereas in Auschwitz showering, washing, and *Entlausungen*—disinfection treatments against lice—were part of the regimen of the camp, at Bergen-Belsen there was no washing or cleansing of any kind. The inmates lived in total filth. Lice bred so profusely in Bergen-Belsen that everyone who placed a hand under his or her arm or clothing drew out a handful of the pesky insects at any time. The inmates were left merely to exist—and either survive, or die.

Food rations in Auschwitz were already far below the most minimal subsistence levels, and people there continually lost weight, became increasingly emaciated, and frequently died of starvation. We received still less food in Bergen-Belsen, where only one serving of bread was distributed per day. The only inmates who had any more food were those few who found work in the kitchen.

The primary claim to infamy at Auschwitz was its highly efficient crematoria, which were capable of exterminating and burning to ashes the remains of several thousand victims per day. Bergen-Belsen had none of these apparatuses. However, the extreme conditions of overcrowding, starvation, and filth, as well as the illnesses that bred and spread throughout the camp population, brought the daily death toll to numbers that rivaled the average daily death tolls of Auschwitz. People were particularly plagued by onslaughts of dysentery and diarrhea, and they died by the thousands.

The corpses in Bergen-Belsen were not removed and cremated in ovens. Instead, the dead and the dying lay piled up, rapidly growing like heaps of garbage. For our toilet needs, we had to go outside the barracks to a huge, dug-out hole in an adjacent field. In the process, we could not avoid walking over bodies, whether in the severely overcrowded barracks or on the grounds outside. Merely the chore of getting outside necessitated walking over the dead skeletons, reduced by starvation and disease to mere bones, and bulgy-eyed, grimacing corpses.

Given these conditions, the continued existence of every prisoner became increasingly more tenuous. Within our own family, Mother fared worst of all and was fading rapidly. Irka, Rachela, Cousin Rivtche, and I determined to do everything possible we could to help her survive.

Cousin Rivtche managed to get a job in the *Schälküche*, the kitchen where potatoes were being peeled, because she knew that people working there were often able to steal some potatoes. Through this activity, Rivtche felt a sense of fulfillment by being instrumental in obtaining a little food, at least, for her ailing aunt. In addition, Rivtche learned how to judge just when it was relatively safe to steal a few extra potatoes. Lying in the barracks at night, she could hear the Nazis talking among themselves in an adjacent barracks. She would wait until their talking faded into total silence. Then, assuming that they had retired for the night, she would fearlessly run into the kitchen, steal a few potatoes, and run back to the barracks to bring them to Mother. Rivtche managed to bring some food to us almost every day. We all then strove to assist Mother, getting her to eat some of what little food there was. Water was also at a premium at Bergen-Belsen. At times there was none at all. Hence we struggled to obtain water every way we could in a desperate effort to help Mother cling to her life.

Rachela also succeeded in obtaining work in the Schälküche. While she was there, a Jewish woman in charge agreed to allow Rachela to take some potatoes out if she would in turn deliver some food to friends of this woman. Rachela agreed gladly. Thus she, too, was able to bring potatoes to the barracks for us. But bringing the illegally acquired potatoes to the barracks was a dangerous endeavor. On one occasion, a German guard caught Rachela and beat her severely for the "crime." Fortunately, she was not fired and continued working in the kitchen.

But being caught by Nazis was not the only danger one could encounter when stealing potatoes from the kitchen. When walking from the kitchen to the barracks, Rachela and Rivtche had to pass by a barracks where a number of Russian prisoners were interned. These prisoners were husky, gruff, and aggressive women who were on the lookout for people leaving the kitchen with food in their hands. When they found such a person, the Russian women would then boldly walk over and grab the food away and brutally fend off any resistance from the person they were robbing. Both Rachela and Rivtche were on occasion attacked and robbed by them. Neither, however, was deterred, and both continued to brave the hazards to bring their stolen potatoes to our barracks.

The critical food situation was thus slightly mitigated through the courageous initiatives of Rachela and Rivtche. It was also slightly alleviated through the magnanimous efforts of a longtime friend of the family, Mrs. Kornblum, who before the onset of the Holocaust resided on the outskirts of Bodzentyn. Whenever and wherever she was able to find any available source for heating, she put together whatever foods scraps she could lay hold of and cooked a soup. Mrs. Kornblum would then bring some of her soup to share with our family, especially with Mother. There is no adequate expression of gratitude for Mrs. Kornblum's kindness, particularly in view of the extreme deprivation being experienced by all in Bergen-Belsen and the unfathomable difficulties she had to overcome in preparing the soup and sharing it with us.

In addition to the food shortage, I encountered an unexpected, dangerous problem shortly after we arrived in Bergen-Belsen. During the period I had been hospitalized in Auschwitz, I was administered numerous experimental injections, and the upper part of my right arm where the inoculations had been injected somehow never completely healed. Now in Bergen-Belsen, an infection on my arm developed into a huge abscess, and the pus spread all the way into my armpit. Having no other choice, I went to the camp clinic and took my place at the end of a line. The line was incredibly long, and the service seemed so slow. One of the Jewish girls who was assisting as an acting nurse noticed me and the agony I was experiencing. Compassionately, she approached me, escorted me from the line, and treated me out of turn. She first cut open the abscess and allowed the pus to drain out. Then she applied a salve to the affected area. Afterward, she gave me an additional supply of the salve to apply myself as needed. From that point on, the infection gradually abated. Although a permanent, ugly scar remained on my arm, the infection did eventually heal.

As the weeks passed, the acute food situation became even worse. By the beginning of April 1945, there was almost no food to be had anywhere, and the water was said to be contaminated or even deliberately poisoned. The deaths increased. Even Rachela and Rivtche were unable to get food; nor were the young women from Starachowice, who had been initially sent from Auschwitz to construct the Bergen-Belsen camp and who knew the ins and outs of the camp, in any better position to help. There were days when absolutely no food was distributed.

Hunger, however, was not our most serious problem. Worse were the numbing sensations, the feelings of weakness and lightheadedness, as well as instability as we began to lose our equilibrium. In desperation, people attempted to drink water from filthy ponds and reservoirs. People were dying by the thousands. Clearly, none of us could remain alive for more than a few weeks at most. We were now in the midst of a tight race with death. Our only hope of salvation was through freedom. The critical question was: Would liberation come before it was too late?

V

THE LIBERATION
AND ITS AFTERMATH

35

The British Enter Bergen-Belsen

FROM approximately the beginning of the week of April 8, 1945, bomb explosions began to be heard from afar. As they drew closer, our barracks began to shake from the vibrations. We knew that the hour of liberation was at hand.

On Sunday, April 15, an inmate was suddenly heard shouting, "I just saw a tank!" Soon, tank after tank rolled by, and Nazis were seen retreating and being shot at. The Germans were finally being driven out of Bergen-Belsen by British armed forces. Our hour of liberation had arrived. Finally, two years and almost seven months after we had abandoned our home in Bodzentyn for the Starachowice labor camp, we were at last free people. Under normal circumstances, the moment of liberation would have evoked spontaneous expressions of rejoicing, dancing, and singing in the streets. But circumstances in Bergen-Belsen were not normal. Even the healthiest of the liberated victims were far too exhausted physically and emotionally to celebrate.

Our British liberators were in near disbelief when they observed the conditions of the camp and the surviving inmates. No civilized human being could imagine finding approximately 14,000 corpses and another 14,000 dying victims heaped in piles all about, discarded like garbage. No one could imagine finding approximately sixty thousand more deathly ill, starved, and emaciated people with bulging eyes, nothing but skin and bones. No one could imagine finding inmates crowded so miserably together with filth, infectious diseases, and lice all about.

The British were so outraged that for a day or two they brought captured German prisoners from Bergen-Belsen on a truck and allowed the inmates to throw stones at them, or wreak our revenge on them in whatever ways we pleased. Some of the men were able to muster up enough strength to go out and strike a few righteous blows at their former persecutors, but most of the women were too ill and too indifferent to respond. Soon, however, the British were ordered by their superiors to discontinue their mistreatment of prisoners of war, explaining that such abuse constituted a violation of the internationally recognized Geneva Convention.

The British immediately began implementing a five-pronged program of rehabilitation for the liberated inmates:

1. They poured handfuls of DDT disinfectant on everything, on people as well as on objects.
2. They brought in truckloads of supplies, of water, bread, and condensed milk. The enriched milk, however, as well as the sudden intake of normal amounts of food, caused the death toll to rise dramatically because our shrunken stomachs were unable to digest that much food.
3. The British began setting up a new camp a short distance away, and in between the old and new camps, a place was set up where the inmates were cleansed and disinfected. A special powder was also put into clothes to disinfect them as well.
4. The British brought in doctors and medical students from Belgium, who set up a makeshift hospital in the new camp area, where the curably ill were transferred immediately. Those appearing hopelessly ill were simply left to die. Their numbers continued to soar into the thousands. Medical supplies of all kinds were brought in, and hosts of volunteer nurses' aides from Belgium and Sweden came also to help the sick and bury the dead.
5. The healthy inmates were gradually taken from the barracks in the old camp and, after undergoing the disinfection procedure, were transferred to small apartments and houses being prepared in the new camp, which had formerly been occupied by Nazi soldiers.

Mother's condition had deteriorated by now to a critical state. However, the ill were being transferred to the new hospital in alphabetical order. We realized that by the time they got to the S's it would likely be too late to save Mother. Irka approached every person she knew connected with the hospital to see if they could get Mother transferred there immediately, but no one seemed to have the authority. Irka finally approached the head doctor of the hospital, Dr. Hadassah Bimko, and described Mother's condition to her. Irka pleaded with Dr. Bimko, insisting that if nothing was done for Mother before her letter of the alphabet came up, she would probably no longer be alive. Dr. Bimko agreed and ordered that Mother be brought to the hospital out of turn.

Soon a Red Cross ambulance arrived, and Mother was placed in it along with a number of other gravely ill inmates. When Irka jumped onto the ambulance to accompany Mother, a British soldier ordered her off, declaring, "There is no room for you. Only the sick can go on this ambulance."

"You will have to shoot me. I am not getting off," Irka answered. "My mother is deathly ill, and I fear she may die. I must remain with her."

The soldier then responded, "We will have to take you to be disinfected. Are you willing to undergo the procedure?"

Irka replied, "Yes, I'll undergo anything."

The British soldier then yielded and granted his approval by declaring to a subordinate, "Okay, let her go, too."

Irka then accompanied Mother to the hospital, as Rachela, Rivtche, and I remained in the barracks to wait our turn to be disinfected and transferred to the new camp. Irka remained at Mother's bedside day and night. Although it was vitally important that Mother begin to eat more, she seemed able to eat less and less. Irka strongly encouraged Mother to try to eat more, but apparently Mother was simply unable to digest the food.

There were two young women at the hospital, named Karola and Rachela, who had worked in the camp clinic even before the liberation and who resided in the attic of the hospital. They were not professional nurses, but they had had some clinical experience, and what they lacked in training they more than compensated for in industriousness and compassion. As they observed Irka, constantly at Mother's bedside, and noted how she was ever struggling to induce Mother to eat, they empathized with Irka and attempted to assist her in every way they could. They brought food to Irka and insisted that she eat and rest a bit herself. They also encouraged Mother to eat as much as possible.

In addition to her rapidly deteriorating health, however, Mother had apparently lost the will to live. At one point she said to Irka, "My mother came to me in a dream last night. She sat me up and told me that Father, Moishe, and Shloime are no longer alive." Although Irka, Rachela, and I knew that Father and Shloime had perished on the train journey from Starachowice to Auschwitz, none of us had ever breathed a word of it to Mother. Irka now strove vehemently to convince her that soon the war would be over, and that there was every reason to hope that Father, Moishe, and Shloime had survived, and that we would be together again.

Mother countered, somewhat annoyed, "What are you talking about? My mother came to me in my dream last night to tell me that they are not alive. So what kind of life can there be for me now?" Nothing Irka said could alter Mother's train of thought.

The war was now rapidly coming to a close. By April 21, a Russian army had entered Berlin. Four days later, the Nazi capital lay under siege. On May 1, it was learned that Adolf Hitler had committed suicide and that he had been replaced by Admiral Karl Dönitz as Nazi Commander-in-Chief. Berlin was surrendered to the Russians on May 2, and all Nazi armed forces in northwest Germany surrendered to the British two days later.

On Tuesday, May 8, the announcement came over the radio that Nazi Germany had surrendered unconditionally to the Allied forces of Great Britain, Soviet Russia, and the United States of America. The Nazis, their armed forces, their government structure, and all their political programs were at last crushed. The radios were blasting with performances of the national anthems of the victorious Allies and with other music and the sounds of rejoicing the world over.

Through the windows of Mother's hospital room came more sounds of blasting radios and rejoicing soldiers, volunteers, and former inmates. Mother asked that the windows be closed. The noise seemed to be too shrill for her abused and weakened nervous system. Irka closed the windows, causing the sounds from outdoors to be at least partially muted, and the quiet tranquility that Mother needed was somewhat restored. Irka then worked, with assistance from Karola and Rachela, to persuade Mother to eat some rice soup that had been brought for her from the hospital kitchen. Mother insisted she simply could not eat it. Instead, alluding to the war's end, she spoke with quiet resignation: "Now I can die in peace."

Irka protested desperately, demanding, "Mother, don't talk like that! I need you, and Rachela and Golda need you!"

But Mother seemed disinterested and uttered no reply. She was fully aware of the fact that the war had ended in total victory for the Allies, and at no point had she lost an iota of her lucidity. She gave Irka the last gold coin, which our brother Moishe had given Rachela and Irka on the one occasion they had met at Auschwitz, and which constituted the last tangible link to our family's past in Bodzentyn.

Mother's only response to Irka, however, was one simple request, "Please look after Goldeleh." And with that request, she breathed her last words—and expired.

The crushing blow of Mother's death was thus left to be shouldered by

Irka alone. She had no idea where she might find Rachela, Cousin Rivtche, or me. She had neither the physical nor the emotional strength to attempt to locate us, nor could we have done anything if she had found us. Irka was fortunate to have her two friends in the hospital, Karola and Rachela, who did all in their power to console and help her in her terrible grief and loneliness.

The hospital doctors also attempted to console Irka. They explained to Irka that it was only Mother's heart that had kept her alive for as long as she had endured, for all her other vital organs had apparently ceased to function. Their assumption was that Mother had been suffering from tuberculosis of the bones. She was all of forty-two years old.

Later that day, Irka was informed that Mother would be buried in a mass grave following a mass funeral service to be held the next day. In tears, she pleaded that Mother at least be given an individual grave. Unfortunately, Irka was told, countless people were dying daily, and therefore getting an individual grave was out of the question.

Irka, who was still a young, inexperienced girl of nineteen, alone, grief-stricken, and heartbroken, did not know to whom she could turn for help, nor did she have the emotional strength to resist the bureaucracy. The next day, May 9, 1945, a mass funeral service was conducted for the multitudes who had perished the preceding day, and Mother was buried in a mass grave in the new camp cemetery. When the service and the mass burials were completed, Irka placed a marker over Mother's grave site so that she would know its location when she returned to visit it. She came to check it every few days.

After the funeral service, Irka remained in the hospital, where she assisted her new friends in caring for the ill. In the meantime, Rachela, Cousin Rivtche, and I were still in our old barracks. The new camp hospital was nearby, but we had no contact with Irka and did not know where she and Mother had gone. The old camp had been roped off with wires and had become one huge hospital of sorts.

Finally our turn came, and we were taken from our old barracks and went through the disinfection procedure. Then we were transferred to a small apartment house in the new camp. As soon as we were settled in our new apartment, the three of us set out to find Mother and Irka.

On a warm May day, we walked to the fence surrounding the hospital. We had no idea in which building we might locate them, so we walked along the hospital grounds calling, "Irka, Irka. Szachter, Szachter." Finally we caught sight of Irka laying by an open window, her head resting on her crossed arms over the window sill. From the expression on her face and her nonresponse to our calling, we all realized, without saying a word to one another, that Mother was no longer alive.

We entered the hospital and soon found Irka with her two friends. When Irka informed us that Mother had passed away, we were heartbroken. Karola and Rachela attempted to console us and brought us food, but none of us could eat. When tragedy had struck previously, claiming the lives of so many of our dear ones during the Holocaust, the unrelenting persecution had deprived us of time to grieve. This time, our feelings were overpowering. We wept and mourned. Our grief persisted, and only abated after several months.

Soon printed lists of survivors began being published and distributed wherever surviving Jews were to be found. We did not even bother to look for the names of Father or Shloime. We did, however, look for the name of our brother Moishe. Unfortunately, our search was in vain. His name did not appear on any of the lists.

We inquired from men who had survived Auschwitz and learned that Moishe, as well as our cousin Shloime Biderman, had been sent to Camp Dachau shortly before the Germans evacuated Auschwitz. Upon learning that lists of survivors from Dachau were circulating in Munich, Rachela braved the trip, only to learn that neither Moishe's nor Shloime's name was on any of the lists. Mother's intuition was once again proved correct. Moishe had obviously not survived.

Back in Bergen-Belsen, we learned from other men who had survived Auschwitz that only one day before the death march began from Auschwitz to Bergen-Belsen, our Uncle Froyim Biderman had been caught attempting to steal a potato from a large pile and was shot dead on the spot. Thus, the entire Biderman family had been wiped out. His wife, our aunt Gitteleh, and their two sons, Moishe and Itche, it will be remembered, had all perished back in Starachowice.

We learned that our uncle Pintche Greenbaum had also perished at Auschwitz. Thus, the entire Greenbaum family had also been completely wiped out. Our aunt Brucheleh had perished together with her two children, K'silush and Moisheleh, in Starachowice.

Cousin Rivtche learned from a friend from her hometown of Szydłowiec that her sister, Chantche Ehrlich, had been transported from Auschwitz to Ravensbruck Concentration Camp, and from there to Malchow Concentration Camp, where she perished from maltreatment and starvation.

We learned from friends in Bergen-Belsen that Uncle Yoss'l Schreibman, who had successfully escaped from the Starachowice labor camp at the time we were being sent to Auschwitz, had been shot in the forest by a Pole.

We learned that Uncle Leib'l, who had escaped from the Starachowice labor camp with Uncle Yank'l, also at the time we were being sent to Auschwitz, was alive and well and was residing in Poland, in Kielce.

Cousin Rivtche soon learned that a group in Bergen-Belsen was going to Poland in September. Fearlessly, she decided to go with them in order to meet Uncle Leib'l there. She traveled to Kielce, where she found him and visited with him for several weeks. While she was there, he told her that he and Uncle Yank'l had escaped to a forest near Starachowice, where they had survived from the last days of July 1944 until the first weeks in 1945, when the Russian army overran that area of Poland. It is noteworthy that Mme Zofia Surowjecka, who had sacrificed so much and had continually endangered her own life to save mine, also aided Uncles Leib'l and Yank'l in their struggle for survival in the forest.

Then, during the waning weeks of the German occupation, Uncle Leib'l and Uncle Yank'l resided together as Poles in Kielce. One day, Uncle Leib'l said, he left their apartment for a short while to purchase some food. When he returned, he found Uncle Yank'l on the floor—lying in a pool of blood. Upon investigation, he learned that Uncle Yank'l's assassin was a Pole and a onetime schoolmate of Uncle Yank'l. After the Nazis had been driven out of Kielce, Uncle Leib'l did indeed strive to bring the despicable culprit to justice, and in all probability he could have succeeded. However, the anti-Semitic climate in Kielce at that time was so flammable that Uncle Leib'l could not continue pressing charges against Uncle Yank'l's murderer because his own life was in jeopardy also. He was forced to accept the reality that a Jew in Poland could not safely achieve justice against a non-Jewish Pole. He dropped charges.

After several weeks, Rivtche returned to Bergen-Belsen, while Uncle Leib'l remained in Poland, in an effort to retrieve as much as possible of the once-great value of the family estate in Bodzentyn. Although the buried fortunes had disappeared, Uncle Leib'l did succeed in selling some of the family property. He soon moved to Germany, near Bergen-Belsen, so he could be close to us and visit with us frequently.

Epilogue

As ROSH HASHANA of 1945 approached, almost four months had passed since Mother had died, and we felt the time had come for us to prepare and erect a monument for Mother's grave site. In this endeavor, we were fortunate in having the assistance of our lifelong friend and townsman, Shmiel Weintraub. Shmiel had also survived through all the camp experiences of Starachowice, Auschwitz, and Bergen-Belsen, and, like ourselves, was now residing in the new camp in Bergen-Belsen. Moreover, in keeping with his past leadership in the communal Jewish life of Bodzentyn, he was now active in the Jewish community in postwar Bergen-Belsen.

Through him and a friend of his, a handsome monument of stone was arranged for and was prepared to be placed over Mother's grave site. The monument was unveiled in a ceremony that was conducted in Yiddish by a rabbi from the Jewish Palestinian Brigade of the British Army. The unveiled monument revealed an engraved, Hebrew epitaph, which translates:

Here lies

MIRYAM RIVKAH SZACHTER

Daughter of Irah

Born in the year 1902

in Bodzentyn

Laid to rest 3 Sivan*

in Bergen-Belsen

May her soul be bound in the bonds

of eternal life.

*Irka maintains Mother was buried May 9 (26 Iyar), six days before 3 Sivan. The cause of the discrepancy is unknown to me.

With Mother's death, twenty-eight of our thirty-three closest loved ones from our generations-long home of Bodzentyn had fallen victim to the most cataclysmic tragedy in Jewish history. Not included in that number are our innumerable second and third cousins and distant relatives, none of whom was known to have survived. The twenty-eight who perished are:

Grandfather Meier—who perished from hunger and typhus in Starachowice;

Grandfather Nus'n—who perished in a crematorium at Auschwitz;

Father—who perished on the train journey from Starachowice to Auschwitz;

Mother—who perished at Bergen-Belsen from extreme maltreatment and malnutrition in the camps in Starachowice, Auschwitz, and Bergen-Belsen;

Our brother Moishe—who perished at Camp Dachau;

Our brother Shloime—who perished on the train journey from Starachowice to Auschwitz.

Of the Ehrlich family:

Aunt Feigeleh and Uncle Y'shia—who perished in the liquidation of Szydłowiec;

Cousin Chantche—who perished in Camp Malchow from extreme maltreatment, malnutrition, and starvation in the camps at Starachowice, Auschwitz, Ravensbruck, and Malchow;

Cousin Ruchtcheleh—who perished together with her parents in the liquidation of Szydłowiec.

Of the Biderman family:

Aunt Gitteleh—who perished in the liquidation of Starachowice;

Uncle Froyim—who was shot when stealing a potato the day before Auschwitz was abandoned;

Cousin Moishe—who perished with his mother in the liquidation of Starachowice;

Cousin Itche—who was killed when a giant mallet fell on him in the factory at the Starachowice labor camp;

Cousin Shloime—who perished at Camp Dachau.

Of the Greenbaum family:

Aunt Brucheleh—who perished in the liquidation of Starachowice;

Uncle Pintche—who perished in a crematorium at Auschwitz;

Cousin Moisheleh and Cousin K'silush—who both perished with their mother in the liquidation of Starachowice.

Of the Schreibman family:

Aunt Dineleh—who perished in the liquidation of Starachowice;

Uncle Yoss'l—who was shot by a Pole in a forest near Starachowice;

Cousin Lalunya and Cousin Moisheniu—who both perished with their mother in the liquidation of Starachowice.

Of the Uncles Szachter:

Uncle Moishe—who perished in a crematorium at Auschwitz;

Uncle Moishe's wife, our aunt Chavtche, and Samush, their baby boy, who both perished in the liquidation of Starachowice;

Uncle Froyim—who was sent to Auschwitz in 1941 and presumably perished in a crematorium there;

and Uncle Yank'l—who was shot by a Pole and former classmate in Kielce.

The five survivors of our entire family included Uncle Leib'l, the lone survivor of his generation; Cousin Rivtche Ehrlich, the lone survivor of our eleven first cousins; my sisters Irka and Rachela; and me.

Individually and collectively, we set our sights toward the future, toward building a new life. And in so doing, we hoped to sanctify, to some extent at least, the memory of those who did not survive.

List of Close Relatives

Great grandfather Alter Szachter
Grandfather Meier Szachter (Father's father)
Grandfather Nus'n Szachter (Mother's father)

FATHER
Y'chiel Szachter

MOTHER
Miryam Rivkah Szachter

SIBLINGS
Moishe
Irka
Shloime
Rachela

AUNTS AND UNCLES
Aunt Gitteleh and Uncle Froyim Biderman
Aunt Feigeleh and Uncle Y'shia Ehrlich
Aunt Brucheleh and Uncle Pintche Greenbaum
Aunt Dineleh and Uncle Yoss'l Schreibman
Uncle Moishe and Aunt Chavtche Szachter
Uncle Froyim Szachter
Uncle Leib'l Szachter
Uncle Yank'l Szachter

FIRST COUSINS
Moishe, Itche, and Shloime Biderman
Chantche, Rivtche, and Ruchtcheleh Ehrlich
Moisheleh and K'silush Greenbaum
Irka (Lalunya) and Moisheniu Schreibman
Samush Szachter